WAR

IS NOT A GAME

WAR CULTURE
Edited by Daniel Leonard Bernardi

Books in this new series address the myriad ways
in which warfare informs diverse cultural practices,
as well as the way cultural practices—from cinema
to social media—inform the practice of warfare.
They illuminate the insights and limitations
of critical theories that describe, explain,
and politicize the phenomena of war culture.
Traversing both national and intellectual borders,
authors from a wide range of fields and disciplines
collectively examine the articulation of war, its
everyday practices, and its impact on individuals
and societies throughout modern history.

WAR
IS NOT A GAME

The New Antiwar Soldiers and
the Movement They Built

Nan Levinson

RUTGERS UNIVERSITY PRESS

NEW BRUNSWICK, NEW JERSEY, AND LONDON

Library of Congress Cataloging-in-Publication Data

Levinson, Nan, 1949–

War is not a game : the new antiwar soldiers and the movement they built / Nan Levinson.

pages cm

Includes bibliographical references and index.

ISBN 978–0–8135–7113–3 (hardcover : alk. paper)

ISBN 978–0–8135–7115–7 (e-book)

1. Iraq Veterans Against the War. 2. Iraq War, 2003–2011—Veterans—United States—Political activity. 3. Iraq War, 2003–2011—Protest movements. 4. Soldiers—Political activity—United States—History—21st century. 5. Veterans—Political activity—United States—History—21st century. 6. Peace movements—United States—History—21st century. I. Title.

DS79.767.P76L48 2014

956.7044'31—dc23

2014004945

A British Cataloging-in-Publication record for this book
is available from the British Library.

Visit our website: http://rutgerspress.rutgers.edu

Manufactured in the United States of America

for Phyllis Levinson and for Alan Lebowitz

CONTENTS

ACKNOWLEDGMENTS

My deep and abiding gratitude goes to the people in this book, who gave me their stories, time, wisdom, and patience. I couldn't have written it without them—and what a fine way to discover that a cliché is true. This is their book, and I hope I've done right by them. A special nod goes to Aaron Hughes, Anne and Andy Sapp, Nick Jehlen, Nancy Lessin, the late, missed Charley Richardson, Winston Warfield, Amadee Braxton, Liam Madden, and Kelly Dougherty, who time and again provided explanations, answers, and insight.

I'm sure I will miss a number of people who deserve a thank you, and an even greater number whose ears I've talked off in my immersion in the subject, so picture me slapping my forehead and saying, damn! as I rue the omission. Those I haven't forgotten include my readers, Anthony Hixon, Julie Levinson, and Lanie Zera; my editors, Leslie Mitchner and Daniel Bernardi for their enthusiasm, smarts, and kindness; my indexer and pal, Martha Berg; my copy editor with a sense of language and of humor, Beth Gianfagna, and all the good people at Rutgers University Press who made this book a book; my encouragers, Mary Susan DeLaura, Neil Miller, Tom Engelhardt, Joe Hurka, Michael Bennett (who gave me my first, indelible introduction to basic training), and Richard and Georgia-Jean Hollander (who gave me a place to stay, though they didn't always agree with me); my good neighbor Mark Giles (who shoveled snow and took care of us so I could sit at my desk and finish the book); and my mother, Phyllis Levinson—how lucky I am to have had her to guide, sustain, and root for me all these years.

Finally, a mere thanks is inadequate for Alan Lebowitz, my supporter, mentor, exemplar, advocate, companion, laugh-sharer, dinner-maker, my husband, my love.

PROLOGUE

War Is Not a Game

"We're going over now. You ready?" a young veteran with a soul patch and a quicksilver smile asks a fellow vet who's grabbing a smoke outside the Holiday Inn in downtown St. Louis in August 2007. They exchange a short nod. The heat wave, close to one hundred degrees all week, has finally broken, so it's no longer punishing to venture beyond air conditioning. The two veterans, one lanky, the other solid as a door jamb, climb into a car, where a few others wait, and they all head down the street to the Missouri Black Expo job fair, now in full swing.

The exhibition hall is big, echoing, overlit, packed with job recruiters and seekers, but the clump of young men and women in black T-shirts with "Iraq Veterans Against the War" stenciled on the front is hard to miss as they make their way to the booth with "Go Army!" splayed across its canopy. A Humvee, decked out with fancy twenty-inch rims, is parked next to a table laden with brochures and sign-up sheets. There, military recruiters and civilian contractors chat with teens and encourage them to take turns playing "America's Army," a simulation game proclaiming itself to be "The Only Game Based on the Experience of Real U.S. Army Soldiers."

For the antiwar veterans, the buzz has begun the day before, when a handful of IVAW members are hanging around the hotel lobby on a break from the panel sessions at their third annual meeting. "There's a job fair going on across the street," someone says. "The army's got a recruiting booth, I saw them unloading a truck, we gotta do something." They bat ideas around until someone—probably Steve Mortillo or Jabbar Magruder—suggests a sound-off, and it clicks. The plan spreads with a quiet signaling among the veterans. Now, at the expo, they're ready for action.

"Fall in," comes the command, and the veterans do. Ninety people with real U.S. Army and Marine experience stand at attention in mass company formation four rows deep, their arms rigid at their sides. There's Camilo Mejia, the first soldier to be court-martialed for refusing to return to Iraq, and Kelly Dougherty, one of IVAW's founders and now its executive director. Liam Madden, who helped launch an Appeal for Redress to Congress and in three months got more than one thousand active-duty personnel to sign it, is there. Also Garett Reppenhagen, who co-hosted the first antiwar blog by an active-duty soldier, and Aaron Hughes, an artist-activist, who's about to spearhead IVAW's most ambitious project, the Winter Soldier investigation, which will offer grunt-level testimony about the wars next March.

Magruder takes his stance at the head of the formation and shouts, "Iraq veterans against the war, what have you learned?"

"War is not a game!" the veterans yell in unison.

Again comes the call and the response, "War is not a game."

Then a third exchange. And "War is not a game!" even louder now, caroms around the trusses of the ceiling.

Fernando Suarez, whose stepson, Jesus, had the dubious honor of being the first Mexican American to die in Iraq, stands in front, snapping photos and pumping his fist in the air, while the veterans applaud and cheer and high-five one another. As they disperse, a few police officers arrive. It's unclear who called them, but it doesn't matter. The veterans did their action, and they are stoked.

IVAW likes to talk about a "consent theory of power," in which the war in Iraq is depicted as an upside-down triangle balanced precariously on its tip and shored up by "pillars," including the military, the government, the education system, and public opinion. The goal is to topple the triangle by eroding the most vulnerable pillar, and that, the vets have decided, is support for the war among those who are fighting it. Today wasn't about theory, though. They saw an opportunity, they were nimble enough to seize it, they did something new, something big, and they didn't need anyone else to help them do it. "This is a new era of what action is and what protest is," announces Steve Mortillo, who served as an army cavalry scout near Samarra. It's evening now and he is introducing a video of the protest to the older veterans attending the Veterans For Peace annual convention. "With a small amount of people you can be so powerful to stop something like the U.S. recruiting machine in its tracks."

War Is Not a Game grew out of a feature I wrote for the *Boston Globe* in 2005, which grew out of the inquiry into resistance within the military that I had embarked on a couple of years earlier, when the invasion of Iraq seemed preordained. I had written about a small but prominent group of conscientious objectors in the First Gulf War, and I figured that if there was dissent in a volunteer military during that brief and surgical operation, there had to be something going on when a full-scale war, based on sketchier pretexts and prospects, loomed. With a mix of disbelief, anger, and despair, I watched my country tumble headlong into a war that seemed so pointless and wrong on so many levels—political, strategic, economic, moral—and as much as I like to be right, it only made it worse when all the dire predictions came to pass. But back at the beginning, what I needed was to look at the situation through other eyes, so I started talking with military counselors, soldiers about to be mobilized, soldiers gone AWOL, families caught in conflicting loyalties, and veterans groups. Somewhere along the way, I was hooked.

When Iraq Veterans Against the War emerged as a force in the antiwar movement, I realized that these veterans and active-duty solders were at the heart of the story I wanted to tell. I was intrigued by the paradox of warriors at the vanguard of an antiwar movement, attracted to their challenges to conventional pieties, moved that they had found a way to use their frustration, fury, and sorrow to try to force change, and, as always, curious about what propels people beyond bellyaching and onto the barricades. I liked their refusal to be reasonable, to shut up and behave as expected, especially the ones who no longer gave a damn about propriety, though the reason in too many cases—that the worst that could happen did—is hard to bear.

Yet, even as I watched the group evolve, I can't say exactly why these soldiers appealed to my very civilian soul. I'm not quite a pacifist, although my category of "just wars" is small; not quite a patriot, although I am plainly American and cherish much about my country; not quite antimilitary, although the closest I came to that world before I first reported on it twenty years ago was when the Russian army arrived at the front door to conscript my grandfather, who ran out the back door and didn't stop running until he got to America. And yet I am strongly drawn to these veterans.

Some of it is a shared weariness of perpetual war, some that I too am bored with chanting the same slogans over and over as Joan Baez, bless her ever-committed soul, warbles in the background—and making so little difference. These veterans may have exasperated and baffled me;

they could be disorganized, defensive, insular, self-dramatizing, and impossible to get on the phone, but they were seldom boring. And although they were never more than a tiny portion of the military and never came close to stopping the army from doing what it wanted, they caused people in the army to stop and reconsider, and that changed many lives.

So maybe it comes down to this: There is a golden season in the life of a political movement when it is poised between obscurity and banality, inchoate impulse and ossified routine, a time so full of hope, so electric, it practically crackles. The poet Seamus Heaney wrote of a rare historical moment when "hope and history rhyme." For IVAW, that moment came early in 2007 and lasted for about eighteen glorious months. *War Is Not a Game* is the story of that time.

AUTHOR'S NOTE

I often use "soldiers" throughout this book to stand in for members of all branches of the military. Anyone who has ever tried to construct a graceful sentence around soldiers, marines, sailors, airmen, reservists, National Guard, and Coast Guard of both genders will understand this as a purely practical decision.

Second, at a dinner party in Washington, DC, I was seated next to a marine general who corrected a term I had used while describing my book, saying gently, "You're never an *ex*-marine." Many veterans of the marines I talked with disagreed, however, and were adamant about being finished with the Corps forever. So with a nod to my authoritative dinner companion, I do refer to "former" and "ex-"marines.

∼ *Somerville, Massachusetts, 13 November 2007* ∼

"Tell everyone you know not to say, 'Thank you for your sacrifice.'"
A slight pause. "And don't ask if they've killed someone," adds Ian
LaVallee, who hasn't, unless you count the time he tried to slit his wrists
in the bathroom of New York's Port Authority one drunken night after
he returned from four months outside of Mosul with the army's 82nd
Airborne. It's that second instruction that stops me. Why would you
ask something so personal of someone you hardly know? Is it simple
prurience? Or is it because veterans are seen as public property,
available for probing and patting, like puppies or the bellies of pregnant
women?

Ian is twenty-three, dark-eyed, handsome, well-defended—kind of.
He slings an overstuffed bicycle bag over his shoulder and tells me a joke
he's borrowed from the older vets.

"How many Vietnam veterans does it take to screw in a light bulb?" he
asks.

I start to oblige with, "How many?" but he's already jabbing a finger in
my face and shouting, "You can't know, man! You weren't there!"

"Just tell them to say, 'Welcome home,'" he concludes and hugs me
goodbye.

1

MAIMED FOR BULLSHIT (WITH GALLANTRY ON THE SIDE)

It was a sultry summer's evening in 2004 when six, seven, or eight veterans of the U.S. military—the number varies depending on who's doing the telling—gathered in Boston's historic Faneuil Hall and declared themselves Iraq Veterans Against the War. They were a little fuzzy on what that entailed—being against something is a few planks short of a platform, and they had much to learn about the fine points of geopolitics and strategic campaigns—but this they knew: they and the rest of the American public had been lied to, they had been sent to war woefully unprepared and ill-equipped, victory wasn't around any foreseeable corner, and the bloodshed (growing, not receding) would ensnare American soldiers in shameful acts, which would haunt them for years and create a generation of enemies among the people they were mistreating. Most important, as comrades-against-arms, they would do whatever it took to bring an end to the ugly, misbegotten war they believed would change them and their country forever.

The group was in town, along with some four hundred other American veterans from perhaps as far back as the Spanish Civil War, for the annual convention of Veterans For Peace (VFP), a nineteen-year-old organization, drawing renewed vigor from its opposition to the war in Iraq. VFP had chosen Boston as its convention site to dovetail with the Democratic National Convention, where Barack Obama, a junior senator from Illinois, would introduce John Kerry, a Vietnam veteran who had once pleaded compellingly for peace, as the party's presidential nominee. That's the birth narrative, repeated whenever IVAW's story is told: the convention, the cradle of American liberty, the passing of the torch from veterans who had sworn that they would never let what had happened to them happen to another generation of soldiers. Now that history was repeating itself, they regretted how little had been learned.

Most accounts cite eight founding members of IVAW, but only six made it to Boston for the launch. "It was July 23rd, my birthday. There were six of us," says Michael Hoffman, proceeding to name seven—himself, Kelly Dougherty, Tim Goodrich, Alex Ryabov, Diana Morrison, Jimmy Massey, and Rob Sarra—who announced to the packed hall that they were starting an organization of veterans who had served since September 11, 2001, and who opposed the war in Iraq.[1] Six of the founders had met for the first time as a group that day at a workshop called "Iraq Veterans Sound Off," where an audience of about 150 heard them tell of their experiences in Iraq and Afghanistan. Some had never spoken in public before, but made eloquent by the rawness and urgency of their message, they had stunned their listeners, and emotions were running high. Now it was time to take their stories to a larger audience.

Hoffman, a former marine, who had participated in the initial invasion of Iraq, spoke first. Stocky, barrel-chested, voluble, and boisterous, he was so revved up in this, his first year back from Iraq, that he seemed to generate enough energy to light up the hall singlehandedly. Dressed in a T-shirt featuring a wanted poster for George W. Bush and shorts that bagged to the middle of his calves, he stood flanked by Massey, Dougherty, Ryabov, and Goodrich. Over their heads hung a massive painting of Daniel Webster addressing the U.S. Congress and a frieze proclaiming, "Liberty and Union Now and Forever."

Hoffman was a crisp and dynamic speaker who looked as if he meant to skewer you with his deep-set eyes. He launched into a version of what was to become his signature tale about his sergeant, a man with twenty years' experience in the Corps, who announced to his squad that they weren't going over to liberate Iraq or kill Saddam or find weapons of mass destruction. "You will be going to Iraq for one reason and one reason only," Hoffman quoted his sergeant as saying: "Oil." But, the sergeant added, they were going also because they had signed a contract and, more important—nods and murmurs of recognition rippled through the hall—they had an obligation to take care of their buddies. Most of his fellow warriors were still on active duty and couldn't tell their own stories, Hoffman continued, so the veterans on the stage that night would speak for them until they could come home and speak for themselves.

"We still have that obligation, so that's why we have come together to form Iraq Veterans Against the War," he told the crowd, who rose in acclimation, cheering, clapping, whistling, stomping, and crying. This is a group that jumps readily to its feet, conventions being part pep rally and part confirmation, especially for these old antiwar pros, that they had not become irrelevant. Even so, the applause went on and on for what seemed to Hoffman like five minutes.

Rumors had been circulating, but the launch of a new organization was a closely held secret. Frank Corcoran, a veteran of the Vietnam War and member of the Philadelphia chapter of VFP, who would volunteer with IVAW through its first year, was in the audience. Five years later, he remembered it as a defining moment. "Michael Hoffman, oh, man, he's good on stage," he said. "Then, watching the young vets *terrified* out there, feeling their way, putting their stories out there. It was really quite a moment. I thought that whole building was going to collapse. It felt like, we're gonna do this, we're finally gonna make the breakthrough and we're gonna get people to listen to us. I remember distinctly feeling very"—he sucked in his breath—"deeply that this is the beginning of something that's going to matter. We're going to organize in a way that we haven't before."

Corcoran's optimism was more than just the excitement of the moment. The national conversation about the Iraq War seldom involved those who were fighting it, but at the time of the IVAW launch, if GIs or marines made it into the American consciousness, it was through war-glory tales of heroism and sacrifice or laundry lists of misery and victimhood. IVAW's founders may have been heroes, victims, or pawns (and at times all three), but what brought them together—and set them apart—was that they had decided to become activists.

This was not the first time the United States had met the paradox of soldiers opposing a war, nor is it uncommon for one generation to reject the political touchstones of previous ones, but with the active-duty military constituting less than 1 percent of the U.S. population, soldiers who actively oppose any war are a minority within that minority, which appears on the average American's radar only when somebody screws up or gets killed. Unlike World War II, where the burden was distributed more evenly across the population, or Vietnam, where all men of a certain age had to reckon with the draft, the Iraq War was being fought by a professional military. That military filled its ranks through recruitment based on economic, and not always truthful, inducements; involuntary retention under an open-ended stop-loss policy; and an unprecedented call-up of citizen-soldiers in the National Guard and reserves. Children of the military, raised in the tradition of soldiering, helped to fill out the ranks. "One lesson learned from Vietnam," observed Charley Richardson, a founder of Military Families Speak Out, "is if you're going to start a war, don't even pretend to threaten the sons and daughters of the upper middle class and the rich."

And apparently, if you're going to start a movement, don't even call it that. While identity politics once made it cool to feel disenfranchised, by this time, a backlash against "political correctness" had made people wary of being reduced to the causes they embraced, while new social media made it possible to air a gripe or assume a political stance without leaving home. "The watchword of political discourse has degenerated from 'movement' to 'spin,'" the historian Taylor Branch wrote.[2] "Movement" is a term invoked hopefully or bestowed retrospectively, but the veterans on the stage that July night, and the others who followed, weren't interested in being spun for anyone else's purpose. They had had enough of that to last a lifetime. Despite the necessary irreverence and occasional Che T-shirt, most of them weren't trying to start a revolution. They meant to challenge and provoke, and IVAW would always struggle with the question of how radical it wanted to be, but their strongest feeling from the start seemed to be one of betrayal—by their government, politicians, and commanders—and to feel betrayed, you have to have had some faith to begin with. What the IVAWs wanted was to set the record straight, and they wanted to be heard.

They also wanted to end the war in Iraq, but people with little political standing or financial muscle have limited options for influencing public policy. Recognizing this, the veterans who signed on to IVAW in the early days cast around for the right model of political engagement. One example was Veterans For Peace. Most of those vets had become politically active during the Vietnam War, when the energizing spirit came from kids of draft age from all classes taking to the barricades out of self-interest, as well as idealism; in doing so, they added fuel to a social revolution that dominated America for decades. But that was a different era, in Bob Dylan's resonant phrase, one of "music in the cafés at night and revolution in the air."

In contrast, the model that dominated the decade when the Iraq veterans were coming of age was identified with the political Right: smart, accomplished, conservative kids raised in suburban comfort and entitlement, whose vitality came from an establishment philosophy and a sense of persecution by the Left. Complaining of powerlessness, they empowered themselves through networks formed at religion-affiliated colleges and law schools and university-based publications. They also drew on the ground-level organizing of talk radio hosts and mentors who had entered government during the Reagan era and were eager to groom a new generation for a counterrevolution. They may have been less sanctimonious than activists on the Left, but their brand of political engagement was no more appealing to the army grunts. Though different in philosophy, goals, and style, organizations on the Right and Left were both based on the assumption that it would be a well-connected, college-educated elite who would set the terms of debate and provide the debaters.

Iraq Veterans Against the War envisioned something different: a movement that would arise not from those predictable quarters, but from working-class, high school graduates, who had once bet their future on the military. And at a time when "change" (mostly about things that wouldn't) was the mantra of every politician, tactician, causist, and malcontent, these budding antiwarriors aimed to change the way that change came about. Their organization would be resolutely grassroots and nonviolent, and, if it couldn't be totally leaderless, then at least it would break with the "great man" idea of history, which Americans embrace and then need to debunk—as if democracy requires taking greatness down a peg. The veterans would spurn partisan politics and traditional pressure tactics, such as lobbying, and instead take to the streets and cyberways to organize, particularly within the military. They would speak directly to GIs to counter the belief that an attack on the war was an attack on them. For civilians, they would point to the plastic yellow ribbons on the rumps of SUVs and explain that the problem was not the military strategy, but the political policy that led to the invasion; not a few bad apples, but a situation that made ordinary soldiers act from their worst instincts. They would testify that the war was not a glorious campaign of liberation, but a dreary slog of an occupation that could not be won because occupations never are and because no one knew what winning would look like.

Most important, IVAW members would tell their stories. While veterans from World War II, Korea, and, to a large extent, Vietnam wanted *not* to talk about their war experiences, the Iraq vets ached for a reckoning of what relatively few Americans were being asked to bear or even acknowledge. It was also a good strategy. They recognized that what they had going for them was their sheer ordinariness and their authority of having been there; they took the abstractions of patriotism, protest, courage, and sacrifice and made them flesh. After all, a clean-cut soldier just back from policing a Baghdad neighborhood was much harder to dismiss than a scruffy student bused in from God-knows-where. So from its earliest days, IVAW did double duty. By testifying to the grunt-level reality in Iraq, its members alerted the American public to what was being done in its name. By speaking out, they alerted their fellow soldiers, marines, sailors, airmen, and veterans to what it was possible to do in their name.[3]

"Someone sees me and says, I agree with that guy. I just don't have the courage to do it alone," explains former marine Joseph Turcotte, an early IVAW member. "So now he comes, stands next to me. I'm not alone, he's not alone. And more people come. It just takes one person to start a movement."

In the fall of 2003, that person was Michael Hoffman. Hoffman had joined the marines in 1999, when he was nineteen, having grown up in a small town outside Allentown, Pennsylvania, where his father was a steelworker and his mother drove a bakery truck. After high school, he bounced around dead-end jobs until he met up with a persuasive military recruiter who convinced him that the marine corps was his only option. That made sense to Hoffman, whose description of Allentown would make a good Bruce Springsteen song. "It's a city that isn't exactly going places," he said about a year after he returned from Iraq. "For people in a position like mine, [enlisting] really seems like the way to go."

And there was something else, a remnant maybe of that stubborn loyalty to your buddies, if not to the Corps. In a conversation five years later, he elaborated, "There's this idea that you join the military because you want to kill people and go to war. Granted, there's a few that think that way, but it's a small minority. Overall, people join the military because they want a better life for themselves and to help people. The military is sold as a good influence in the world, either by providing aid or taking out dictators. Just because we realize that the military's not really doing it doesn't mean that we're going to stop looking for ways to do that."

It took a while for Hoffman to come to that insight. The country was at peace during his first years in the marines, and his stints at Camp Lejeune in North Carolina and Camp Hansen in Japan were quiet ones. While home on leave about two years into his service, he visited a friend who worked at a bookstore where, as he tells it, a copy of *Chomsky for Beginners* leaped out at him from the shelves. He had long been a self-described "recreational politics watcher," following politics as others follow football, but that book, he said, "blew my mind, literally." Soon he was reading more Chomsky—*Manufacturing Consent, Propaganda of the Public Mind*—then tackling other leftist thinkers, such as Howard Zinn and Daniel Ellsberg. He reported with pride that he came to be known as the radical in his unit.

Those books got passed around a group of eight marines, who coalesced around their reading and their music, particularly alternative rock groups, such as Rage Against the Machine, with its radical politics and in-your-face lyrics, like, "Fuck you, I won't do what you tell me," which Hoffman remembered screaming, half-drunk and half-comprehending, when they were at a strip joint during training. But mostly it was the new ideas they were discovering that excited them. Chomsky, neither popularizer nor stylist, is not an easy read, so there's something beguiling about a bunch of marines debating the fine points of media filters and American hegemony. "It was a really odd reading group," Hoffman said. "We'd drink beer instead of coffee and talk till 3:00 a.m. on weekends, but that's what I guess it pretty much was."

In December 2002, a few days short of the end of his active-duty contract—the date he was slated to return to civilian life—Hoffman's first sergeant called him into his office and informed him that he had been stop-lossed; that is, retained involuntarily past the end of his contract.[4] That meant he was going to Iraq. Even then, Hoffman doubted the official rhetoric about the 9/11 attacks, and he didn't see much point in invading Iraq. He considered refusing deployment, but quickly realized that he wasn't a conscientious objector. More to the point, he couldn't ditch his friends. "When you go into combat, you're not thinking of the president or a cause or anything," he pointed out. "You're thinking about your life and your friend's life and getting home alive."

So he went, first to Kuwait, then into Iraq, taking part in the ground invasion, which began on 20 March 2003. As a lance corporal with a marine artillery outfit, he provided cover for coalition forces moving north toward Baghdad. He was in-country for two months, leaving Iraq when the war at first appeared to be over and a brief drawdown of troops ensued. He left the marines that August, having served the four years he had signed on for plus an extra six months under stop-loss. "After seeing what happened there, it changed for me. I asked myself, why are we there, and there was no good reason for it," he told me. Why did he think the United States went into Iraq? "Oil, plain and simple," he replied, having found nothing to contradict what his sergeant had told him before they left.

Almost as soon as he got back home, Hoffman found his way to the Philadelphia chapter of Veterans For Peace. There, Dave Cline, a much-decorated, much-admired, disabled Vietnam War veteran, and then president of VFP, invited him to speak at a meeting. Hoffman gave what Cline called an "experiential rap," and the older veterans, most of whom had fought in and against the Vietnam War, listened to echoes of their experiences. Hoffman, ever the student of politics, prevailed on them to teach him about that time and that fight. "There was a significant number of people who had learned lessons from Vietnam, also a number of young people who knew nothing," Cline told me. "Part of our job is to teach them. We had hoped the country had learned from Vietnam. It didn't."

A mess of inchoate impulses at that time, Hoffman was drinking too much, sleeping too little, and feeling isolated by his inability to explain to civilians, who didn't want to hear anyway, what had happened in Iraq—to him and to the Iraqi people. "I felt like I was the only one," he said, a plaint repeated over and over as disillusioned veterans found their way, haltingly, to each other. "The Philadelphia chapter took me in at the beginning, showed me the ropes, got me on my feet, pretty much saved me from myself." But the brotherhood of older veterans—old war horses, ready to go when they heard that bugle blow, by Cline's description—wasn't quite enough. Hoffman realized that the grunts who had been to Iraq had a unique perspective. He envisioned an organization in his generation's image, one that would give them standing in the antiwar movement. To hear him describe its gestation, IVAW sprang into being almost by spontaneous combustion. Cline, however, remembered it a little differently. You can't start a group until you have at least two members, he reminded Hoffman; how else can you hold meetings? He urged him to slow down, find other veterans who felt as he did, test the waters a little. And so, on Veterans Day 2003, the first after U.S. troops invaded Iraq, Hoffman took the microphone at an antiwar rally in Philadelphia and publicly denounced the occupation.

By the following July, when IVAW was born, more than nine hundred U.S. troops had been killed in Iraq, and approximately $150 billion had been appropriated for the invasion and occupation. (It would be another year before anyone kept somewhat reliable records of how many Iraqis had been killed or displaced.) In the fourteen months since George W. Bush had declared "Mission Accomplished," no weapons of mass destruction had been found, evidence that they had ever existed was increasingly suspect, the United Nations had pulled out of Iraq after its headquarters was bombed and its chief envoy killed, and Saddam Hussein had been yanked from a hole in the ground and taken into custody. What had at first seemed like a welcome for liberators had turned toxic, as coalition forces fought for control of Fallujah, Ramadi, Samarra, Najaf, and other cities. Iraq had turned into a 360-degree, 24/7 battlefield with no end in sight.

The toll on the American fighters was becoming obvious: a study published in the *New England Journal of Medicine* reported significant mental health problems among returning soldiers and marines,[5] and the army was alarmed enough by the rise in suicides among active-duty troops to beef up its prevention program.[6] It was around this time that an army sergeant, who was about to be sent back to Iraq for his second tour, told me bitterly, "This war cannot be won. It won't be won, not now, not ever. We're getting maimed for bullshit."

Polls showed that an increasing percentage of Americans preferred not to have their soldiers in Iraq, but most Americans apparently also preferred to be ignorant of whatever it was they were doing there.[7] To gloss over the doubt, frustration, and guilt, which dominated the reception of American soldiers by American civilians, the latter sentimentalized the former, while their government spent vastly more on defense than any other nation and salted the world with military bases.[8] Everyone seemed to agree to a willful blindness, taking it as a given that all international problems have a military solution, that the United States has the best prepared soldiers in the world, that a marine never leaves a buddy behind, that the army will make a man of you, and that anyone becomes a hero just by donning a uniform and making it through basic training.[9]

At the same time, America fancies itself a peace-loving nation and clings to the belief that soldiers hate war and go to great lengths to avoid it. We quote Douglas MacArthur telling West Point cadets that "the soldier above all other people prays for peace" and nod knowingly at William Tecumseh Sherman's proclamation that "War is hell." (We're less familiar with what came before that in his speech: "I am tired and sick of war. Its glory is all moonshine.") Yet, the United States has been involved in wars for more than half of the past fifty years (not counting off-the-record incursions into countries such as Angola, Somalia, and Haiti), and it is open to question whether all of those wars were unavoidable. In other words, someone has wanted war, albeit on other people's turf, and it isn't just the politicians.

An annual poll of military personnel conducted by the *Military Times* at the end of 2004 reported that 60 percent of its active-duty subscribers agreed that the United States was right to go to war in Iraq, and 84 percent believed that U.S. forces were somewhat or very likely to succeed, though most thought it would take the troops three to ten more years to do that.[10] Subscribers to *Military Times* tend to be older, more experienced, more career-oriented, and more likely to be officers, so it's unclear how many enlistees shared this faith in the mission. Jim Worlein, who joined IVAW after returning from Iraq, wrote in a blog post, "Few things get me going like someone saying, 'Well, you signed up for stuff like this.' . . . I volunteered to serve my country, not to throw my life away for nothing. That is how I felt the entire time I was in Iraq. There were no notions of some glorious idea of a mission."

Soldiers bellyache all the time, voicing their dissatisfaction by indirection or all-purpose sneers such as "bullshit." Only a very few turn complaint into defiance, fewer still into concerted resistance. No more than a small percentage of the American public takes part in active political protest at any given time, either, but in the military, the forces working against activism are particularly powerful. Service people are restricted in what they are permitted to say while in uniform and even more so in combat zones, where soldiers talk to the public through the filter of journalists, if at all. (Mandatory "media awareness" training before they're shipped out and censorship of blogs from the front don't do much for candor either.)

The military's core values of loyalty, obedience, and duty form a very effective buffer against dissent, discouraging people with military affiliations from expressing disaffection or doubt. "There's this invisible line," David Wilson, an army sergeant, e-mailed me from Kuwait as the war began. "If you cross it, you could end up washing a lot of dishes." Only the price is usually higher than dishpan hands. Dissidents are routinely ostracized by their peers or threatened with reprisals or dangerous assignments. They are seen as unreliable, and in a world where nothing matters more than having your buddy's back, no lapse is more unforgivable.

Those intense bonds, which the military relies on in combat, continue after people get out of uniform; even those who reject the military's mission often feel proud of their service and affiliation. "I grew up in the army," explains IVAW member Adrienne Kinne, a sergeant who enlisted in the army out of high school and got her education during her two terms of duty. Three years after leaving the service, she still sounds slightly amazed that she nearly reupped again, even after she decided the war was wrong.

Then there are the injuries, physical, psychological, and moral. Large numbers of soldiers return with their bodies and minds shattered, leaving them unable or unwilling to revisit their months in combat, as this kind of activism would compel them to do. Shame silences too. Best-selling memoirs may revel in the confessional mode, but people who have done or acquiesced to things they are deeply ashamed of aren't likely to call attention to their actions—or to dissent. When they get home, many Iraq vets are eager to stash their war memories away with their uniforms and get on with their civilian lives. Many don't have the time for political activism or the money to travel to protests.

Finally, so many soldiers are recruited when they are young and uninformed and don't count themselves part of the class that assumes its voice should be heard. "Military people feel their opinion doesn't matter," explained John Hustad, when he and a fellow army reservist, Todd Arena, posted a "To whom it should concern" letter on PunkPlanet.com as the war began. It read in part, "We were US citizens prior to our enlistment oath, since then we have become something greater and lesser, citizen-soldiers." Intended to make other GIs question their motives and actions, the letter concluded, "We ask you to stand up and act now. . . . Shake off your apathy and exercise your rights and duties as Americans to ensure a better future. Speak out, any way you know how and any way you can."[11]

The late historian Howard Zinn, a World War II veteran and patron saint of the GI rights movement, called war resistance "breaking out of the stranglehold the military has on one's mind." Veteran-activists are continually pressed to pinpoint a defining moment that broke that stranglehold, but most balk at that question. What they will describe instead is an uneasy awakening. They will tell you that it was gradual, confusing, and very, very hard.

Soon after Hoffman began speaking out, he started attracting a smattering of other disaffected vets around the country, who eventually came together to form IVAW. Unusual for openly opposing the Iraq War so soon after they returned home, IVAW's founding members were nonetheless typical of the troops who were fighting it. Alex Ryabov and Isaiah Pallos had been in Hoffman's marine unit, part of that discussion group, or "clique," as he labeled it for want of a better word. Pallos, a working-class kid from Ohio, had been stop-lossed and released from the marines along with Hoffman. Ryabov had immigrated from Ukraine to Brooklyn, New York, when he was seven. He was still active-duty, doing desert training in California when, according to Hoffman, "He called me up out of the blue and said, 'I don't know what you're doing, but I know you've got something cooking, and whatever it is, I want in.'" So after Ryabov got out of the marines, he was ready to join Hoffman in whatever he was cooking up.

Others were passed on to Hoffman, usually through the ever-resourceful Dave Cline. That's how he heard about Jimmy Massey, another combat veteran, who was also speaking publicly against the war. Massey, a North Carolinian, had made his career in the marines for eleven years, rising to staff sergeant and working as a recruiter before switching to combat duty and taking part in the invasion of Iraq. While fighting there, he questioned the rules of engagement, claiming to have told his commanding officer, "We're committing genocide." Diagnosed with depression and post-traumatic stress disorder (PTSD), he was medevacked back to the States, where he received an honorable medical discharge in December 2003. Early on, he went public with his antiwar stance, not an easy thing to do in a region that is home to one of the greatest concentrations of military installations in the country. Hoffman recalled Massey arriving at the Veterans For Peace convention, looking around and saying, "I'm home."

Massey had a flair for attracting press—and controversy—as he told detailed, disturbing stories with a lilting Carolina accent and well-timed pauses, stories about bullets to the heads of small children and unarmed Iraqi civilians killed at checkpoints, counting as many as thirty kills for his unit within a matter of days. In 2005, a *St. Louis Post-Dispatch* reporter, who had been embedded with another unit nearby, mounted a convincing case that Massey had fabricated or embellished his more incendiary charges.[12] Massey's struggle to substantiate the specifics undermined his credibility, but the essence of his stories was corroborated soon enough by other returning troops.[13]

One of those was Rob Sarra, a nine-year veteran of the marines. Six days into the invasion, he fired on an unarmed Iraqi woman who carried a white flag he had failed to see. It was a story he would repeat in speeches and interviews, as if to exorcize a ghost. (The woman died, though an official report determined it wasn't by Sarra's bullet.) Traumatized, he refused orders to fight, even as he continued on with his platoon to Baghdad. His subsequent request to transfer to a noncombat position was denied, as was a later bid for reenlistment, and he left the marines in April 2004. Sarra made his way to IVAW through Vietnam Veterans Against the War, which is based in Chicago, his hometown.[14]

Hoffman met Tim Goodrich, an air force veteran from California (by way of Buffalo, New York), on a two-day march from Dover Air Force Base to the White House to mark the first anniversary of the invasion. Goodrich had participated in an intensified bombing campaign over Iraq in the fall of 2002 at the time President Bush maintained that he was working through diplomatic channels. Goodrich was discharged shortly after the ground war began.

Diana Morrison was in Boston as a member of Veterans For Peace. She had joined the army in 1986, when she was seventeen, and served with the military police in Iraq for six months in 2003. Still in the California National Guard that August, she was only IVAW founding member who was active-duty at the time. "She went out on a limb," said Hoffman with admiration.

"Kelly is probably the most interesting story," he continued, recalling how Kelly Dougherty joined the group. "One or two weeks before Boston, I got an e-mail from her dad saying, 'My daughter is just back from Iraq.' He said, 'I'm going to bring her to Boston and I want her to join you guys when you start IVAW.' I get there and there's Sean and he's got Kelly and Kelly's kind of looking around, like, what's going on here? She kind of got drug into it kicking and screaming by her father."[15] Dougherty, who would become IVAW's first executive director, recalled that she was excited but nervous. She had been back from Iraq about five months and, without warning, her father had signed her up for the panel of Iraq vets speaking about their experiences, something she hadn't done before. She had enlisted in the Colorado National Guard in 1996 while still in high school under a buddy system, which allowed friends who joined at the same time to complete their basic and job training together. She trained as a medic on weekends, deployed to the Balkans, and was back studying at the University of Colorado in Colorado Springs when her unit got sent to Iraq to do patrols and convoy escorts near Nasiriyah. Dougherty wasn't pleased to be an MP rather than a medic, especially because she had opposed the war since before it began. She told the VFP audience that day that she had never had lofty aspirations about freeing the Iraqi people, though she thought many of her fellow soldiers hung onto that belief even after they knew it wasn't true because all the other reasons for the invasion had proved to be false.

Doughtery was then twenty-six, with big, dark eyes; short, unruly hair that she kept tucking behind her ear; and a deceptively diffident manner, especially in those first public appearances, when she smiled nervously and rushed her words. There was nothing tentative about her analysis or report, though, as she insisted that U.S. forces were not helping the Iraqis and could not possibly help, because they were "occupiers in bulletproof vests." Her story, one she would polish as she toured the country over the coming months, involved what happened on those convoy missions. She was assigned to guard vehicles, most of them contracted to Kellogg Brown and Root, that had broken down somewhere on the road. Often, after hours of standing around trying to look menacing, the soldiers were told to burn the trucks so the Iraqis wouldn't have access to whatever was on them, be it fuel or food. "I'm not proud of burning flatbed trucks filled with food while hungry Iraqis looked on. I'm not proud of burning ambulances," she told an interviewer some months later.[16]

By the time they got to Boston, none of the veterans were feeling much pride about their months in Iraq. Massey, Hoffman, Ryabov, and Morrison reported symptoms or diagnoses of PTSD, and all of the founders reiterated their need to find a haven with others who thought and felt as they did. "[For] anyone who has been in combat, there is nothing that compares to it and then you are plopped back into civilian life. It's like running at the speed of light, then suddenly just stopping," Morrison told a reporter on Veterans Day 2005. "Like most soldiers, you expect people to read your mind and know you just went through hell."[17]

"Returning soldiers always try to make it not a waste," Dave Cline told me matter-of-factly. He had probably said it many times before. I would guess that most people prefer not to waste their lives, but soldiers, fresh from proximity to death, may feel a particularly strong need to make their lives meaningful. Some do it by identifying with the military or joining veterans organizations or marching in parades, some by repudiating war and killing. Many of the young, recently returned veterans took advantage of their GI benefits and enrolled in college; many found succor in helping other veterans readjust to civilian life. Hoffman made plans.

With the combination of naïveté and arrogance required to start an ambitious national organization, he prevailed on the Philadelphia chapter of Veterans For Peace to raise money to fly the vets he had contacted to the convention. On his way to Boston, he visited a Web developer friend in New Jersey. They created a website and a logo, modeled on an old Vietnam Veterans Against the War design, of a down-turned rifle with a helmet atop and the outline of Iraq in the background. Meanwhile, Daniel Ellsberg, a VFP member, suggested the name, Iraq Veterans Against the War, as an echo of the older organization.

The board of Veterans For Peace met just before the convention started. Hoffman got on the agenda, presenting the brief mission statement he had drafted and asking them to sponsor IVAW as a project and allow it to piggyback on VFP's nonprofit status. Most of the board had never met him before, but, as Hoffman told it, "Dave Cline stood up and said, 'Listen, this is a no-brainer for us. This is what Vets for Peace is about. Those of us who are Vietnam veterans said when we were VVAW that when this happened again, we would step forward to these guys.' After Dave spoke, there were no questions asked. They said, 'Okay, you got it.'"

On Friday morning, the second day of the convention, the Iraq Veterans Sound Off workshop was held in a crowded, windowless room at Emerson College in downtown Boston. One by one, Hoffman, Dougherty, Morrison, Ryabov, Massey, and Goodrich talked about troops being inadequately equipped and trained. They described the futility of the mission and their frustration, embarrassment, and despair that they could offer so little to the people whose lives they were turning upside down. Often, the U.S. troops got in the Iraqis' way, said Morrison, "treating them like criminals in their own country." She held up a graceful hand to illustrate that the signal Americans use to mean "stop" is read by Iraqis as a gesture of greeting. She had just recently learned about that simple point of miscommunication, she said, long after it might have saved Iraqi lives.

Ryabov, whose family had left Ukraine shortly after the collapse of the Soviet Union, said that, in that country, when the government lied, the people knew what was going on, whereas in the United States, the government "tries to sweep things under the rug [and] convince people that they're part of these great causes and stuff to bring democracy to the rest of the world." And Massey, apologizing for being a long-winded southerner, undermined that demurral with the zinger, "I was trained to be a killer, and I loved my job."

The testimony of the six Iraq veterans was a litany of horrors and regrets, but also of determination to do better. For them, ending war was not one choice from a smorgasbord of causes, but *the* cause. When they volunteered for the military, they may have been among the last people of their generation to believe in duty and honor and the grand idea of America, but by the time they got to Boston, they were disillusioned with the pretexts and promises of their leaders, military and civilian. Political activism feeds on the energy of common purpose; it may also give meaning to experience or loss, and, especially important for these young veterans, it could return to them some sense of control over their lives. In putting their anger and resentment to use, they began to feel that they would accomplish something, as they had seldom felt in Iraq. "You could hear a pin drop," recalled Frank Corcoran, the older vet, who was in the audience for the Iraq Vets Sound Off. "I remember having to leave just to catch my breath."

And then it was Friday evening, time for the big announcement. The Great Hall, the second-floor meeting room in Faneuil Hall, is the kind of soaring public space that makes you want to be a better citizen. Designed by Charles Bullfinch, the architect of Federal-style elegance, it has tall windows, galleries on three sides, ornate brass sconces, a rostrum decorated with pilasters and busts of great men, and a podium carved of oak. The hall holds upward of eight hundred people, and that night it was nearly full. Someone played the guitar, someone sang, a Vietnam veteran in a wheelchair spoke, two city councilors presented a proclamation welcoming the vets, a member of the group 9/11 Families for a Peaceful Tomorrow talked about peace, a therapist talked about rape in the military, members of Military Families Speak Out held photo collages of the nine hundred U.S. war dead, while behind them, a woman dressed in colonial garb hoisted an American flag on a pole until she got tired and plopped it on the floor like a mop.

Finally, two and a half hours into the program, the five young veterans mounted the stage. Hoffman took the microphone and announced the launch of Iraq Veterans Against the War to a wall of applause. When it died down, he iterated the organization's three goals: Bring the troops home now, see that those who served receive the benefits promised them when they enlisted, and ensure that Iraq be rebuilt and its governance returned to its people. Those goals were honed over time and accomplished only sporadically, but they remained a remarkably consistent beacon since that first night when anything seemed possible.

Over the coming year, this tiny group multiplied. By September, 40 veterans had joined; by October, it was 60; and when IVAW met the following summer at another VFP convention, 137 members were on the books. Feeling their way, these newly minted activists would testify in public, commiserate in private, persuade over late-night beers, sometimes even speak from beyond the grave. *This is what happened; this is what matters*, they insisted to anyone who would listen. *Do something!* And as they challenged policy, refused orders, bore witness, collected injustices, risked arrest, reckoned the costs, and laid on a little harmony for their fellow whistlers in the dark, they came to realize that they were creating a political movement. They called it the new GI resistance.

⌘ Boston, Massachusetts, 28 February 2007 ⌘

The Smedleys are occupying John Kerry's Boston office. Or at least I think they are.

A smattering of posts on the online forum of the Smedley Butler Brigade, the Boston chapter of Veterans For Peace, have outlined the plan. It's part of something called the Occupation Project, a civil disobedience campaign aimed at getting members of Congress to pledge to vote against the $100 billion supplemental appropriation to fund a "surge" in U.S. troops in Iraq. The argument is that although a bill must be veto-proof to pass—an impossibility, given the current makeup of Congress—blocking the appropriation is within reach. Veterans For Peace has endorsed the project, and, as one of its most active chapters, the Smedleys are out in force, prepared to occupy politicians' offices and risk arrest, if that's what it takes.

Last week, the vets and other antiwar activists staged a sit-in at the office of Democratic Representative Ed Markey. As the group read the names of the war dead and rang a bell for each, Markey's staff welcomed them with coffee and doughnuts, and Markey agreed to sign the pledge. Buoyed by their success, they have decided to take on Kerry, who is particularly irksome to the Smedleys, because several of them knew him back when he was a fellow antiwarrior in Vietnam Veterans Against the War. Problem is, they're not likely to get to his office. The elevator has to be set to go to the tenth floor, where his office is, and the guard probably won't do that if they don't have an appointment. So the plan is to meet in the lobby and try to get some media play out of Kerry's refusal to meet with veterans.

It's ten o'clock on a crisp, late February morning, and I'm about a block from Kerry's office when I see five scruffy-looking men in winter jackets and caps walking toward me. "Stop," I say, "I'm coming to meet you. What happened?" Jesse Perrier, a videographer and Vietnam vet, takes charge of the report. Twelve Smedleys had a half-hour conference call yesterday with Kerry, who was in Washington, but he declined to sign the pledge, saying he was following a different strategy—Perrier dismisses this with a wave of his hand—so a bunch of them (twenty? twenty-five?) stood around this morning waiting for something to happen.

"I was ready to sleep there," announces Severyn Bruyn, a retired sociology professor, who did intelligence work in World War II. Weeks later, on the Smedley forum, Bruyn will suggest a silent parade of the war wounded past the White House, organized row by row: first the blind veterans with their white canes, followed by the veterans in wheelchairs, next the veterans without arms, then the veterans with brain injuries, then all the veterans who have been mistreated at VA hospitals, and on and on.

Like these men, I think it should be a no-brainer for Kerry to support their position: the moral high ground, a clear refutation of his flip-flop image and Swift Boat smears. But one of democracy's design flaws is that when people who challenge power get power, they stop challenging. Kerry has spoken against the war in Iraq, but he doesn't appear to be leading the charge to end it soon. "I pledged to myself long ago to be informed by Vietnam, not imprisoned by it," he would tell *Newsweek* later. But these vets haven't been able to compartmentalize as successfully, and anything less than total opposition to the war will not wash.

A few of them peel off toward Ted Kennedy's office, though it's not clear why, as he has already signaled that he will vote against the surge supplement. Three stand with me and talk, eager to expand on their philosophies.

"Okay," I say, trying to head off the lectures on the folly of the war. I've heard too many, and I'd guess that Kerry has too. "Why are you doing this?"

"You see the thousand-mile stare in their eyes," Perrier says of the soldiers returning from Iraq. Other vets recognize it and relive their own battles.

"Martin Luther King said you do it because it's the right thing to do," Bruyn reminds us. "Gandhi said you do it regardless of the consequences."

"The damn thing is so idiotic," concludes John Manheim, a Korea-era vet.

"Do you think you can be effective?" I ask.

"We can piss and moan and raise hell," Manheim answers with satisfaction. And off they go.

2

BOOTS ON THE GROUND

A good convention can be a high; the aftermath is something else. All those good ideas that get generated now need to be put into practice, and that's hard work. The Veterans For Peace had been through it before, but for the nascent Iraq Veterans Against the War, the challenge was figuring out just what this creature was that Michael Hoffman and company had birthed in Boston. Fortunately, they found two stalwart supporters to help: Amadee Braxton, a civilian activist, and veteran Frank Corcoran. When you return from a convention, says Corcoran, "You come back to reality. And then you get back to work and try to get going."

The first official headquarters of IVAW was a one-bedroom apartment Hoffman shared with his wife about a half-hour from Philadelphia. He supported himself with unemployment compensation and terminal-leave pay from the marines, and when that ran out, he worked at a Halloween store. He tried going back to school, but his PTSD interfered, so he channeled his considerable energy into IVAW, becoming its national coordinator and earning a princely $1,000 a month. Hoffman spent most of his time on the road, speaking, inspiring, and recruiting new members, which is where his talent lay. He wasn't much interested in the details of organizing, so some of the older vets started to look around for someone who was.

Enter Braxton, an independent filmmaker in her mid-thirties, who had been organizing for social justice for a couple of decades. She was between projects and casting about for part-time work when a friend introduced her to Hoffman. Braxton recalls, "At the time, I was seeking a meaningful way to express my frustration and anger about the fact that we were continuing in this war. A friend in New York involved in Vets For Peace said, there's this new vets organization. They really need an office and help thanking donors and getting situated. Maybe you can help them do that for a few months." "As usual, she didn't know what she was getting herself into," Hoffman says and laughs.

Braxton's first activity was finding space at the national office of the American Friends Service Committee, the Quaker-sponsored peace and justice organization. There, she shared a single desk with Hoffman and Corcoran, who had retired from teaching and was available to volunteer nearly full-time with IVAW. Hoffman had recruited Corcoran the morning after George W. Bush was reelected in 2004. Dismayed, Corcoran declared that he would have to leave the country, but Hoffman, who knew him from VFP meetings, had other plans. "You know Michael," Corcoran continues. "He said, 'You're not going anywhere, old man. We need you here.' And that's when he asked me [to help]."

Corcoran, then in his early fifties, speaks in a slightly hoarse and burry voice, dropping his g's and studding his sentences with "whoa!" and "man!" He enlisted in the marines at eighteen for want of something better to do: "Not an unusual story," he comments. He got sent to Vietnam in 1968, saw a lot of combat, got badly wounded. "They couldn't send me back [to Vietnam] because it took so long to fix me up." After the marines, he tried college, and when that didn't take, he worked with a street crew for the Philadelphia Electric Company. At twenty-eight, encouraged by his wife, he returned to school to become an elementary school teacher, a career he followed wholeheartedly for the next twenty years. He had two daughters, kept busy. Life was good, but he couldn't leave Vietnam behind. "I followed the classic path. I avoided anything to do with military vets for the next twenty years," he says, and then, in the next breath, acknowledges that the avoidance didn't work. "Jumping around, all tensed up in my stomach and having to go up into the mountains on the Fourth of July—like other vets."[1]

In the 1980s, he got involved in peace groups, hiding that he was a veteran until the United States starting bombing Iraq in the First Gulf War. "That blew it all apart. What happened to a lot of vets in 2003 happened to me in '91. That's when I found Vets For Peace and joined." With other members, he founded Project Hearts and Minds to bring medical supplies to Vietnam. He traveled to impoverished rural communities there on a few short trips, then spent a year in Saigon, volunteering with International Mission of Hope to help families adopting Vietnamese children. Corcoran's work in Vietnam gave him experience in managing a new organization and an understanding of how hard it is for veterans to evolve from warriors to peacemakers, both valuable assets to bring to IVAW then.

While Corcoran answered the phone and ran an ad hoc speakers bureau, Braxton got to work thanking donors, creating a filing system, and looking for money to fund the operation. "I did a lot of behind-the-scenes stuff, and Amadee was the brains of the outfit," Corcoran says. "No Amadee Braxton, no IVAW. As it exists, Amadee was responsible for it." By this time, they were up to about sixty members, with more joining weekly. Hoffman was the East Coast operation; Tim Goodrich covered the West Coast; and Jimmy Massey, Rob Sarra, and Kelly Dougherty spoke about their new organization to whomever would listen. Braxton says, "Basically the criteria for membership at that point was a handshake and maybe to exchange e-mails and phone numbers." So she came up with a membership form that made members a little easier to track. Soon, she was working a part-time, sixty-hour-a-week job; Corcoran was in the office most days; two other staff members were brought on; and Hoffman dropped by when he wasn't on the road.

"We pretty much ended up taking over the entire office," Hoffman recalls. "The Quaker work ethic—kind of quiet, studious—and then there's us. They kept giving us bigger offices until we realized that we were getting moved farther away from everyone else." They eventually landed in the basement near the printing room, where they could make all the noise they wanted.

For all the hubbub, IVAW was a very small group of recently returned veterans, who spoke and marched and operated as a kind of rent-a-vet service for any antiwar activity needing a little battle cred. Telling their stories was their primary activity. Historian Paul Cohen, speaking about China, points out that in moments of unresolved crises, cultures often try to find stories from their past that resonate in the present, offering a model of either the right spirit or a desired outcome.[2] For the United States, mired in an occupation of Iraq, the Vietnam War was the obvious story-from-the-past, but it is a story of failure on multiple levels. The success story coming out of Vietnam was of GIs organizing against the war and joining with civilian activists to hasten its end. The Iraq vets may have been determined to create their own movement, but the right story for them, the one that prefigured and helped explain their trajectory more often than they may have cared to recognize, is what happened thirty-five years earlier

It's a truism that generals fight the last war, focusing on strategies that were important in the past rather than the present; as war in Iraq loomed, the American public seemed to be fighting the last antiwar movement. The prevailing image of Vietnam veterans returning to the States is one of hostile civilian protesters squaring off against alienated grunts. Antiwar activists still bring up the probably apocryphal story of demonstrators spitting on returning soldiers, mostly to discredit it, but the division still haunts.[3] It may haunt no one more than the Vietnam veterans themselves. So, they appreciated it when the civilian campaign to stop the invasion of Iraq made a point of reaching out to them. Among the first to respond were those who had fueled that earlier antiwar movement, making use of their status as veterans to stage the kind of highly visible and dramatic protests that have been a part of American life since the Boston Tea Party.

David S. Meyer, a political scientist who studies political protest movements, argues that the Constitution and Bill of Rights were intended to institutionalize dissent. The theory was that it is better for a country to have conflict within its government than revolution against it. However, a central goal of protest is to keep opponents off-balance and uncertain about what will happen next, so while the capacity to absorb and blunt dissent may be the genius of American democracy, it also tends to push political movements toward ever more radical actions in a bid for attention to their claims. Political change comes about through an unpredictable mix of radical demands, moderate compromises, and a long, hard slog (the Vietnam and Iraq GI resistance movements both struggled to find the right balance), but the change begins when someone or something captures the public imagination. Meyer quotes Samuel Adams as saying, "It does not require a majority to prevail, but rather an irate, tireless minority keen to set brush fires in people's minds."[4]

About three years into the Vietnam War, certain irate veterans began to fill that role, and soon brush fires also burned in the minds of active-duty GIs fighting in Southeast Asia. By 1969, there was unprecedented, open rebellion from the rank and file; officers could no longer depend on their orders being carried out; and the United States faced the most prolonged and organized GI resistance it had known.

The United States has a history of sporadic veteran involvement in political movements, from Shays' Rebellion after the Revolutionary War up through the nuclear freeze movement in the mid-twentieth century.[5] In 1932, in what came to be known as the Bonus March, some seventeen thousand jobless World War I veterans and their families set up encampments in Washington and demanded immediate payment of certificates they had been given as bonuses for their service. (President Herbert Hoover sent in General Douglas MacArthur, who brought in the infantry, the cavalry, and six tanks to remove them brutally.) In January 1946, soldiers eager to return home from World War II rioted on overseas military bases to protest delays in their demobilization. This was the culmination of the "Bring 'Em Home" movement, in which GIs and their families pressured politicians to do just that through petitions, letter-writing campaigns, and tugs at the heartstrings to "bring back daddy."[6] The Vietnam GI resistance movement, however, was something different. It focused on ending a war, and that was unprecedented in America.

During the Vietnam War, it was widely assumed that GI resistance was led and fed by an elite; that is, middle-class college graduates who had been drafted. The army published two studies in 1971 and 1972, which divided resistance within the military into acts of dissidence and acts of disobedience. Dissidence included publishing underground newspapers, visiting coffeehouses, and joining such protests as "Armed Farces Day," a spoof of the militaristic pomp of Armed Forces Day.[7] In other words, dissidence was political activism. Disobedience ranged from refusing to obey orders to sabotaging equipment—that is, resistance or rebellion. ("Combat avoidance," widely practiced in both Vietnam and Iraq, falls somewhere in between.) The studies found that the rebels came from lower-income backgrounds and had less education than the dissidents. That shouldn't have been surprising; people with good prospects for prospering within the economic system are more likely to push for change through the political system. What did come as a surprise, at least to army officials, was the finding that the dissidents were more likely to be enlisted men than draftees.[8] That discovery, and maybe the attendant surprise, would find echoes three decades later in IVAW.

Many of those dissidents were active in Vietnam Veterans Against the War (VVAW), an organization that began in 1967 and still exists in much-truncated form. It was an active and coherent organization for only about two years, however, starting around the time of the November 1969 antiwar march on Washington, known as the Moratorium, and more or less imploding late in 1971. A majority of Americans had turned against the Vietnam War about two years before the Moratorium, when the Tet offensive had shown the war to be essentially unwinnable, and the march attracted about a half-million people in a highly effective protest.

In its early days, VVAW invested heavily in partisan politics, supporting Eugene McCarthy's failed 1968 presidential bid, and then foundering after demonstrations at the Democratic National Convention in Chicago that summer turned violent. About a year later, VVAW regrouped and reoriented itself to serve veterans: providing information on resistance, lobbying for GI rights and benefits, organizing on campuses, and running a recruiting ad in the February 1970 issue of *Playboy*, which brought in thousands of new members. (It was a very male organization.)

According to Gerald Nicosia's history of the Vietnam veterans resistance movement, *Home to War*, VVAW originally saw itself as a civilian, educational organization. It wrote into its charter that it would disband when the war ended, but its members' veteran status gave them special legitimacy and put VVAW in the spotlight. Membership grew quickly: six hundred in April 1970, more than two thousand by that fall, and at its peak, some twenty-five thousand on the rolls, including five thousand service members in Vietnam. This was the heyday of the civil rights, feminist, and gay liberation movements, all taking their demands for social and economic equality to the streets, and the veterans were in the thick of it. They staged attention-grabbing, emotionally charged events, such as Operation RAW, or Rapid American Withdrawal. Unfolding over Labor Day weekend in 1970, RAW was a hard-hitting piece of street theater, in which about two hundred vets, dressed in combat fatigues and armed with toy rifles, marched through towns between Morristown, New Jersey, and Valley Forge, Pennsylvania, simulating the search-and-destroy missions they had undertaken in Vietnam.

A few months later, VVAW convened the first Winter Soldier investigation, distilling the name from Thomas Paine's praise for soldiers who stood by their country in its darkest hours. From 31 January to 2 February in 1971, at the Howard Johnson's New Center Motor Lodge in downtown Detroit, more than one hundred veterans testified about the transgressions they had witnessed or committed as combatants in Vietnam. As the Iraq vets would do thirty-seven years later, they insisted that the problems were systemic. They were not the isolated actions of a few "bad apples" (the language didn't change much over the years), but a consequence of the criminal underpinning of the war. Another five hundred to seven hundred veterans came to hear the testimony, many joining the antiwar movement for the first time. The mainstream press beyond the Midwest ignored them all. But, again like the Iraq veterans, these testifiers aimed their stories and confessions at active-duty troops and fellow vets, and for them, the message carried across the country.[9] Membership ballooned to about twelve thousand.

VVAW was on a roll. That April, it followed up Winter Soldier with Dewey Canyon III, a five-day protest in Washington, where some 1,200 veterans and supporters camped out on the National Mall.[10] Dewey Canyon III may be remembered today primarily as the launching pad for John Kerry's political career, because it was during that week that he demanded of the Senate Foreign Relations Committee, "How do you ask a man to be the last man to die for a mistake?" But it was also a week crammed with marches, petitions, lobbying, press conferences, guerrilla theater, provocations, arrests, ceremonies honoring the dead, and down-to-the-wire negotiations over whether the government would evict the veterans from the Mall by force. (The Nixon administration backed down, though not before riling the courts, Congress, and the local police, and the vets stayed put, entertained by a road company of the musical *Hair*.)

Dewey Canyon III's grand finale was the returning of medals, an angry, sad, potent ritual that unfolded over a couple of hours on 23 April 1971. Hunter S. Thompson would describe it as "perhaps the most eloquent anti-war statement ever made in this country,"[11] and years later, Barry Romo, an early VVAW organizer, would highlight its significance by pointing out that "for working-class people, putting on a uniform and getting a medal really is the highlight of your life. When you get buried, you're supposed to have medals."[12]

Winston Warfield, a member of VVAW's Philadelphia chapter with a year in Vietnam under his belt, lined up that day along with some eight hundred other veterans waiting their turn to hurl the medals they had earned over a six-foot-high fence made of chicken wire and wood, which had been erected at the base of the Capitol steps to keep the protesters out. "That was an extremely moving thing to be involved in," he says. "I was struck by how emotionally devastated the guys were who were throwing away their medals. To me it was a big thing because I was still kind of getting acclimated to radical movement politics." Over the fence went Warfield's medals, including a bronze star. "These were guys who had lost eyes, arms, legs and had sacrificed a tremendous amount, and they were sobbing. I still remember that. The pile of medals just grew higher and deeper behind the fence."

Warfield, a longtime member of Veterans For Peace, is in his early sixties when we first meet. He is tall and square-chinned, with salt-and-pepper hair and mustache, greenish eyes behind gold-rimmed glasses, the hint of a belly, and a habit of calling all veterans "brother" or "sister." Four decades after he lobbed his medals over that fence, he sits on his front porch in Dorchester, Massachusetts, as a summer day lingers to a close, greeting neighbors as they walk dogs or return from work. He is a computer program analyst who coaches Little League for his two sons and who once described himself to me as "an all-American antiwar protester."

Warfield grew up in Tucson, enlisting in the army after two troublesome years of college. "I joined for this raft of confused reasons," he explains. "One of the reasons was that they were drafting a huge number of individuals at that time. If you did not have a college deferment, you were going to get drafted, so one of the notions was, if you joined, you would have more choice." This was referred to as "draft-induced enlistment," a common strategy that didn't always pan out as the enlistee hoped. Opting for the corps of engineers, Warfield worked as a mapmaker from 1968 to 1969 in a tactical operations center at the brigade level in Vietnam's Quang Tri province, about twelve miles south of the demilitarized zone.

As with the IVAWs, Warfield's views on the Vietnam War and his place within it evolved gradually. "I do remember starting to have questions about Vietnam while I was Stateside in the army before I went," he says. This was 1967, when debate about the legitimacy of the war was still limited and, although he was aware of antiwar activity, he wasn't involved. By the time he got to Fort Carson in Colorado for training, he was growing more troubled. "At that point we knew we were all going. I even at one point thought about refusing to go and going to the chaplain, but my buddies talked me out of it. So I did not have the courage of my convictions, doing what a lot of other guys did. I have a lot of respect for them. I also had mixed feelings like everybody does in the military. I didn't think it was right for me to stay home while other people had to go. That's a powerful incentive in the military: you feel guilty about insulating yourself from risk when others can't."

Warfield's misgivings heightened when he got to Vietnam and saw the ravages of twenty years of war. They grew more acute as he read about the radical politics of Malcolm X and listened to the psychedelic rock of Jimi Hendrix. "There was a cultural rift in the military that was characterized by what you put inside yourself to kill the pain and what you listened to," he says. "I was with the dopers." He avoided getting high on guard duty or outside the wire because it was dangerous, but he knew a lot of guys who were perpetually stoned in an attempt to dull their fear and horror. Warfield, instead, got radical. "I hung out with the black soldiers. The fact that you were a white guy hanging out with black guys was a political statement in itself." That was particularly true in the rear, he notes, where racism was ugly and sharp.[13] "They were all very radical, very antimilitary, and we all kind of adopted that attitude." Warfield and his pals let their hair grow long, refused to salute officers, shrugged off threats of punishment. "What are they gonna do, send us to 'Nam?" he says, quoting a common taunt. Others went further: in his unit, he knew of two instances of fragging, a grenade attack, usually by an enlisted man, against an officer.[14]

Warfield got involved with VVAW after he was discharged and back at college. "That was an organization that scared the crap out of the government," he says, boasting that Richard Nixon called VVAW the single most dangerous group in the United States. (It was Attorney General John Mitchell who made that charge, but former VVAW members like to remember it as Nixon, probably because that makes a better story.) As an organization, VVAW never really threatened the government, but its members had been hardened by their time in Vietnam to the point where they were pretty much immune to both rewards and punishments, making them hard to control and potentially dangerous.

Ironically, the success of Dewey Canyon III exposed the schisms within VVAW, and over the next several months, the organization began to unravel. A core group kept it alive, but GI resistance failed to cohere as a national movement. Infighting—ideological, personal, and racial—highlighted the difficulty of balancing political goals with antiauthoritarian anger. The group struggled to maintain discipline and focus and to keep members engaged in the mundane business of movement-building between major actions, but cadres hardened and bickered, leaders grew weary, members went rogue, and government infiltrators capitalized on the turmoil to stir up more trouble. Meanwhile, funding was drying up, members were moving on to other ambitions, national politics and the nature of the war were shifting, and the organization couldn't adapt to these changes quickly enough. Decades later, IVAW would grapple with the same, nearly crippling issues.

Nonetheless, VVAW had an impact. Like IVAW, it brought to the antiwar movement a moral authority no other group could equal. Though it didn't end the Vietnam War single-handedly, it did a lot to subvert the military mission, and, on a practical level, that war ended because enough soldiers refused to fight. Assessing VVAW and the GI resistance of his day, Warfield weighs the balance. "I don't want to take too much credit because the civilian antiwar movement was big and huge and powerful in those days. The counterculture aspect of it was very important. There was a de facto mass boycott of established mores and cultural values. It's not like that government was afraid that we were going to stage a military coup. What they were afraid of was, by that point in time, resistance within the military was so strong that they couldn't use the military against us."

He cites a story, corroborated by several historians, which made its way through the encampment during Dewey Canyon III. The government had to ditch plans to send soldiers from Fort Bragg to remove the veterans from the National Mall because so many of the active-duty soldiers assigned to that task refused orders to evict their brothers. A group of them showed up on the Mall to assure the vets that trucks from the base weren't going anywhere because they had poured sand into their gas tanks.[15] "There were some very significant things going on in the military," Warfield continues. "That was more important than whether VVAW was bad or not. The military does not succeed unless it has fighting spirit, particularly if it's up against a powerful foe. The American military in Vietnam lost its fighting spirit."

In the end, though, the most significant effect of the GI resistance movements, then and now, is on the resisters themselves. It allows them to turn the largely negative experience of war and their role in it into a set of positive values and goals to replace the warrior values they ultimately shed. VVAW also created a generation of politically active and politically savvy citizens with direct knowledge and understanding of the military and war and an abiding commitment to passing that insight on.

Comparisons between VVAW and IVAW are inevitable, given that the war in Vietnam was the last U.S. conflict that lasted long enough for a significant GI resistance to emerge. "Same as Vietnam only with more sand," was Warfield's summation of the Iraq War. Yet, in *The Turning: A History of Vietnam Veterans Against the War*, Andrew E. Hunt observes, "VVAW was simultaneously unique and a product of the times."[16] The same can be said of IVAW, which is why, for all the parallels, the two organizations diverge in significant ways.

VVAW didn't begin to get organized until the Vietnam War was nearly three years old, whereas IVAW was launched sixteen months into the Iraq War. Troop strength in Vietnam peaked at nearly 543,500, and a total of about 3.5 million U.S. servicepeople served in Southeast Asia during the eleven years of the Vietnam War.[17] In contrast, there were never more than about 160,000 U.S. troops in Iraq at a given time, and many served multiple tours of increasing length.[18] Slightly more than fifty-eight thousand American troops died in the Vietnam War between 1959 and 1975, nearly thirteen times the number who died in Iraq. Something the two wars do share, however, is the absence of accurate counts of civilians killed as "collateral damage."

During the Vietnam War, GIs spent one year in-country, which meant that individuals rotated in and out at different times, rather than in intact units. When the military switched to volunteers, it addressed the lack of cohesion by training and deploying units together, so that, like Michael Hoffman, many soldiers and marines went to Iraq despite misgivings because, if they didn't go, someone else—often someone they knew—would have to go in their stead. Of course, the biggest difference in the way the wars were staffed was the draft, which loomed over young American men during most of the war in Vietnam.[19] Of the troops who served there, about a third were conscripts, and uncounted others were draft-induced enlistees like Warfield. Conversely, the Iraq War was fought by professional soldiers who joined the military voluntarily. It may be, as critics charge, that recruiting tactics targeting the poor and uninformed created an economic draft and that stop-loss amounted to a backdoor draft. (David Cortright, who compiled probably the most comprehensive account of GI resistance during the Vietnam War, later observed that soldiers fighting in that war couldn't wait to get out of the army, whereas soldiers fighting in Iraq couldn't afford to leave.[20]) Nonetheless, today's military is made up of people who chose at one point and for whatever reasons to be there.

According to Cortright, "The GI movement had always been primarily a movement of enlistees," but the Vietnam and Iraq GI movements evolved differently for a number of reasons.[21] Greater troop strength in Vietnam meant that VVAW had a vastly larger pool of veterans to draw on for members than IVAW; the draft kept soldiers circulating through civilian society during Vietnam, making it more likely that Americans would come in contact with the people fighting their wars; the ethos of a volunteer army made it harder for Iraq vets to turn their backs on the military and, when they did, ensured that their conversion would be even more intense.

In the years since the Vietnam War, civil society also changed. The prevalence of new technologies has made widespread dissemination of images, information, misinformation, and opinion almost instantaneous. As any activist knows, this is a mixed blessing, offering unprecedented tools for organizing on one hand and creating an increasingly competitive market for attention on the other. That political activism is now a marketplace, where brand recognition triumphs, speaks volumes. Hardly a week goes by without a march for or against something, making it hard to attract the notice of politicians, the news media, or the public. (Maybe this isn't all that different from 1971, when a VVAW member who contacted the *Washington Post* about covering Dewey Canyon III was directed to the Style section of the paper.[22])

So the most obvious difference may be that, while the government viewed the Vietnam antiwar movement as a threat and retaliated against VVAW with spies, agents provocateur, and dirty tricks, when it came to the Iraq antiwar movement, what was notable about the Bush administration was its lack of response.[23] Those in power tend to view protesters less as engaged citizens than as unruly mobs and often respond by cracking down on them, or at least trying to undermine their credibility. Yet on 15 and 16 February 2003, in what was likely the largest political protest in history, at least six million people took to the streets of hundreds of cities around the world to oppose a military invasion of Iraq—and the U.S. government thumbed its nose at them all.[24]

Different wars, different armies, different times. Still, IVAW and VVAW echo each other in ways that can make it seem as if they were following the same script. The newer veterans could have saved themselves some heartache by reading a few scenes ahead, but maybe organizations like VVAW and IVAW—composed mostly of young, newly politicized people drawn to extreme measures and organizing around opposition to a specific war—are meant to have a cyclical and limited lifespan. They arrive as a flash of lightning, burn brightly for a year or two, then fade as events overtake them or public sentiment catches up. Their impact during their glory days is apparent, if only because they remind civilians vividly that there are costs to war. Their lasting influence takes much longer to sort out.

Sometimes the fire isn't out, but merely banked. When Veterans For Peace began in 1985, it recognized that stopping a war is different from protecting peace. "Our collective experience tells us wars are easy to start and hard to stop and that those hurt are often the innocent," reads the organization's official statement. This more expansive goal may be a reason for its longevity. In 2005, twenty years after it began, VFP's membership stood at about 6,500 veterans from as far back as the Spanish Civil War. Dedicated to nonviolence and democratic process (the latter sometimes as elusive as lasting peace), VFP organized much of its activity through some 120 independent chapters around the country, including one in a California prison; it also worked on national campaigns and was officially represented at the United Nations. Over the years, members had taught, lobbied, counter-recruited, raised money, raised hell, launched projects to rebuild Vietnam, and engaged in campaigns aimed at limiting interference in Central American politics, closing the infamous School of the Americas, getting the U.S. Navy out of Vieques, and exposing the effects of Agent Orange and depleted uranium.

The organization grew from a core group of Boston veterans who had cut their political teeth on the GI resistance during Vietnam and who coalesced around opposition to the Reagan administration's Central America policies in the 1980s.[25] They called themselves the Smedley Butler Brigade. Shortly after the Smedleys formed, Jerry Genesio, a former marine who had lost a brother in Vietnam, proposed a working relationship between the three hundred–some Smedley veterans and three hundred–some other veterans in northern New England. With his wife and three other vets, he organized Veterans For Peace. An office was set up in Portland, Maine, where it remained until 1995, when it moved to Washington, DC.

A few years later, Lee Vander Laan volunteered to serve as executive director. Vander Laan, who works in the computer industry, had been a radio specialist with the air force in Vietnam. In an e-mail about those early days, he wrote, "I was on the Board of Directors at the time, and was increasingly concerned that VFP was going down the tubes, as they say. The treasury was very sparse, and the president reminded the board that it was their fiduciary responsibility to carry VFP, if it fell into arrears. There was going to be a vote to determine whether or not to close VFP." To forestall that eventuality, Vander Laan took charge, commuting between Boston and Washington for about a year to represent the organization and serve the membership, which was then about 1,200 veterans and supporters.

In the summer of 2001, the board voted to move the operation to St. Louis, where Woody Powell, a Korea-era air force veteran, would take over as executive director. Vander Laan loaded the contents of the VFP office onto a U-Haul and drove it to St. Louis, arriving on Sunday, 9 September 2001. "The truck was unloaded and the entire office set up over the next day or two," his e-mail continued. "As Woody and I arrived at the office on Tuesday, September 11, we received a call from Woody's wife, Joan. She said to turn on the TV. We both saw the second tower explode from the aircraft we witnessed flying into it." They immediately put out a press release with a statement from the VFP board and followed it up with a series of national ads. The first, pursued with (and mostly financed by) the Japan-based Global Peace Campaign, appeared in the *New York Times* and referred to the 2001 military campaign in Afghanistan and read, "Stop the Bombing to Save a People"—an echo of the pretext for destroying hamlets in Vietnam.

VFP found renewed purpose and a burgeoning membership as hostilities heated up in the Middle East, so it was prepared to jump-start the campaign to stop the invasion of Iraq.[26] Having spent the years since Vietnam butting up against the caprices of power, these older activist-vets had seen how a large enough number of people taking to the streets could alter history. "After Vietnam, people came home, got tired, thought we won't do this again," said Gulf War veteran Michael McPhearson, VFP's executive director from 2005 to 2010. "But we did do it again. This time we can't go home."

From the earliest days, VFP was instrumental in IVAW's development, helping with funding, supporting chapters and individual members, collaborating on projects, and offering perspective. As IVAW was setting up shop, the psychiatrist Robert J. Lifton, who had organized rap groups for Vietnam vets in the 1970s, wrote, "Generational transmission of war

experience has always had enormous psychological importance. . . .
Above all, war survivors hunger for meaning. . . . In this quest for
understanding, it turns out that Iraq veterans have much in common
with their older compatriots who fought in Vietnam."[27] Or, as Barry
Romo of VVAW put it during IVAW's Winter Soldier hearings, "What
you give a generation when we're dead is the organization that you leave
behind."

The antiwar veterans, old and young, recognized this and spoke
often and movingly about the bonds they shared, but day-to-day
interactions could be less harmonious, especially as IVAW grew in size
and confidence. Some of the differences were stylistic: aging hippies
singing plaintive ballads didn't cut it with the Rage Against the Machine
generation. Other tensions—how to support without interfering, or how
to claim independence without disrespect—mirrored conflicts between
anxious parents and offspring setting out on their own. VFP provided an
example of ongoing resistance that the younger veterans both emulated
and pushed against. At times, it was hard to know which was more
productive.

"We're not antiwar, we're pro-peace," Ken Farr insisted in 2005, just after
the moment of silence for all victims of war which begins each meeting of the Smedley Butler Brigade. The brigade, the Boston chapter of
Veterans For Peace, took its name in honor of Major-General Smedley
Darlington Butler, whose thirty-four years in the marine corps took him
to all the hotspots of the early twentieth century: China during the Boxer
Rebellion, and Honduras, Nicaragua, Haiti, and Mexico during their uprisings. In another loop of history, he would write that he helped make
Mexico and China safe for American oil interests.[28] At the time of his
death in 1940, he was the most decorated marine in U.S. history. (Maybe
equally important, he created the first marine football team.)

Then, in retirement, Butler did an about-face and became a staunch
anti-interventionist. In 1933, the year after he visited the Bonus Marchers'
encampment in Washington to show his support, he toured the country
to tell about his conversion in blunt and highly quotable language. He
had been well rewarded, he said, as "a racketeer, a gangster for capitalism
. . . who could have given Al Capone a few hints."[29] He felt he had also
been a dupe. "Like all the members of the military profession, I never had
a thought of my own until I left the service. My mental faculties remained

in suspended animation while I obeyed the orders of higher-ups. This is typical with everyone in the military service."[30] His short book, *War Is a Racket*, was published a couple of years later, and every Smedley quotes from it at the drop of a hat: "War is a racket. It is conducted for the benefit of the very few, at the expense of the very many."[31] Warfield, one of the brigade's earliest members, says, "General Smedley Butler had a similar reawakening as we have had." How could the Smedley veterans not love him?

Shortly after it began in 1985, the Smedley Brigade undertook its first major action: a peace convoy to Nicaragua. The point, says Warfield, was "to dramatize that there were war veterans who were against what Reagan was doing to people in Central America. Even if we weren't doing it directly, it was the same as we were in Vietnam." Dramatize they did. After the Boston vets hatched the idea, word of the convoy raced across the country. Within a few months, organizers had collected 140 tons of food, medical supplies, and clothing for the Nicaraguan people, who had been caught in a civil war for nearly a decade. Workers in Maine gave oats; the city of Newton, Massachusetts, gave a school bus; the Robert Kennedy Foundation gave money; someone donated a dentist chair; and someone else contributed four dozen baseballs. Convinced that the government had planted operatives, but convinced also that they were doing nothing wrong, the veterans put the moles to work loading supplies and painting the slogan "Feed the children, not the war" on banners and vehicles.

Most of the goods were shipped ahead, but about thirty tons were loaded onto thirty-seven buses, trucks, vans, and cars, and on 21 May 1998, a group of veterans, fifteen Smedleys among them, set off from northern Maine with friends and family members on a 2,500-mile journey to Managua, Nicaragua. A couple of weeks later, they met up in Austin with three other convoys from across the country and headed for the Mexican border. Warfield reports that the convoy was harassed "by a group of heavies trying to break it up," but twenty years on, Smedleys still get a kick out of reimagining all those high-adrenaline Santas trucking down the highway with banners flapping, as they carried Christmas in June to the people of Nicaragua.

When they got to the border at Laredo, U.S. customs officials stopped them. The Reagan administration had planted false stories in Texas newspapers claiming that the veterans were smuggling antiaircraft and other weapons to insurgents in Central America. When Representative Mickey Leland visited the encampment to inspect the vehicles and reported back that they were "clean," the government objected that the veterans' plan to donate the vehicles to Nicaragua violated a 1985 export ban. Some trucks were impounded, and some veterans were arrested. Others headed to Washington to lobby for the convoy's release, while others stayed in Texas and found different crossings, where they slipped across the border unimpeded. Truckers, many of them veterans themselves, honked their horns in raucous support, newspapers wrote sympathetic editorials, and, overnight, what had been a humanitarian mission ballooned into a political protest. By the time what remained of the convoy got to Managua the following month, another 300 tons of supplies had been donated.[32]

The convoy was the kind of grand gesture the Smedleys like and the IVAW vets wanted to emulate, but for a while afterward, the group went dormant. "We're a brigade," explained Warfield. "A brigade by definition is something that comes together out of necessity and when that necessity is gone, it shrinks. So when there wasn't a need, we just went back to our everyday lives. But when there's a need, we feel disturbed, upset, the PTSD starts haunting us again, which started up right away when Gulf War One exploded. That's when we started making trouble in Boston again. We tacked ourselves onto the end of the Veterans Day parade and made a big stink. We did that every year and pissed off all the flag wavers. We established a new style where we do antiwar military cadences and response, thanks to the creativity and organizing."

Like VVAW earlier, Veterans For Peace and IVAW took the traditions of war and refashioned them into traditions of peace. One such tradition was the military cadence, the call-and-response soldiers sing while marching in formation, which the Smedleys and the IVAWs reworked for their own purposes. "They wave the flag when you attack/When you come home, they turn their back/Sound off/One, two . . . ," Warfield singsongs. "And the crowd loved it. That's our style."

The crowd may have loved it, but the parade organizers didn't. The Smedleys' petitions to the Boston chapter of the American Legion to carry the Veterans For Peace banner and antiwar signs in the Veterans Day parade were turned down consistently from 2003 on. They marched anyway, bringing up the rear behind the street sweepers, and when the parade was cancelled in 2005, purportedly for lack of an audience, they took credit. "The American Legion does not want us to be in the parade, so they canceled it," Tony Flaherty, a retired navy lieutenant, boasted to the *Boston Globe* on behalf of the Smedleys. "No one wants to hear about peace."[33]

Flaherty's real crusade, however, is to get the Smedleys into the Saint Patrick's Day parade, the second-largest in the country, which oompahs its way through his native South Boston every March 17. The organizers— "pet vets," he calls them dismissively—are his nemesis. At seventy-six when we meet in 2007, Flaherty is Irish-handsome, a short, trim, bantam rooster, with curly, steel-grey hair and very blue eyes made bluer by tinted, rimless glasses. His speech is pure Southie, with its stretched vowels and swaddled r's, his gestures expansive for a small man. He flings his arms open and upward, grabs at my elbow to hold my attention, and gives quick barks of unamused laughter when he's uncomfortable. By turns dyspeptic, despairing, and determined, he's an embodiment of the implacability of these older veterans who think the world is a mess but can't quite stop trying to make it better.

"Yesterday, I could have just jumped off the top of a building a couple of times," Flaherty announces over lunch as a sweet spring breeze wafts in from the harbor. He repeats that he's the wrong person to talk to, that he's too depressing, that it's too late for an antiwar movement, that Noam Chomsky is right when he claims that 80 percent of the population is gripped by calculated ignorance and the other 20 percent are pimps. "I'm not good at macro," he says. What he is good at, whether he chooses to acknowledge it or not, is building community and crafting strategy. He cofounded South Boston Residents for Peace, remains one of the Smedley Brigade's most committed members, and logs countless hours pursuing meetings with city officials, writing letters to editors, and protesting political perfidy. He is what people who don't want to deal with his complaints call a crank. But recognizing that parades are nothing if not symbolic, he has solid reasons for demanding that the Smedleys and other peace groups get to walk alongside the mounted police, military color guards, and JROTC marching bands.[34]

Flaherty describes himself as a child of South Boston, raised by Irish immigrants with "a magnificent sense of justice" and a penchant for fighting over politics at the kitchen table. He enlisted in the navy after high school in 1949. "I was working six days a week for $19. I knew there's got to be something more than this," he recalls. But he didn't join up just for the paycheck. "We were injected with God and country. We had John Wayne. My father was in the service. We had gone through the demonization of Germany and the Nazis. I thought I was saving the world. I was saving my sister, I was saving you women from being raped by the communists. And saving our country. The bullshit. We believed that."

In his twenty-five years with the navy, he rose through the enlisted ranks, got his commission as a lieutenant, and was decorated for combat service in Vietnam, where he took men and supplies upriver in I Corps. "I was in Vietnam when the protests started. Our younger kids would mutiny—that you don't hear much about. We had an officer on deck pistol-whipped to death on Christmas Eve. We disarmed all of our corps once because of the uprisings we had with the black soldiers. We were having racial revolution. They painted those kids coming back [from Vietnam] as druggies and everything else. I had two hundred kids, they were all college, they were magnificent. Then they started fraggin' us. You couldn't walk the ships to get to our carriers." Flaherty responded by staying drunk a good half of the time.

One day in 1969, he was walking along the Cau Viet River near the demilitarized zone. "I saw this girl, maybe about ten, a little bit older. She was carrying a baby, she had a little kid holding onto her leg, he had a crutch, and another little child holding onto her. And I looked. How long, I don't even know because it was the first time ever that I saw a Vietnamese as a human being. I said, 'Holy Mary, mother of God, I've got five children myself, what the fuck am I doing?' Nothing happened. Didn't change things," he concludes, then pauses to reassess. "It did change something. It probably began to change me."

That image continues to haunt Flaherty. He returned from Vietnam feeling alienated and abandoned and kept drinking heavily until he retired from the navy in 1974. Finally, he had a breakdown and was hospitalized. "I had no understanding of what they say is PTSD. I would be in these therapy sessions and I'd be screaming, and they'd say, 'Well, Tony, you're angry.' 'Waddya mean, I'm angry?'" he shouts in demonstration. To admit to pain and remorse was to be weak, not an officer, not a leader, not a man. It's a lesson today's soldiers were to take to heart too, sometimes with tragic consequences. "I tried to commit suicide several times," Flaherty continues. "I was doing it several ways—through the booze. I ended up in the gutter, lost the family, lost everything."

Back in Boston, as he recovered, he studied political science at Suffolk University, where three women professors adopted him and introduced him to philosophy, feminism, and the avant-garde. "They were tough on me. They spun my head around," he says admiringly. He got a job setting up model programs for people with addictions, particularly women. "That woman in Vietnam might have opened a way for me later on to, ah…" The silence stretches on too long. "Move into pain," he finally says and gives a short laugh. "Some recognition of collusion. Because they were not human to me. I would have just as soon killed them."

Tony joined Veterans For Peace, got involved in the peace convoy, met other veterans who became close friends and allies, and, each year, he tries to insert some peace into his city's celebrations of war. But he demurs that his time is past and worries that a proliferation of organizations may undermine the unity needed to achieve peace. "Every other day now, there's another veterans group, so we're always dealing with egos," he says. Why do demonstrations need to cover every cause de jour, which confuses and turns people off? "There is no concerted purpose, other than a grandiose language," he says sadly.

Flaherty is hardly alone in despairing that all of VFP's activity and arguments go nowhere. If your goal is world peace, it's a safe bet that you're setting yourself up for failure. Yet he keeps at it because, as he says, he can't not. Riffing on the possibilities for change, he notes, "It's like a recovery program. You have to admit there's a problem. You have to make amends. You have to put the drink down, you have to put the gun down. Everybody says everybody's got good and bad. I don't know if I fuckin' believe that anymore. They have good in them as long as it's comfortable."

Our lunch ends, our talk has gone long, it's getting late. Tony launches into a final story that his sister, a Mother Superior, is fond of telling: Christ is on the cross—he extends his arms and droops his head forlornly to illustrate—looking down at the sprinkling of disciples and Roman soldiers and citizens milling around, none paying him much attention. Abandoned by God and man, Christ turns his gaze heavenward and mutters, "This shit is *not* working."

"I expect results," Tony concludes. "Biggest joke in the world. Maybe I'll change. As a manifestation of peace, I'm hardly it. I'd kill you for peace."

∼ St. Louis, Missouri, 17 August 2007 ∼

They're our brothers, they're our sisters, we support war resisters.
They're our brothers, they're our sisters, we support war resisters. Over
and over the veterans chant, shouting it from the balcony and pews of
the Centenary Methodist Church in St. Louis, preaching, literally, to the
choir. Their collective voice is heaviest on the bass notes and not entirely
aligned in rhythm, so the exact words of the cadence are hard to make
out, but the message is heartfelt and clear.

Agustin Aguayo, a bespectacled, thirty-five-year-old, Mexican American
soldier, has just finished telling his story. In contrast to the shoulder-
shimmying music and rousing speeches of the evening's public speak-out,
his sentences are halting, his words touched with a Spanish inflection and
punctuated with open-handed gestures. He tells how he joined the army
as a way to take care of his family and how he was sent to Tikrit in Iraq two
years later as a medic with the 1st Infantry Division. How he applied for a
discharge as a conscientious objector, but was sent back to Iraq while his
petition was considered. How, while he was there, he refused to load his
weapon, even when he was on guard duty, an action that damned him as
not to be trusted. How, when the army denied his CO and a federal court
upheld the army's ruling, he went AWOL to avoid redeployment because
he didn't want to take part in war anymore.

"When you know better, you do better," he wrote to the District of
Columbia federal court, explaining why he would not return to Iraq.

Twenty-four days after going AWOL to avoid redeployment, he
surrendered to military authorities, who flew him to Germany in
handcuffs, court-martialed him, and sentenced him to eight months
in prison. It is only a few weeks now since he has been released and
reunited with his wife and young daughters.

44

"I'm glad I'm not just the crazy person the army paints me as," Aguayo tells his audience with a careful smile. He turned himself in, knowing he would be punished, because, he says, "I felt I didn't do the wrong thing, so I never felt like running." What he felt when he refused to fight was joy.

"Because I have taken this stand," he concludes, "I am free."

3

EXIT A FREE MAN

Antiwar veterans like the Smedley Butlers can resist war through symbolic actions, such as protests or civil disobedience. Antiwar soldiers can do it directly by refusing to fight.

In the build-up leading up to the invasion of Iraq in March 2003, the majority of soldiers who didn't want to deploy sought to get out of the army with a minimum of fuss, and the army seemed inclined to oblige. As hostilities heated up, though, so did the response. That January, the GI Rights Hotline, a coalition of antiwar groups, recorded about 3,500 calls—more than double the monthly rate the year before. Callers from all branches of the military tried to get discharged on medical or technical grounds or by making themselves undesirable to keep around. Many simply fled and then stayed away long enough to be classified as deserters.[1] When Private Wilfredo Torres, who had deserted about a year before, turned himself in at Fort Myer, Virginia, in November 2002, he was told that six thousand soldiers had already gone AWOL and that the army expected ten thousand more that year.[2]

The military is not a debating society for good reason, and soldiers don't get to pick their battles. Moreover, this was an all-volunteer military, so presumably enlistees knew that soldiers fight wars, even if recruiters tended to play that down when wooing them. But there was a small group of soldiers and marines who felt moral or political revulsion about this particular war, and for them the issue became just how much of their conscience they had signed away when they had signed up. At first a dribble, then a handful, then scores of dissidents refused to slip away quietly, instead demanding attention to their argument with the very underpinnings of the war.

There are many ways to resist—ranging from rejiggering a duty roster to turning patrols into search-and-avoid missions to refusing or sabotaging orders to the extremes of mutinying or murdering officers—but perhaps the most direct, individual, and controversial is conscientious objection, or CO.[3] Pacifist resistance and the right of soldiers to adhere to their moral sense have had legal recognition since the American colonies set up their first militias, and the courageous individual heeding his conscience and damning the consequences is a staple of American mythology.[4] Still, Americans have been ambivalent about claims to pacifist imperatives, even during the Vietnam War, when at least seventeen thousand enlistees filed for CO and approval rates went as high as 77 percent. By 1972, there were more COs than draftees, a contributing factor to the demise of the draft.[5] But here now was a different war with no conscription, which made the idea of a soldier claiming conscientious objection particularly mystifying. The typical response to doubts about the war was, "You signed up, you shut up," and most did.

Wes Sudbury, who got discharged from the army as a conscientious objector just before the invasion of Iraq, observed, "In the military, I think people just shut their brains down. You don't want to decide that what you're doing is wrong. Then you have to figure out what you're going to do about it."

The right to conscientious objection doesn't exist in any law, but it has been included in military personnel regulations since 1962. The Uniform Code of Military Justice defines it as "a firm, fixed, and sincere objection to war in any form or the bearing of arms by reason of religious training and belief." Since the Vietnam era, "religious" has been interpreted to include deeply held moral and ethical convictions not necessarily based on God, though a history of religious observance helps. Applicants must convince their commanders that they changed their beliefs after they signed up, that their objection is not based on politics, and that they oppose all wars. (In contrast, many other countries allow for selective objection.) These standards are meant to be stringent, in part as a weeding-out process. "The army recognizes that people can have a change of heart, but the burden of proof is on the soldier making the application," army public affairs officer Martha Rudd said. "I know of a chaplain who did CO interviews and says that he can tell if the applicant is sincere within the first five minutes."

CO counselors talk about "crystallization," a moment of blinding clarity, but for the young and questing enlistees who became conscientious objectors to the Iraq and Afghanistan wars, the process of shedding a warrior identity was long and convoluted. The decision to turn your back on all that you have believed and trusted is never easy, but these soldiers reached a point where they could no longer make compromises with their reality.

Mark Wilkerson, who applied for CO in 2004 after returning from a tour in Iraq, told me, "When I was eighteen, I got a scrapbook with all our military family history going back to the Revolutionary War—sketches, photographs, journals kept by these soldiers. I tried to justify what I was doing every way I could, and then I could no longer justify it, so I had to take my pride, everything I thought I knew about life and the war in Iraq, and change it around to fit what I was seeing and what I was experiencing." Wilkerson's CO—admittedly, "a rant-filled, angry, scathing statement about everything"—was denied. He went AWOL to avoid redeployment and was sentenced to seven months in prison after he turned himself in. When he got out, he joined IVAW.

Turning themselves into students of history, political science, and philosophy, the dissident soldiers read widely: Ralph Waldo Emerson, Seymour Hersh, the ubiquitous Noam Chomsky, the libertarian economics writer Richard J. Maybury, Morihei Ueshiba, the founder of aikido. Armed with new perspectives, they confronted the old ideas and values that had formed them and the communities that had nurtured them. They grew angry at being used in the service of lies, political opportunism, and bad judgment, and by whatever unlikely route, they concluded that war in Iraq would protect neither their country nor its Constitution. In short, they decided that this was not what they had signed up for and not where their duty lay.

It may be in the interest of the military to get rid of soldiers who don't want to fight, but conscientious objection is a direct challenge to the core beliefs of the officers who control the CO process and who are well positioned to fetter and punish those they perceive as apostates. For this and other reasons, there is no reliable count of how many service members consider themselves conscientious objectors. According to army statistics, which are notoriously incomplete, sixty active-duty soldiers applied for CO in 2003, the first year of the Iraq War, and thirty-one were approved.[6] The marines reported receiving thirty-two applications and approving twenty-two.[7] The military counts only the applications that make it to headquarters, and each branch of the service gathers, classifies, and interprets its figures individually and without independent review, so military counselors estimate that the real number of applicants is many times the official number.

"No one could give a definitive number on applications (no matter what anyone may tell you)," J. E. McNeil, then at the Center on Conscience and War, wrote in an e-mail in January 2003. Several years later, Chuck Fager, then director of Quaker House in Fayetteville, North Carolina, wrote that he operated under the maxim, "There are Lies, Damn Lies, Statistics, and Pentagon Numbers." By his estimate, only about 15 percent of the CO applications his organization shepherded to the end of the process succeeded.

By any reckoning, the number of genuine conscientious objectors in an army of recruits is very small, yet they are seen as a threat. Some of this is a knee-jerk response to criticism, but the unease COs create within the military structure is not without basis. Resisters can be a match to the tinder of growing resentment, especially during an unpopular war. Sometimes, their influence is just a matter of passing on information, but more often, the force of a CO's convictions and the appreciation for the guts it takes to act on them can lead others to doubt the value of the mission. The greatest threat, however, may be that resisters show the rank-and-file soldier that resistance is possible.

The military created multiple barriers—some intentional, some inherent in the system—to conscientious objection. Service members reported finding it hard to get accurate information about the process and being actively discouraged from applying. Early in 2003, websites classified as "advocacy groups" by Websense and SmartFilter, Internet filtering systems the military used, were often blocked.[8] David Wilson, an army sergeant stationed in Kuwait at the beginning of the war, confirmed that he couldn't get to websites for the GI Rights Hotline, War Resisters League, or American Civil Liberties Union, groups that assist CO applicants. The Internet became more available as GIs found ways to get online outside the army's system and Iraqi techies found ways to make money helping them, but even with better access to information, resisters were surprised to learn that conscientious objection was an option.

Then there was the process, which usually took six months to a year, during which time an applicant was expected to comply with all orders and regulations, including deployment to a war zone. CO applicants had a better chance of succeeding if they had legal counsel, but it was hard to find lawyers versed in military law and expensive to enlist their services; from the battlefield, it was nearly impossible. The CO process was controlled by commanding officers, who, despite often being unfamiliar with the regulations, had considerable leeway to manipulate how things went, including turning an application aside, conveniently "losing" it, or stopping it at any of several steps along the way. For Jose Vasquez, a staff sergeant in the Army Reserve, it took two and a half years—something of a record—for his application to be approved, and then it was only because his congresswoman stepped in to help.

While a CO petition was under consideration, applicants were supposed to be reassigned to noncombat duties, but this didn't always happen, at least not without a struggle. While Vasquez's case was pending, he was sent to Fort Sam Houston in Texas to prepare for deployment to Iraq until military lawyers figured out that he wasn't supposed to be there. Agustin Aguayo, sent to Iraq while his CO was under review, received assurances from the army that he would not be required to carry a loaded weapon, but he was twice "counseled" and issued an Article 15, or nonjudicial punishment, for refusing to bear arms. Regardless of the official response, nearly all applicants for conscientious objection describe being shunned by their peers and officers and isolated at a particularly stressful time of their lives.

Obviously, there are easier ways to get out of the military.

David Wilson's story, like all the stories in this book, is his alone, but it follows a familiar trajectory for soldiers who applied for CO early in the war—from his navigation of the process without the guidance of knowledgeable counselors, through the army's maze of obstacles, to the disdain he came to have for the military mission in Iraq and the politicians who sanctioned it. He was also typical of so many CO applicants in that he ultimately didn't succeed.

Wilson grew up in Charleston, South Carolina, where his father taught at the Citadel, his mother was a vocational high school principal, and his family worshiped at the Baptist church. (Wilson's faith later shifted to mountain biking.) Looking for money to pay off debt and return to school, he enlisted in the army in 2000 at the relatively late age of thirty. He was self-reliant, fit, and sure of himself, so he had no difficulty holding his own with the younger enlistees. By the time he was sent to Kuwait in February 2003, he had risen to sergeant and was assigned to the 32nd

Army Air and Missile Defense Command as an electronic warfare techni-
cian.

Wilson and I were introduced by a soldier in his unit, who had gotten
out as a CO before the invasion. We exchanged e-mails in March and
April 2003 and resumed e-mailing (his preferred mode of communication) six years later. He had nothing to gain by answering my questions,
but answer he did, diligently, promptly, and fully, even when his personal
time was limited on army computers in Kuwait. Six weeks after he arrived there and one week before the invasion of Iraq, he wrote: "My position on going to war with Iraq is difficult to describe. I have no problem
fighting off an oppressive govt. I have no problem blowing someone's
head off if they are trying to rob my house or harm my family. I do have
a problem with a govt. that uses its army to achieve those goals. I have
a problem with a govt. that does not pay attention to actions it is taking
that harm the Constitution that I was sworn to defend."

A month later, still in Kuwait, it was a different story, as he wrote on
drunkcyclist, a friend's blog. "I hear missiles flying overhead and I get interviewed by CNN as they do a documentary. I feel relief when the A10s
hit the persistent launcher in Basra with a missile. Then I get real angry.
I wish bad things on those who do what they think is right for America."
By then, Wilson was angry at his chaplain, "who tries to be a cheerleader
for this war by quoting Old Testament scripture." He was angry at his
fellow soldiers, who lumped all Iraqis together as the enemy and called
antiwar protesters unpatriotic. He was angry at a general he heard of
who didn't care how many soldiers he lost in battle, angry at the contractors who talked nonstop about job security, and angry at an AP reporter,
"this poor girl [who] was obviously quite excited to be around so many
men." Most of all, he was angry at himself. "Why did I let it go this far?"
he asked plaintively. He concluded that he was a conscientious objector.

He informed his immediate chain of command of his intention to
apply for CO. "A couple were pissed, but they understood." He told his
first sergeant and battery commander (the latter would determine the
fate of his application), and they were furious. He didn't draw on any of
the GI rights counseling groups because he thought—inaccurately—that
he didn't qualify for their help because his objection wasn't on religious
grounds. Instead, he found the relevant regulation online and worked
feverishly on his packet, basing his claim on his conclusion that he could
fulfill the military's values only by objecting to its actions. He named

specific commanders and cited intelligence he was privy to as evidence that information was falsified and then promoted as truth. "It was my way of defying orders without being seen as a dissenter," he explained several years later.

A talk with a chaplain strengthened Wilson's resolve. A colonel who read his packet cried. Another asked how he would feel when he told his nieces and nephews that he was a CO. A psychiatrist recommended that he get counseling to deal with the "tragedies"—his quotation marks— that he had seen. In the thick of this ordeal, he e-mailed me, "My unit's job here is done. But there will be more actions before my time is up. I don't want to be a part of any more violence. This is all too big for me. I don't belong in this mess."

His commanders urged him to ride it out, because his unit would be going home soon, but a week later, Wilson reported that he had been "coerced" into turning in his CO packet. His security clearance was revoked, and he "went from being the go-to guy in my unit for electronics and comms, to being the head count at the chow hall." Like other COs, he insisted that his resistance could not be dismissed as combat stress or bad faith. He wanted to get out of the army because he believed that what the army was doing in Iraq was wrong.

Things improved when he got back to Fort Bliss in Texas, where he was assigned to Operation Santa Claus, an on-post charity, rebuilt bicycles for kids, lived at home with his wife, and tried to distance himself from the war by unplugging his television. He hadn't been in combat, but he was disappointed to have been part of the war apparatus, since it seemed so obvious to him that the invasion could have been avoided. Meanwhile, his CO application worked its way through the system for about a year and was then denied; he suspected that there was pressure to reject it within the chain of command, but he wasn't sure who made the decision. He could have appealed, but with less than six months left on his contract, he stayed at the charity and did his best to rattle the brass with wisecracks about their war bravado, while sowing doubt among younger soldiers with tales of military stupidity and false intelligence reports.

His views on the war didn't change much, except for sour amusement that the situation had turned so bad so fast. On his blog, he called the army "the greatest terrorist network in the world," but his anger seemed to subside, probably because he had never considered himself much of a soldier to begin with. "I was just a guy looking for an adventure and a way to continue my education," he e-mailed me when I got back in touch in the spring of 2009. He had added IVAW to his Myspace page, thought about bicycling across Texas to join the antiwar protest of Gold Star Mother Cindy Sheehan, and that was the extent of his activism. Glad to be back in civilian life, he resumed the intensive mountain biking he loved and used the GI bill to study for a master's degree in exercise physiology.

Then on April Fool's Day 2006, he was recalled for Individual Ready Reserve (IRR) duty. Typically, soldiers sign a contract for four years active duty and four years inactive; after they are discharged from active duty, they go on the IRR rolls for the remaining years, but receive no pay and are essentially done with the army. In 2004, however, when the army started having trouble filling its ranks, it began ordering those in IRR to report again for duty. When the fat packet of orders arrived in Wilson's mailbox, he freaked out. He was fairly confident that a bad knee would save him from redeployment, but the orders required him to report to Fort Jackson in South Carolina and put his life on hold while the army determined his fate. At Jackson, he got lucky: the doctor who interviewed him had also been called back on IRR and wasn't happy about it. Wilson convinced the doctor that releasing him was in the best interest of the army, and he was sent home. But the recall process had forced him to pull out of his graduate program, and he never finished his thesis. Instead, he returned to his original plan and got certified to teach science in high school.

So in the end, he got out of the army the way most soldiers do: by completing his contract. Not sorry he enlisted, he's not sorry he applied for CO either. "I wanted to serve my country," he concluded in one e-mail, then added in another, "I just wanted to do what was right. I wanted to maintain my integrity and the only way I saw to do that (other than requesting that they throw me in jail) was to file as a CO."

Like most of the early resisters, Wilson said goodbye to the army and melted back into civilian life. But soon, others chose to make their resistance public—which was when military officials reacted as people usually do when they think they're losing control: they aimed for more control. One tool at their disposal was to meet public resistance with swift and unblinking punishment.

Members of the military have the right to say, write, publish, and read what they want—with restrictions, some of which date back to the Civil

War. Statements disloyal to the military or intended to encourage others to disobey orders are forbidden; limits can be placed on the distribution of reading matter and the organizations service members are permitted to join; and while soldiers are allowed to attend demonstrations, they may do so only in the United States, off base, off duty, and out of uniform. They cannot encourage violence, show up at an event likely to become violent, or join any organization whose purpose is violence—except, of course, the military.[9] Officers are held to a somewhat higher standard under articles of the Uniform Code of Military Justice, which forbid "contemptuous words" against a list of public officials and "conduct unbecoming an officer."

Prosecutions for speech infractions are uncommon, especially for officers, but courts-martial for other offenses, such as missing deployment, allow the military to crack down on resistance by giving harsh punishments to GIs who take their dissent public. It may be true that military courts are to justice as military bands are to music, but civilian courts are also reluctant to defend justice if that requires second-guessing military policy, especially during wartime. From 2003 on, the judiciary became another venue closed to debate about the legitimacy of the war. Not that GI dissidents didn't try.

On 1 April 2003, Stephen Funk, a twenty-one-year-old marine reservist from Seattle, called a press conference outside Camp Pendleton, California, where he was stationed, to announce that he was refusing to go to Iraq with his unit, thereby becoming the first serviceperson to resist deployment publicly. Funk, a lance corporal, had told his commanding officer that he was applying for CO and would not report for duty when his unit was mobilized. Then he went AWOL for forty-seven days. He attended antiwar rallies and, when his CO packet was ready, turned himself in. Funk was charged with desertion, which in wartime carries a potential death penalty, and was sent to New Orleans for his court-martial, far from family and supporters. His lawyer, Stephen Collier, believed that Funk was singled out precisely because he had sought publicity. "They're definitely not making it easy for my client," he said. But publicity is double-edged. The mainstream media covered his press conference and trial, the first time it reported on disaffection within the ranks since the country began to mobilize for war, and Funk's supporters capitalized on the marines' harsh response to organize a defense committee to raise money and morale. Perhaps because the public was watching, Funk was convicted of a lesser charge and sentenced to six months in the brig. He too joined IVAW after he got out.

Funk's resistance was groundbreaking in that it pushed dissent from a private and solitary struggle into the public sphere, and it became a model for resisters who followed: deliberately missing deployment and filing for CO, then surrendering to military authorities with a public explanation of the reasons and circumstances for the resistance and a hope the press would cover it. Antiwar activists, who understood the symbolic power of a protester in uniform, were eager to display any soldier willing to proclaim disagreement with the war or the military. The antiwar movement liked to portray these resisters as victims, but by the time they were ready to speak to rallies or reporters, most knew what they were getting into. They were aware that their actions, if not their speech, would have consequences, and they were generally willing to follow the script. The military also followed a routine—arrest, punitive confinement, unsympathetic trials, relatively harsh sentencing—as did the defense committees, who worked to rally support in the court of public opinion.

As the war turned into an occupation and more GIs filed for CO or fled, not only did the strategy for effective public resistance become clearer, but more resources became available. Deciding to resist was still hard, and many who did it chose to stay out of the limelight, but once someone was ready to go public, he or she found networks of well-informed supporters ready to help. Many were veterans who had resisted in previous wars—or who wished they had. Among Funk's advocates was an ex-marine named Jeff Paterson, who, in 1991, sat down on the tarmac of an air station in Hawaii and refused to board a plane bound for the Persian Gulf, thus becoming the first service member to resist deployment in the First Gulf War. Paterson and others had been organizing political and legal support for Funk since the February before he turned himself in, and eventually that effort grew into the group Courage to Resist.

As the new kid on the block, Courage joined several civilian organizations that had been assisting military resisters for decades. The oldest U.S. organization was the American Friends Service Committee (AFSC), founded by Quakers in 1917 to organize alternative service for conscientious objectors in World War I, who would assist civilian victims in battle zones. The War Resisters League, a secular, pacifist group, began in 1923; the faith-based Center on Conscience and War (formerly NISBCO) in 1940; and the Central Committee for Conscientious Objectors (CCCO), a counseling network, in 1948. (CCCO suspended operations in October 2009.) The Vietnam War engendered the Military Law Task Force at the National Lawyers Guild, Citizen Soldier, and veterans groups, including Vietnam Veterans Against the War. In 1994, about twenty organizations banded together to formed the GI Rights Hotline.[10] The purpose of these counseling programs was to inform members of the military about regulations and their rights, but because they were sponsored by antiwar or pacifist groups, they were poised to help resisters resist.

Despite a growing disaffection among troops being sent to Iraq, it wasn't until the spring of 2004 that a soldier who had fought there refused to return and made a big enough deal of it that the army was forced to respond. Camilo Ernesto Mejia was a twenty-eight-year-old staff sergeant in the Florida Army National Guard, when he spent about five months in Ramadi with the 1st Battalion, 124th Infantry, guarding prisoners on base and undertaking risky patrols in and around that city. In his memoir, *The Road to Ar Ramadi*, Mejia charts his journey from an unhappy-but-conscientious squad leader to a leading dissident. His case was complicated, as most are. It involved a citizenship status in flux, misleading information from the army, and his decision—which he seems to have arrived at more by default than volition—not to return to his unit in Iraq when his two-week furlough ended in October 2003. At the core of Mejia's story was his conclusion that he could no longer participate in a war he had come to see as wrong in both concept and practice.

Mejia brought solid revolutionary credentials to the cause. Born in Nicaragua a few years before that country's populist uprising, he was named in tribute to Camilo Torres, a radical Colombian priest, and Ernesto "Che" Guevara. His mother was a prominent political activist, his father a popular folk singer, and for a while, he lived the privileged life of the Sandinista elite. After his parents separated, he moved around Central America with his mother and brother, until they finally landed in Miami. He joined the U.S. Army at nineteen, drawn by twin needs: for college tuition and for a sense of belonging. Mejia did three years active duty, then joined the Florida National Guard while he was studying psychology at the University of Miami. That's where things stood in March 2003, when he was stop-lossed and sent first to Jordan and then to Iraq. He got a promotion, took care of the men serving under him, and was a good soldier—until he couldn't be one anymore.

Weeks after his leave ended and he had missed every flight back to Iraq, he finally acknowledged to himself that he did not intend to return to his unit. He fled to the anonymity of New York, where he lived a fugitive existence for the next five months. Someone in the peace movement connected him with an attorney named Tod Ensign, whose bootstrap organization, Citizen Soldier, has helped resisters since the Vietnam War. Ensign introduced Mejia to Louis Font, a lawyer in Boston, who had defended resisters during the First Gulf War. Ensign was eager to highlight Mejia's resistance, and Font knew the legalities, so the three of them worked out a strategy: Mejia would complete his CO application, then hold a press conference and turn himself in.

Mejia had been giving anonymous interviews for months, telling how he had seen Iraqi prisoners tortured and American soldiers sent on patrols with Vietnam-era flak jackets and repeating regularly that it was not right to die for oil. So by the time of the press conference on 15 March 2004, he had become something of a cause célèbre. His mother had joined Military Families Speak Out, which helped organize more than sixty supporters to stand with him at the Peace Abbey in Sherborn, Massachusetts, as he gave a statement to a bank of reporters. The group then escorted Mejia to Hanscom Air Force Base, where he turned himself in to military authorities.

His case continued to get coverage through his court-martial at Fort Stewart, Georgia, where his attorneys were barred from raising questions about the legality of the war. This so-called Nuremberg defense—the principle that soldiers have a right and obligation to refuse to participate in war crimes—was a key element of their defense strategy, but in Mejia's trial, and nearly all the resister trials that followed, it was disallowed. It took little time for the military jury to find Mejia guilty of desertion, and his punishment was set at the maximum of a year in prison, plus reduction in rank, forfeiture of pay, and a bad conduct discharge. While he was imprisoned, Amnesty International adopted him as a prisoner of conscience. He received some twenty thousand letters of support, and Daniel Ellsberg, who had leaked the Pentagon Papers to the press during the Vietnam War, visited him in jail and introduced him to IVAW, which was just then being born. "I knew I was going to be a part of it," Mejia told me several years later.

Mejia's stand brought recognition and admiration, but it also required him to put his life on hold for a year while he was separated from his young daughter, blocked from continuing his education, and denied his freedom. Still, he closes his book with a brave refrain echoed by other resisters and their supporters. "I learned that there is no greater freedom than the freedom to follow one's conscience," he writes of the moment he was sentenced to prison. "That day I was free, in a way I had never been free before."[11]

After Mejia, the list of early, notable resisters grew apace. In February 2004, Army Sergeant First Class Abdullah Webster refused to deploy to Iraq as his CO was being considered, becoming the highest-ranking noncommissioned officer to do so. His application was eventually denied, and he was sentenced to fourteen months' imprisonment for refusing orders and missing movement. In January 2005, Kevin Benderman, a forty-year-old sergeant with ten years in the army, one tour in Iraq, and a family tradition in the military dating back to the American Revolution, applied for CO and refused redeployment while his application was being processed. Going public with his resistance, he told reporters that of the twenty-two people in his unit, seventeen had gone AWOL and two had attempted suicide, apparently to avoid returning to Iraq.[12] At his court-martial that July, Benderman was acquitted of desertion, but was found guilty on the lesser charge of missing movement and received a fifteen-month sentence, the longest for any resister. That November, Katherine Jashinski, a specialist in the Texas National Guard, became the first woman to announce her resistance after the army denied her CO application, which had been pending for a year and a half. Court-martialed for refusing to train with weapons, she received a relatively light sentence of four months in prison.

Meanwhile, resisters began fleeing to Canada, seeking political asylum there. The first to apply for refugee status was Jeremy Hinzman, who had been an army infantryman in Afghanistan before filing for CO. After his application was denied, he moved to Toronto with his family in January 2004 and began his petition for refuge.[13] Hinzman was soon joined by more war resisters, who got support from U.S. veterans who had dodged the draft or fled the military during the Vietnam War.[14] By the sixth year of the Iraq War, however, when about 250 U.S. deserters were believed to be living in Canada, that government was considerably less welcoming. Though there appeared to be strong support for the Iraq and Afghanistan resisters among the Canadian public and parliament, the politically appointed Immigration and Refugee Board disagreed.[15] In July 2008, it deported an American war resister, Robin Long, for the first time since the Vietnam era.[16]

Resistance was growing, not just among grunts, but apparently among junior officers as well. Ehren Watada, a twenty-seven-year-old, highly accomplished first lieutenant from Hawaii, announced that he would not go when his unit of the army's 3rd Stryker Brigade was sent to Iraq in June 2006, thus becoming the first commissioned officer to refuse deployment publicly. Officers can leave the military by resigning their commission, and a handful had done that during this war, but when Watada tried—three times—to resign his commission, his petition was denied. He explained that he could not consider conscientious objection because he didn't oppose all wars, only the Iraq War, and had concluded that his only option was to refuse to deploy.

Watada, a former Eagle Scout and magna cum laude graduate of Hawaii Pacific University, came across as a self-possessed and thoughtful man. He wasn't a rabble-rouser, but he was clearly a fighter, just the wrong kind. That kind—a valued officer challenging the very basis of an unpopular war—was apparently intolerable to the army, and retaliation was immediate, harsh, and prolonged. In the first such prosecution in forty years, Watada was charged with missing movement, as well as contempt toward officials and conduct unbecoming an officer for publicly criticizing government policy and the president. The latter charges stemmed in part from a speech he had made to the Veterans For Peace Convention in Seattle that year. His evermore Byzantine case looped back and around for nearly four years.

Watada, like other resisters, wanted to explain why he believed the war in Iraq was criminal, making it a dereliction of duty for him to carry out orders related to it; that is, he wanted to evoke the Nuremberg defense. Antiwar and soldiers rights groups rallied round, eager to give him a platform, and his case was widely reported, usually with the prediction—exaggerated, as it turned out—that he would become a lightning rod for dissent against the war. When Watada got his day in court, army judge Lt. Col. John Head declared that this was a conduct case, not a free speech one. He ruled that Watada's beliefs were irrelevant, and he disallowed any discussion of the legality of the war. The army, for its part, argued that Watada had been insubordinate, citing interviews he gave about his beliefs, and, in what could only be read as an attempt to

intimidate the press, subpoenaing two journalists who had interviewed him.[17]

Then on the third day of the proceedings, Head confounded everyone
by declaring a mistrial. At issue was a pretrial agreement Watada had
signed in exchange for the army's dropping two charges against him. The
agreement acknowledged that he had given the interviews and had not
boarded the plane to Iraq with his brigade, but whenever the judge tried
to get him to concede that this was an admission of guilt, he insisted
on trying to explain his motives. Judge Head consistently rejected those
attempts, deciding instead that Watada didn't fully understand the document he had signed. Courage to Resist's Jeff Paterson, who attended the
trial, described the puzzle palace the judge had built: "The fundamental
problem for the judge was that while he had clearly ruled that Lt. Watada
could not legally defend his actions based on his belief that the war was
illegal, the judge had also allowed the prosecution to bring to trial charges against Lt. Watada for publicly expressing his opinions that the war
was illegal."[18] Unable to find a way out, Head declared a mistrial.

Head avoided putting the war on trial, but he handed a legal and
moral triumph to Watada, who had always insisted that the reasons for
his actions were at the heart of his defense. More legal machinations followed until a federal district court judge ruled that a retrial would vio-
late Watada's protection from double jeopardy. The army wasn't ready
to let go, however; it appealed the ruling, but took no further action for
eighteen months, leaving Watada in legal limbo. He was transferred to a
desk job at Fort Lewis, Washington, and kept on active duty far past the
end of his term of service. In the spring of 2009, with a new administration in Washington, two members of Veterans For Peace, Mike Wong
and Gerry Condon, initiated an online campaign to pressure the Justice
Department to withdraw the appeal, and in May, the solicitor general so
ordered. The army continued to threaten to reinstate the conduct unbecoming charges, but finally granted Watada an other-than-honorable
discharge and let him go in October of that year.

By that time, more than thirty resisters had been court-martialed after
publicizing their opposition to the Iraq War.[19] They received sentences
for various offenses averaging six to eight months, though a few were
much longer. Their punishment usually included bad paper discharges,
such as dishonorable discharges, which could mean a loss of benefits.
In comparison, several of the soldiers who mistreated detainees at Abu

Gharib prison were sentenced to less than a year in prison, and a sniper convicted of planting an AK47 on the body of a dead, unarmed Iraqi civilian to make him look like an insurgent was given a 135-day sentence, letter of reprimand, and reduction in rank.[20]

There is joy in fighting the right fight and some security in numbers, but dissent, by definition, is a lonely undertaking. In 2004, when IVAW began, public resisters were few and seldom in a position to speak for themselves and the tendency to set individual resisters on a pedestal implied that only a saintly few had the courage to say no to war. The early resisters were significant as indicators and precursors of unease within the military, but their influence would be limited unless their individual acts of conscience spurred others on to concerted action. Recognizing that need, many of these early dissidents joined IVAW as soon as they were free to, and several went on to leadership positions, including Camilo Mejia, who served two terms as chair of the board, and Jose Vasquez, who became the organization's third executive director. And slowly, as the media—prompted by public, political, and even military weariness with the war—began covering the twists and turns of these cases (if not yet the political ideas that informed them), the resisters were hailed as heroes, as well as victims. Sometimes they were even described as activists.

∼ *August and September 2005* ∼

South Carolina: "My baby was a mama's boy, but the military turned him into a productive young man," Elaine Johnson says with pride. Whenever she visited her son, Darius Jennings, at Fort Carson, Colorado, she cooked meals for him and his six buddies. They made a pact that if one of them didn't come back from Iraq, the others would take care of his mother, so after Darius was killed in Fallujah on 2 November 2003, the surviving six travel to Orangeburg, South Carolina, to spend the weekend of that anniversary with "Mama J." They particularly like her iced tea.

"Sweet?" I ask.

"Sweet," she confirms.

Idaho: "I feel responsible. I feel like I never should have let him join," says Jack Amoureux, of his brother, a twenty-three-year-old marine doing convoy security in Iraq. Raised in a staunchly conservative family in Boise, Idaho, and now a graduate student in political science at Brown University, Jack marvels at the easy ignorance of the students he encounters there. He says, "I want to scream at them, 'Your peers are dying!'"

Vermont: "For me, it's about trust," Nicole Conte suggests, carefully. Her husband is in Iraq with the National Guard, one of the many Vermonters who join because they need a second job. The previous March, a coalition of groups got forty-eight town meetings around the state to pass a resolution asking the legislature to reassess deployment of the Guard to Iraq. "It should be possible to disagree *and* support the troops," Conte adds, her voice turning up at the end, as if maybe there should be a question mark there.

Massachusetts: "Why can't we hold elected officials accountable?"
demands Rose Gonzalez eight months after she stood, very pregnant
and very nervous, before one hundred college students and described
how she felt when her forty-seven-year-old mother was deployed
to Iraq with the National Guard. "I'm thirty years old," she told them,
"but I still need my mother." Now, at her kitchen table in Somerville,
Massachusetts, she cradles her tiny son and tells me a story. Her mother
usually e-mails or calls from her base near Tikrit at least once a week,
so when several days passed in silence, Rose was frantic. Her mother
had been vague on the details of her life there—for self-protection, Rose
thinks—and never explained that when someone on the base is killed,
all communication shuts down to ensure that the victim's family learns
of the death through proper channels. After two weeks of nothing, Rose
e-mailed, "Are you ok?"

The reply came back, "Alive."

4

HOME FIRES BURNING

"That's ours, we created that," boasted Nancy Lessin of Military Families Speak Out (MFSO). She and Charley Richardson, her husband and MFSO cofounder, came up with the name for the Bring Them Home Now campaign, which MFSO and Veterans For Peace launched in August 2003 to demand an immediate end to the American occupation of Iraq. "Bring them home now" was a retort to what struck them as jaw-dropping callousness when George W. Bush challenged Iraqi insurgents to "bring 'em on." "We had always said [the troops] were cannon fodder, but never more than in that moment was that put forward," Lessin said.

MFSO was a national organization composed of relatives of people who had served in the military recently. (The time span was deliberately vague.) It began in 2002 with the aim of preventing the United States from invading Iraq. When that failed, its members, who always maintained that it is possible to oppose the war and still support the troops, continued to press for an end to the occupation so their "loved ones" would no longer have to fight what they believed was a woefully wrongheaded war. To that end, their goals were clear: bring all the troops home immediately, take care of them in Iraq and on their return to the States, and end the policies that led to the war so such a miscalculation would not happen again. They added opposition to the war in Afghanistan to its mission statement in 2009.

MFSO claimed to be the largest organization of its kind in American history, a safe bet, as precedents were few. Women have figured prominently in peace movements throughout America's history, with mothers claiming special rights and responsibilities (along with special abilities to make life difficult for military recruiters).[1] The first Mother's Day was organized in 1873 as a celebration of peace; Women Strike for Peace was active in the Vietnam antiwar movement; and some Gold Star Mothers led a contingent of Vietnam Veterans Against the War to Arlington National Cemetery during Dewey Canyon III.[2] But a sustained, national organization of military-related families working closely with other antiwar activists did seem new. Respectful of soldiers, unabashedly steeped in love of country, eloquent in its ordinariness, and neatly tailored to its historical moment, MFSO presented America with an antiwar movement by way of family values. The result was often startling symbolic and rhetorical power.

For most people, contact with the military in twenty-first-century America is ritualistic—parades, awards, commemorations, funerals—but military families are the civilians closest to war. VFP's Dave Cline called them the transmission belt to active-duty personnel; support for the troops was not optional, but a defining aspect of their lives. As people attuned to the situation on the ground, MFSO members provided a first-alert system for problems within the military, such as lack of body armor for troops in Iraq and inadequate medical care from the Veterans Administration. As concerned parents and spouses, they presented a sympathetic face of the antiwar movement and reminded the public that many soldiers were barely more than kids when they deployed. And as storytellers, the families brought voices that were seldom heard into the national conversation about the war. The veterans in VFP, with their sense of history repeating itself, may have been impatient with talk, but MFSO members, many of whom had never spoken their doubts aloud before, found it exhilarating. "Remember," MFSO instructed in its talking-points memos, "when speaking to the press or public, always speak from your experience and your heart." So maybe it's most accurate to say that they set out to create a conversation where none existed before.

I've had a nodding acquaintance with Lessin and Richardson from MFSO's early days, but it isn't until the summer of 2005 that we sit down for our first extended talk. By then, about 2,500 military families have joined their organization, representing most states and several countries with U.S. military bases. We meet at J. P. Licks, an ice cream parlor and coffee shop featuring a life-sized plaster cow named Clementine. "Welcome to our office," says Richardson, as he greets a stream of neighbors passing our booth. He and Lessin have raised their children from previous marriages—his twin sons, her two daughters—here in Jamaica Plain, a Boston neighborhood divided into half Latino-and-black-working-class and half too-expensive-to-buy-a-house-without-a-trust-fund. They live in the working-class part.

Richardson resembles a graying Hawkeye Pierce with a Fu Manchu mustache. At fifty-two, he is tall and lanky with deep-set eyes and a stud in one ear. He wraps his sunglasses around the back of his neck, checks his cell phone distractedly, then turns back to the conversation with intensity. In contrast, Lessin, fifty-six, talks about her opposition to the war with such equanimity that when she states, "One day longer of the war could transform us from being a military family to a Gold Star family," her flint comes as a surprise. Her ash blond hair is cut in a long shag, her left eyelid droops lazily, her hands are small and delicate. She wears a jeans jacket with a United Steel Workers of America logo on the left pocket, a peace button on the right, and "Women of Steel" embroidered on the back.

She and Richardson talk as a tag team, interlacing each other's sentences with corrections, emendations, reservations, and, ultimately, agreement. Their story, honed by numerous retellings, is presented as a series of way stations along the road to MFSO, which has become the center of their lives. They begin in August 2002, when they spent a bittersweet twenty-four hours at Camp Lejeune, saying goodbye to Richardson's son, Joe, a marine, who was about to deploy to Kosovo. As they walked the beaches of North Carolina's lacy coast, Joe told them he expected to be sent to fight a not-yet-declared war in Iraq. "We knew there was this very dark cloud looming over the horizon," says Lessin, "that he was going to somehow end up being a part of it."

On their return home, they caromed from alarm to anger to anxiety as they anticipated Joe's call-up to war. "Every time there was a knock on the door, when there was a phone call, it took on a different meaning. It could mean that something terrible had happened," she recalls. "As a parent, our job is to keep our children safe, right? So it became very important to me to do everything I could to prevent the war from happening because that was my way to keep Joe and all the other troops and the people of Iraq safe from a disaster." Richardson adds a story about overhearing two men talking at a convenience store shortly after their return from Lejeune. One man was a Democrat, the other a Republican—"It sounds like the start of a joke," he says wryly—and both were in favor of going into Iraq and wiping them out, whoever "them" was. "I realized that what I wanted to do was go in and slap a picture of Joe on the table and say, 'You know, if you're going to have this conversation, at least look at the face of somebody who might be at risk as a result of your bravado.'"

Being a "military family" wasn't a simple proposition for either of them. Both of their fathers had fought in World War II, and Lessin had lived on a military base in Hawaii as a teenager while her father worked with the federal Public Health Service, but their views of the military were formed during the Vietnam War era, and they mistrusted the institution and the ways it had been misused. When Joe Richardson decided to join the marines in 1998 in his junior year of college, his father did his best to dissuade him, but Joe followed through with it. After college, he went to the Defense Language Institute to learn Arabic and was in Iraq during the invasion. He has left the marines and is working in the private sector when we speak.

When I ask why Joe enlisted, Lessin laughs. "You'll have to . . ." she begins before Richardson jumps in with, "I think it's an incredibly complex answer. Basically that's for him to talk about when he wants to talk about it. Joe's always said to us, 'I'm proud of you for what you're doing. Don't ever speak for me.'" Later, he elaborates, "I spoke once in New Bedford at a Quaker meeting house. I said how strange it is that I'm the one in front of you because the reason I'm here is because of a decision my son made, which I opposed."

Richardson and Lessin actively opposed the wars in Vietnam and the Persian Gulf, but they aren't pacifists. "We do believe that, most unfortunately, war is sometimes necessary," Lessin wrote in an e-mail. The impending invasion of Iraq, however, struck them as unnecessary and also illegal. "Somebody I once worked with asked if I knew what a just war was. I started to give a long answer," says Richardson, who tended to speak in enumerated points. "But he interrupted me and said, 'No, Charley, it's much simpler. A just war is one that you'd send your own kids off to fight.'"

He and Lessin concluded that losing a child in war would be tragic, but losing a child in a war that seemed so wrong and not trying to stop it would be unbearable. "We noticed that all of those saying, 'We gotta go to war,' weren't going anywhere, nor were their loved ones," Lessin notes dryly. They also began to notice that when they spoke as parents of a marine, people listened and connected with them differently. Their stories carried weight; with that authority came obligation. "When you can, you must," Richardson insists.

Organizing came readily to them from their years as labor activists: Lessin was working with the Massachusetts AFL-CIO and the United Steel Workers, and Richardson was directing the Labor Extension Program at the University of Massachusetts at Lowell. They sent an open letter to friends, expressing their concerns about the impending war and got responses, not just from people they knew, but from hundreds of others around the world as their letter looped back to them in one of those e-mail Möbius strips.

That October, they gathered a gaggle of family members in Washington to march in their first national antiwar demonstration, each relative carrying a poster. Lessin says, "The very first thing that happened to me as we were waiting, a man about my age, wearing part of a uniform from Vietnam, came up and he hugged me. He said, 'I wish my mom had been doing this for me when I was in Vietnam,' and then he left." The second memorable event at the march was meeting Jeff McKenzie of Gasport, New York, the father of a medevac helicopter pilot who was also facing deployment to Iraq. A letter from McKenzie after they returned to Boston led to a flurry of phone conversations and an agreement that there needed to be a network of military families to offer political, as well as emotional, support. So in November 2002, they teamed up to launch Military Families Speak Out, with a proud membership of three.

At first, MFSO aimed at preventing the United States from invading Iraq. Doing what groups with no political power beyond their voice, vote, and persistence do, they lobbied politicians to oppose military appropriations, waved placards at traffic intersections, wrote letters to editors, and spoke to the media whenever they got the opportunity, which wasn't often. Then, Veterans For Peace invited about ten MFSO families to march with them on a bitter cold day in January 2003 in a large antiwar demonstration in Washington. It felt like a turning point for the organization. "We were home in a community in this larger antiwar movement," Lessin gushes.

Taking a lesson from the Vietnam era, peace activists recognized the importance of including and supporting soldiers, so this time around, organizers put veterans and their families near the front of marches and on the stage at rallies. Highlighting these groups proved to be a smart move. Two and a half years later, Lessin observes, "When the bombs dropped on Baghdad on March 19, 2003, within a week and a half, there were fifty thousand people on the Boston Common to protest. Since then the largest number that has been assembled was two thousand. Where did forty-eight thousand people go?" MFSO, lacking the luxury of discouragement, heeded the president's rhetoric and stayed the course.

Also that January, Veterans for Common Sense, a group then made up primarily of Gulf War veterans, invited Lessin and Richardson to join a press conference at the National Press Club, which was broadcast by CSPAN. They bought a new phone answering machine, created a rudimentary website, and within forty-eight hours, had two hundred new members—and, as Richardson acknowledges, probably had an equal number of detractors. "We were reaching an audience in a way that was, frankly, in their face. It was an uncomfortable place for many of them. For military families it's, my kid's at risk and it better be right, so I don't want to hear anything that challenges that."

Military families keep quiet for many of the same reasons servicepeople do, with the added pressure to "be supportive" and not do anything that might jeopardize a relative's career. They also want to avoid being ostracized themselves. Spouses and children are frequently uprooted and plunked down on military bases far from their families and hometowns, so those bases can become close-knit, if temporary, communities with shared cultures and concerns. For families who don't live in military towns, having a relative go off to war can be even more isolating, especially for those who aren't comfortable in the support groups the military sponsors, such as Family Readiness Groups. Children, prey to peer pressure, may bear the burden in silence. When Lydia Sapp's father was sent to Iraq for a year, no one else in her suburban high school had a close relative in the military, so she felt awkward talking about it, even with her best friends. Talking about her father's deployment would be interpreted as political, she said, like joining the Gay-Straight Alliance or the Conservative Club, and she didn't want to create a label for herself. Her classmates didn't seem eager to talk about it either, though they knew her father because he taught at the school. So she kept quiet about her feelings and this central dislocation in her life and cultivated a parallel life through MFSO and its antiwar activities.

All of these factors create what Richardson and Lessin call a code of silence, which anyone with a military affiliation is expected to follow. "One of the things that Military Families Speak Out has said is the code of silence is wrong," he insists. "It's wrong for military families, but it's also wrong for the nation. If you're talking about war, the people who have something at risk, their voices are important."

Not long after MFSO took to the streets and the airwaves, it went to court, joining a long-shot lawsuit, *John Doe v. Bush*, which challenged the president's authority to go to war without an explicit declaration from Congress. A request for a temporary restraining order was brought by five soldiers (the John and Jane Does of the title); fourteen parents of soldiers, including Lessin and Richardson as lead plaintiffs; and twelve members of Congress. It was heard by the First Circuit Court of Appeals in Boston on 24 February 2003.

The day of the hearing was startlingly clear, making the view from the top floor of the federal courthouse across Boston Harbor almost worth the wait to get into the packed courtroom. In the lobby, scraggily-haired kids carrying bicycle helmets and gray-haired matrons wrapped in hand-knit scarves, all drafted on short notice for a show of support, greeted each other as familiars of vigils and protests. In the courtroom, John Bonifaz, the boyish-looking lawyer for the plaintiffs, argued that it was presumptuous of the president to claim the power to make a pre-emptive strike and occupy another country, because the Constitution as-signs war-making powers to Congress. Or, as he put it at a press confer-ence afterward, "The president is not a king." The government's lawyers responded that the president had both sufficient powers and the bless-ings of Congress, which had adopted a resolution the previous October granting him authority to deploy U.S. armed forces against Iraq "as he determines necessary and appropriate." (Congress has not enacted a for-mal declaration of war since 1942.) The lawyers further argued that it was premature for the court to step in, as the war had not yet begun and, in a preview of courts-martial to come, that it was beyond the court's juris-diction to determine political questions of war.

Oral arguments lasted about fifty minutes, the judge's deliberations about an hour. It came as no surprise to anyone—including the plaintiffs and their lawyer—when he declined to bar the president from going to war. Thirty years earlier, the same judge had ruled in a lawsuit challeng-ing U.S. military actions in Cambodia that his court did not have author-ity to second-guess the executive branch, and he had not changed his mind in the intervening years.[3] After the hearing, Bonifaz warned that the decision basically said that Congress had given the president a blank check, a prediction that would come back to haunt some members of Congress who had voted for the October resolution. The suit failed on appeal on 18 March, the day before the United States began bombing Baghdad. Though it proved futile, this daring legal maneuver brought MFSO to the attention of the national news media for the first time.

Lessin and Richardson leaned to the left in their political sympathies, but they designed MFSO to be scrupulously nonpartisan. (You get the feeling few politicians would have measured up to their standards, anyway.) Its narrow focus on ending the war made it possible to gather under its umbrella people who might agree on little else, and it was a point of pride that the organization encompassed political affinities ranging from John Birchers to Quaker pacifists and much in between. Women predominated, but otherwise the membership mirrored the military: primarily working and middle class and, according to Lessin, about one-third people of color.[4] For the first few years, however, the most visible members tended to be white and economically comfortable, a demographic with the means to travel, the confidence to make themselves heard, and the appeal of sympathetic and quotable victims for the media to highlight.

Most early members opposed the war from the start, but as the occupation dragged on, the group began to attract first-time activists. As if feeling their way in the dark, they stumbled on MFSO and joined out of a need to do something, anything, while the people they cared about were, as Lessin repeated with numbing regularity, "in harm's way." Some members had always had doubts about the justifications for the war but were afraid to say anything. Others believed the United States was right to depose Saddam Hussein but should have pulled out once that was accomplished. Still others changed their minds about the invasion as new information emerged. Nearly all had thought they were alone in their struggle to reconcile their beliefs and their loyalties. MFSO offered them the rare, safe place to honor both.

In January 2005, MFSO, Veterans For Peace, and Iraq Veterans Against the War organized a speaking tour to inform audiences about what they saw as the "ground truth" of the war. Richardson told his listeners—mostly college students and peace activists—that they, the relatives and older vets, were holding a place for the soldiers fighting in Iraq until they could return home and speak for themselves. The tour began at Boston's Faneuil Hall, and among the speakers at the launch were Lydia Sapp, then a high school junior, and her mother, Anne, a special education tutor. Andy Sapp, Lydia's father and Anne's husband, taught English at a high school in suburban Boston, but at that moment, he was in Iraq with the Massachusetts National Guard.

This was Lydia's first time before a large audience. At seventeen, she was a serious, self-possessed young woman with long blond hair and multiple rings, bracelets, and piercings. Nervous at first, she gave in to emotion as she explained to her audience what it was like for her father to leave for Iraq. "There are nights you feel terrible for various reasons and all you want is to hug your daddy, but you cannot. He's ten thousand miles away fighting someone else's war." She concluded, "For too long our families have lived assuming the government is taking care of what we cannot. . . . This conflict can go on no longer and at the cost of not one more life, not one more tear, not one more average citizen."

After that debut, Lydia reported that she, her mother, and her eight-year-old sister, Mary, "went full-throttle," becoming regulars at antiwar events and finding succor among people who shared their circumstances and beliefs. The family had been looking for something positive in the rotten situation they were handed, and in MFSO, they found a base for their commitment to ending the war, a framework for action, and a sense of being a part of something big. In the fall of 2005, Anne e-mailed me about a forum of military families and vets she had attended: "As I observed the reaction of the audience, as I had the reactions of the senators' aides we had met with earlier yesterday, to the information that we presented, I was struck by how little most people really know about what is happening. I know that family and military speaking out are going to make the difference in ending this war. We are not going to go away. And we will have work cut out for us for the rest of our lives."

It's the summer before that e-mail when I visit Anne and her daughters at their home. We sit around a dining table shoved in the corner of the living room, which is cluttered with mismatched furniture, the family computer, a map of Iraq, photos of Andy in uniform, and two bird cages. In one, a bird hangs from a bar by one claw and squawks whenever Lydia speaks, as if to say, "Buy me a drink, sailor?" Mary—moon face, big blue eyes, blond hair that her mother and sister smooth back affectionately— is finishing her lunch and watching *Sponge Bob Square Pants* as Anne clears a space for my tape recorder.

Anne, then fifty, is on summer break from her tutoring. When I arrive, she is puttering in the small garden behind the half of the house the Sapps rent. They had hoped to save enough to buy their own, but Andy's deployment has put all plans on hold. A solidly built woman with glasses and light brown hair, Anne wears an MFSO button on one side of her blouse and a service flag pin, the kind given to military families, on her collar. She laughs often, fidgets with a CD jewel case, looks to the side when she's framing an answer. She sometimes has trouble remembering things, she has told me, and she shakes her head in frustration as she struggles to retrieve a word or checks a detail with Lydia.

After Andy left the previous summer—first for training at Fort Drum in upstate New York, then to Kuwait, and finally to his forward operating base in Iraq—Anne had decided she had to do something other than sit on the sofa and cry, but it was Lydia who got them to MFSO. A friend and teaching colleague of her parents gave her a Post-it Note with the names of antiwar groups, and when she looked into MFSO, something clicked. "My family are all procrastinators," she says. "I knew this was in the back of their minds, but no one did anything." She wrote to Lessin and Richardson, who responded by inviting her and her mother to speak at Faneuil Hall.

The Sapps are in many ways a typical MFSO family, but Anne is unusual in her ease in speaking for her husband, who supports her in turn. When Andy is home on R and R a couple of months later and Anne leaves the room briefly, he turns to me and, beaming like a boy about to burst his buttons, says, "I'm so proud of her. She's found her voice." Perhaps the senior Sapps are in synch because they see themselves as a proud military family. Andy enlisted in the navy in 1976, later switched to the Army Reserve and then the National Guard, where he remained until he retired from the military for good. Still, it came as a shock when he returned from a meeting of his unit in March 2004 and told Anne that he would be called up for duty in Iraq soon. As it turned out, he didn't get called up until fall, didn't leave the country until that Veterans Day, and didn't arrive in Iraq until January 2005, but they didn't know that then. A few hours later, they told Lydia, who says, "I never knew what it meant to feel like you were punched in the stomach, but that's what it felt like." They waited to tell Mary, whose first response was that her father would miss her birthday. Lydia starts to cry as she tells me this, but it's clear she doesn't want to, so that it's a quiet, embarrassed tearing up. Andy acknowledged that all National Guardsmen know they may have to go to war, but he and Anne had hoped that, at forty-eight and nearing retirement, he could avoid it. Yet, as a staff sergeant, he felt responsibility to his men, many of whom were not much older than his students, so when he was called up, he knew he would go.

The Army National Guard is a reserve force of part-time soldiers who usually muster one weekend a month, plus two weeks in the summer. For state duties, units come under the command of the governor, but for federal missions, it's the president. The Guard trains for combat duty like the regular army, but it had usually been called up for domestic emergencies and natural disasters, and most people joined with such service in mind. That changed with the Global War on Terror, aka the occupations of Afghanistan and Iraq. In the summer of 2005, when Andy was in Iraq, the National Guard accounted for nearly half of the army's combat forces there, and citizen soldiers were dying at a much higher rate than professional soldiers.[5] Part of the problem was that the Guard was notoriously ill-prepared. A congressional commission reported in 2007 that 88 percent of Guard units were "not ready" to deploy, largely because they were underequipped, but also because they were understaffed.[6]

Andy's National Guard division was the first since World War II to be in charge of active-duty troops. He expected to deploy as part of a chemical company, but he ended up supervising the guard towers at Forward Operating Base Summerall, near Baiji and Iraq's largest oil refinery. As Anne and I talk, the area is becoming a center of the insurgency, but she reports that Andy almost never leaves the base. Soldiers disparage those who stay inside the wire as "fobbits," but the Sapps are grateful that he has avoided combat. They keep in touch any way they can—e-mail, phone calls. Anne sent him seeds for a garden, though only a single cantaloupe survived the ants and heat. Andy sent her a vial of sand, which she keeps on a window sill. "I want a piece of the earth where you are," she had told him. She describes his absence as a huge inconvenience; being a single mother is tough, and the life she and her daughters have constructed in his absence is fragile. Mostly, she misses him. "There's a grieving process every day, but no focus," she explains. She doesn't mention the anxiety until prompted, saying that you stuff it down because you can't live in constant fear. Still, as if hard-wired for it, when Lydia noticed her guidance counselor waiting outside her classroom one day, her first, panicky thought was that something had happened to her father.

The Sapp girls are finding their own ways of coping with Andy's deployment. MFSO gives Lydia something positive to focus on, but she's several years younger than anyone else in the organization, so it isn't really her community, and the vitriol she has encountered at demonstrations disturbs her. She tells of passing a little girl in a group of counterdemonstrators at an antiwar march in Washington: "She was making faces and yelling at us. I thought, you have no idea what we're going through." Of Mary's participation in marches and such, Anne says, "She's just a little activist soul. I wasn't sure at first [if I should take her along], but I thought there's too much at stake." A few months later, though, during Andy's brief home leave, Mary is in her room with a stomachache, anxious that he'll be gone again too soon. "She needs to have it over and life to be normal," says Anne, sadly.

Anne, too, longs for a break from the intensity of her commitment, which seems to exhilarate and unnerve her in equal measure. When we run into each other at a candlelight vigil, she breathlessly describes her day: lobbying the governor, rushing home to pick up one daughter and drop off the other, defrosting pizza for dinner again. "I'm tired," she says. "I want my life back." But in a calmer moment, she assesses her antiwar work positively. "As Americans we can do this, and we should do it. I would like especially my daughters to grow up knowing that when they see something that's not right, they try to change it. I grew up, my dad was alcoholic; he was a factory worker, very controlling and manipulative. Women were little homemakers. I was thirty when I went to college. It's really exciting to me to watch my girls grow up knowing that these are the things you can do." In a later conversation, she elaborates on the excitement of sharing those ideals with people in MFSO. "I don't want to say ordinary, because they're extraordinary, but average people who, when they see there's something that needs to be done will do it. To be part of that, to be involved with a group of people who just want to make things right."

Despite the dedication of a growing number of members like the Sapps, for a long time, MFSO *was* Lessin and Richardson. In the first couple of years, a light week required them to put in eighty hours on top of their day jobs—and they hadn't had a light week since the Iraq War started. A year after we first talked, when I pointed out that they were still keeping up that relentless pace, Richardson replied, "Yes, but we're crazy." Their press releases always put forth an array of members available for interviews, and they talked about inclusiveness and decentralization and chapter building, but it was 2007 before MFSO elected its first working board to provide broader-based guidance, and it was hard for Lessin and Richardson to let go, even as the membership grew to include hundreds of people they had never met. The delay in opening up the organization was partly a function of funding: their time was all unpaid, and MFSO's budget in 2005 was only about $150,000, which they covered through grants and donations.

As MFSO grew, so did the list of problems it tried to address: inadequate equipment for troops in the battlefield, misleading and predatory recruitment practices, involuntary retention through stop-loss, a paucity of jobs and education for returning veterans, the cost of the war, and a host of health problems—suicide, brain injuries, PTSD, lousy medical care—that were just beginning to come to light.[7] The organization took on government funding for the war, organized support groups for on-base military spouses, strung up Christmas lights to spell out "bring them home now," and, for a while, hosted an online forum where members could connect, question, and vent. (It was shut down after a couple of years out of concern that members were too exposed and vulnerable.) Through it all, Lessin liked to think of MFSO as a place to debate things that mattered. "I think it's a model for what needs to be happening in the country at large, and it isn't," she said.

People who value debate usually attract it. Iraq War advocates attacked MFSO's patriotism and accused its members of aiding the enemy. Its most zealous detractors paid them the left-handed compliment of forming groups with similar names—Military Families Voice of Victory, Families United for Our Troops and Their Mission—to counter their message. That was all predictable. What stung was when people in the antiwar community questioned their motives. In March 2005, MFSO joined with other antiwar groups to organize a protest in Fayetteville, North Carolina, on the second anniversary of the invasion of Iraq. There had been a relatively large march there the year before, and similar demonstrations were planned now in the other forty-nine states, but Fayetteville is next to Fort Bragg and abuts one of the largest military complexes in the world, and that made it the center of attention. A few days before the events, Operation Truth, a veterans' advocacy group formed the summer before, charged that demonstrating in "the troops' backyard . . . blames the warriors for the war."[8]

In a phone conversation several months later, Paul Rieckhoff, Operation Truth's founder and executive director, criticized MFSO's emphasis on immediate withdrawal as unrealistic for Americans and irresponsible toward Iraqis. What was needed instead, he argued, was an exit strategy that would be both achievable and "morally symbolic." Rieckhoff, then in his late twenties, had spent ten months in Iraq as a first lieutenant, leading a rifle platoon, before returning to the States and launching Operation Truth. In speeches, he said that he was against the war from the beginning and didn't understand the hurry to invade, but Operation Truth took no position on the legitimacy of the Iraq War. When we spoke, Rieckhoff maintained that most veterans thought both staying and leaving were bad ideas. "It's a false choice between stay the course or go now," he said. "We have a moral obligation to the Iraqi people. Pulling out immediately, as a humanitarian reality, I find appalling." Labeling the strategy of MFSO and affiliated groups as "fringe," he concluded, "I think they lose a lot of Americans when they say, 'Bring them home now.'"

Operation Truth later changed its name to Iraq and Afghanistan Veterans of America or IAVA. The inevitable confusion between IAVA and IVAW caused chagrin in both organizations (and confused more than one reporter), but as groups of veterans, they shared a mutual respect. There was little love lost between Rieckhoff and MFSO, however. His reluctance to ruffle political feathers got in his way of doing what needed to be done, claimed Richardson, who had no interest in placating the power structure.

To some extent, the dispute was a question of pragmatism versus radicalism, but the tension between the organizations seemed to be one of style as well as tactics. Lessin pointed out that Operation Truth was not a grassroots, member-driven organization and implied that because Rieckhoff had worked on Wall Street and served as an officer, he had different ambitions and priorities from the grunts MFSO meant to represent. Rieckhoff had an elite education (he graduated from Amherst College) and had worked in investment banking in New York while he was in the National Guard, but he was the first in his family to go to college and had worked to support himself all the way through, and, as the war approached, had switched to active duty and volunteered for deployment.

The division was also generational. Arguing that pressure tactics had to evolve, Rieckhoff charged that the Bring Them Home Now groups were stuck in an outmoded model of protest that had been superseded by online organizing and appearances on talk shows.[9] "We think the media is our battleground," he told me and, there, he proved to be an effective tactician. As Operation Truth evolved into IAVA, it focused on passing legislation favorable to soldiers and veterans, such as a revised GI bill in 2009, and it set up a useful interactive website to help veterans figure out their benefits. At the time of the Fayetteville march, though, Rieckhoff led the charge against the military-related antiwar crew.

The number of things activists who are basically in sympathy with each other can find to fight about is impressive. As a war of improvised explosive devices and rocket-propelled grenades intensified in Iraq, a war of words burst over North Carolina. Stan Goff, a retired Special Forces master sergeant, Vietnam veteran, father of a soldier then stationed in Iraq, member of VFP and MFSO, and consultant to IVAW, wrote in an impassioned column for *Counterpunch*: "The U.S. military is not in Iraq to do a damned thing for the Iraqi people. What particular brand of cheap magical-mystery acid does someone take when he implies that Pizarro should be nominated to help the Incas with reconstruction? WE are the barbarians here!"[10] Responding to what was known as the Pottery Barn rule—If you break it, you bought it—IVAW member Patrick Resta said, "If you break something in a store, you don't keep breaking things. You give them a check and get out of there."[11] (MFSO, IVAW, and VFP later riffed on the Pottery Barn rule by creating a Certificate of Ownership for the war in Iraq, which they sent to Congress with the message, "In dubious recognition of your vote to continue funding the War in Iraq, We the undersigned do hereby bestow upon you this Deed of Ownership.")

After the acrimony had abated somewhat, Richardson argued that demonstrating near an army base was not a matter of taking advantage of a hapless audience, but of taking their end-the-war message to people who were ready to hear it. As evidence, he cited a survey in the *Fayetteville Observer*, which found that only half the residents polled in this military town said the war in Iraq was worth fighting, while 44 percent said it was not.[12] As for Rieckhoff's claim that courting politicians and withdrawing troops gradually were the more realistic strategies, Lessin retorted, "We say very clearly that we are not about making deals with the lives of our children and our loved ones."

Underlying this and most debates about MFSO's strategy was a vexing problem no one seemed eager to examine: What does it mean to oppose a war but support the soldiers who are fighting it? The military-related antiwar groups tended to sidestep the apparent contradiction, in part because it highlighted the differences of opinion and sentiment their members held about the military and about America's role internationally, and in part because it's a muddle. After all, if you support soldiers, aren't you supporting armies, and if you support armies, aren't you supporting war?

It is possible, of course, to hate a war and still love a warrior. You can do that without sentimentalizing or sanitizing soldiers as liberators or conveyors of democracy. You can support the autonomy of someone who decides to enlist and recognize the imperatives behind the decision, and you can be reluctant to challenge that decision while danger is imminent. You can know a soldier to be an honorable, kind-hearted, well-intentioned person, and you can recognize what war requires of combatants. As critics of military resisters never tire of reminding us, armies fight wars and soldiers know that when they sign up. To which Lessin, the good labor unionist, responds that they may have enlisted voluntarily, but what they were being ordered to do had nothing to do with the contractual agreement they had signed. So the question still nags: At what level does responsibility for one's actions kick in? Andrew Bacevich, a historian and retired army officer, wrote around the time of the Fayetteville flap, "With few exceptions American soldiers are not warmongers. But soldiers make militarism possible, and soldiers have ended up paying much of the price."[13]

MFSO stuck to its core goals, which, despite Rieckhoff's charges, included assisting the Iraqi people (the situation on the ground rendered most such commitments largely rhetorical anyway), but the issue of immediate withdrawal was controversial, even within MFSO. When I ask Andy Sapp about it during his two-week home leave in 2005, he and Anne look at each other and laugh uncomfortably before he launches into a debate with himself. "I've thought about that at length," he begins. "It's a valid argument that if we pulled out now, the country would collapse. The Iraqi army unit on our base is mediocre at best. The Iraqi police in the village just outside our base, some elements are hand-in-glove with the insurgents. It could easily devolve into a legitimate civil war, rather than a civil war that we're not calling a civil war. On the other hand, all of the reasons that I hear for not pulling out now seem rather weak. Can it get bloodier? Yeah, but it's bloody now. In some ways, we're as much of a hindrance as a help." He ticks off, then dismisses, various justifications. American prestige? "We lost all the good will from 9/11 when we invaded Iraq." To cut and run is cowardly? "We left Vietnam, Lebanon, and no one called us a coward." And concludes, "All these arguments seem at the very least debatable, if not hollow. I think most of them are cynical expressions of an administration that doesn't want to discuss this."

MFSO was not an extremist organization—a solid majority of the American public came to agree that the war in Iraq was not worth fighting—yet, it seems that the more active members were, the more radical they became. The Sapps fall into that category, but "radical" is not quite the right word. They still believe in the idea of America; it's just that the America they believe in is less and less the America they live in.

Both Andy and Anne were raised in conservative, working-class families, "Republicans back to Abraham Lincoln," Andy says of his. His political affinities shifted during the Reagan administration, when he got involved with religion-based activist groups over apartheid and other social justice issues. (The Sapps are devout Roman Catholics, and this informs much of their idealism.) For Anne, the transition came later, but after an initial hesitancy, she has no qualms about stating her position very publicly. At a large rally on the Cambridge Common shortly after Andy returns to Iraq from his R and R, she takes to the stage wearing an army T-shirt, her hand plucking at her pants, as she tells her audience that she worries her husband has changed. She says, "He has a gentle soul," then reads from an e-mail she has just received: "I get angrier and angrier. In fact, I wonder if I will ever NOT be angry."

Andy is angry about a lot of things: the manipulation of grunts by the brass, the waste and profiteering he witnessed in Kuwait, the fanaticism he sees in Iraq, even, it seems, the chirping of sparrows in the morning because they sound so normal and nothing else in Iraq does. When he wrote the e-mail, it wasn't long after an incident that may have brought on his PTSD, though it would take a while for him to understand that. He was taking the midnight meal to the soldiers on guard duty when a bone-rattling explosion shook the tower they stood in and lit up the sky. As he made the round of the other towers, he was able to piece together what was happening. A Pennsylvania National Guard unit stationed at the base had gotten an address in Baiji for a high-value target ("a bad guy," Andy translates), so several Humvees and a Bradley tank convoyed out to raid the house. It turned out to be an ambush, trapping the Humvees in an alley so they could not retreat when IEDs hit. One of these homemade bombs was powerful enough to obliterate the second vehicle and kill four of the five men in it. "They had to pick pieces of them out of trees the next day," Andy tells me later, speaking very softly.

The following evening in the mess hall, he watched a report of the attack on CNN. "They showed the crater and they showed all these [Iraqi] boys, early teens, and they were dancing around. One of them had a piece of uniform with burned flesh on it," he narrates. "This is in August, so it's eight months after we've been in Iraq. I'm exhausted and angry, bitter, all this. It just snapped for me. For the next couple of days, I really, really wanted to . . . to be assigned to a combat patrol. I really wanted to go hurt people. I really came to understand how otherwise ordinary people can commit atrocities. The idea of restraint—at some point, it leaves you."

Andy is a soft-spoken man with a mobile face, a ready laugh, and a tendency to toss his hands in the air as a shrug, but now he speaks with quiet, careful anger. "I've committed a good chunk of my life to serving the military. I'm proud of what I've done, proud to wear the uniform, and proud of the men and women with whom I serve, and it makes me viscerally angry the way the military has been used cynically by people in this administration for vain and venal reasons. We deserve better leadership than this. The men and women who fight under our flag deserve to have civilian leaders who respect them, not as tools of international policy, but as the patriots they claim they believe we are." Part of that respect, he maintains, would be for the chain of command to stop portraying antiwar protest as an attack on the military. "I have yet to run into a soldier in the Middle East who hasn't felt supported. I'm pretty sure that the majority of soldiers over there understand that there's discussion going on back here, some of it heated, about the justness of this war. What Anne is doing is more important than what we're doing in the desert in Iraq, because if we're overseas bringing about democracy at the expense of our own democracy, then we're destroying ourselves."

I had been talking with David Meyer, a sociologist studying political movements, who told me, "Activists keep pitching constantly. They don't know which thing is going to take off." He noted that most actions don't go anywhere and activists seldom get all they want from politicians or the public, but, if they're determined and lucky, they can force those in power to deal with their claims. He suggested that the antiwar families in MFSO could be effective in multiple ways: by giving ammunition to their congressional allies and courage to fence-sitters to join their cause; by spurring journalists to question officials about the war, which would require the officials to keep justifying it; and perhaps most important, by matching the credibility of military spokespeople with their intimate knowledge of the wars and the moral standing that conferred on them.

Andy, fed up with the futility of "making nice through the political system," suggests a more hard-line approach. Citing Vietnam-era activism, he says, "It wasn't until the protests became so widespread and interfered with the way the government conducted business that the pressure finally became so much that either it gave cover to the politicians to do what they should have been doing all along or they did what was right in order to continue in their power." Or, in the tart observation of Abba Eban, the Israeli diplomat and politician who was no stranger to power, self-interest, or political pressure, "History teaches us that men and nations behave wisely when they have exhausted all alternatives."

"To end a war, you have to build a movement," Charley Richardson argued. "Individuals don't end war; movements end wars." It's hard to know what will end a war when you're in the middle of it, but to win anything, a movement needs to do more than amass numbers. It needs to be sexy or stylish or inescapable, and its tactics need to threaten, or at least confuse, those in control. So it took everyone by surprise when, one overheated August, the antiwar movement grabbed the country's attention because a grieving mother in a funny hat took up residence in a Texas ditch and refused to go away.

~ *Cambridge, Massachusetts, 16 September 2005* ~

Carlos Arredondo, a wiry man with expansive gestures and a smile of heartbreaking sweetness, circles the Common in Cambridge, Massachusetts, handing out copies of a letter his son Alexander wrote in January 2003, as he shipped out for his first tour of combat duty. "I feel so lucky to be blessed with the chance to defend my country six months after I joined the military," he wrote to his younger brother. To his parents, he said, "I am not afraid of dying. I am more afraid of what will happen to all the ones that I love if something happens to me."

Alexander enlisted in the marines at seventeen over his father's strong objection and left for training days after his high school graduation. On 25 August 2004, he was shot in the temple by a sniper in Najaf, Iraq. He was twenty years old.

It has been widely reported that when the marines came to Carlos's Florida home to inform him of his son's death, he fled to his garage in panic, grabbed a canister of gasoline, splashed it over their van, and set it aflame, burning more than a quarter of his body in the process.

Carlos comes from Costa Rica, a country, he notes, with no standing army. He had never been involved with politics, save for the two weeks when Somoza's troops caught him as he crossed Nicaragua on his way to the States. "Imagine Carlos Arredondo coming to Boston!" he marvels still. Explaining that he translates from Spanish in his head before speaking, he reports that he moved back to Boston to convalesce and only now is well enough to speak publicly. (He's a quick study: at a rally a week later, he announces, "I know how to spell in two languages, impeach.")

So here he stands a year on, clutching his son's combat boots and telling me that in the run-up to the war, he found himself watching

TV obsessively, trying to glean insight into news that would affect Alexander: Colin Powell's United Nations speech about weapons of mass destruction upset him; George Bush's "Mission Accomplished" brought relief. "They confuse me a lot," he says without irony.

In time, Carlos will bill himself as "Dad on Fire" and crisscross the country in a rickety truck with a coffin in back, becoming an unrelenting, one-man antiwar protest. Alexander will have a post office named for him; under a new law for parents of those killed in war, Carlos will become a U.S. citizen; and when two bombs explode at the finish line of the Boston Marathon, he will rush into the carnage to help save lives and become a local hero. But that's all in the future. Today, his dramatic story is still raw, and everyone wants a piece of him. With the eloquence of imperfect English, he tells it to all comers, until it turns almost soothing in its repetition. He is speaking out now, he enumerates, first, to honor his son; second, to stop the war; and, third, to save other families—"We were torn apart, thrown around"—from knowing such anguish.

"Everyone's story is difficult," observes Melida, Carlos's wife and Alexander's stepmother. "Ours just got more coverage."

Jesus Suarez del Solar, killed 27 March 2003, near Diwaniya, age twenty.

Erik Halvorsen, killed 2 April 2003, near the Karbala River, age forty.

Darius Jennings, killed 2 November 2003, near Fallujah, age twenty-two.

Casey Sheehan, killed 4 April 2004, in Sadr City, age twenty-four.

Sherwood Baker, killed 26 April 2004, in Baghdad, age thirty.

Alexander Arredondo, killed 24 August 2004, in Najaf, age twenty.

5

WHAT NOBLE CAUSE

"Last year when you guys had your convention in Boston, my son had only been dead a few months. I never dreamed I'd be doing this at all, but isn't it weird what life hands you?"

This is Cindy Sheehan, a forty-eight-year-old mother of four from Vacaville, California, speaking at the annual convention of Veterans For Peace in Dallas. It is 5 August 2005, a year since IVAW made its dramatic debut at the previous VFP convention in Boston, and one year, four months, and one day since Sheehan's son, Casey, was killed in combat in Sadr City, a Shiite district of Baghdad. Cindy Sheehan tells her audience that she first heard about Veterans For Peace just before Mother's Day the previous year, when someone on CNN mentioned Arlington West, a kind of transitory Flanders Field for American casualties in the Iraq War, set up each weekend by VFP members and friends. She and her husband drove six hours south to Santa Barbara to see it.

Sheehan told her son not to go to Iraq, but he gave her the soldier's stout-hearted reply that if he didn't go, someone else would have to go in his place and he couldn't do that to his buddies. "So, as you can imagine," she continues, "the grieving parents who lost—lost, I don't like to use that word—whose child was murdered . . ." It's an open wound, she says. There is no time, no way, to heal.

This is hardly the first time Sheehan has made such claims. She is part of a growing group of Gold Star parents—those whose children were killed in Iraq or Afghanistan—who have been making similar statements wherever they can: at antiwar rallies, on radio talk shows, and at community, educational, and religious gatherings. They began organizing the previous October, when several Gold Star parents, who were also MFSO members, got to talking as they carried crosses from Arlington National

Cemetery to the lawn of the White House in what they called a "Trail of Mourning." Sharing sorrow and fury, these parents came together, in part, to counter the hoary image of a Gold Star mother as blue-haired, shawl-draped, heart swollen with pride—and toothless.

Later, someone suggested forming a separate, MFSO-affiliated group, and at the second inauguration of George W. Bush, as the number of U.S. war dead climbed toward 1,500, seven families launched Gold Star Families for Peace, an organization no one wanted to be eligible to join.[1] By the time of the VFP convention, about fifty families were members. Their goals mirrored those of MFSO—take care of the troops in combat, bring them home quickly, and fix a system of disproportionate sacrifice—but they brought the added authenticity of having paid too high a price for what they saw as an unnecessary war. They began to seek justice, a requisite step in the healing of individuals and, apparently, of nations too.

"I believe in the power of collective will," said Celeste Zappala, another founding member. A devout, middle-aged woman from Philadelphia with an open face and a melodious voice, she described herself as "everybody's bleeding-heart liberal." She joined MFSO early on, well before her son, Sherwood Baker, became the first Pennsylvania National Guardsman to be killed in action since World War II. Zappala had opposed the war from the start, and, like Sheehan, had pleaded with her son not to go. Sherwood's life had been an ordinary one: adopted as a baby, he grew tall, played the trumpet, played football, became a social worker, a D.J., and a father, then joined the National Guard to help his community and supplement the minimal salary he earned at a daycare center. He had been raised in a pacifist family, didn't play with toy guns, was taught not to hit back. When he enlisted, he joked with his mother, "What's the worst that could happen? I'd have to arrest you and Daddy at a demonstration?" It is a small comfort to Zappala that her son probably died "with no blood on his soul."

After Baker was killed in a warehouse explosion on 26 April 2004 while providing security for a team of inspectors looking for nonexistent weapons of mass destruction, Zappala became more adamant. "I had no reason to be quiet. In some ways, I live in a different universe than I did before. Because I can speak, I must," she said, "I don't think anyone can be neutral any further. Look me in the face and tell me that it doesn't matter." For a long time, it didn't seem to matter, at least not to the vast majority of Americans, who had no connection to the military and were tired of the protracted war, nor to the mainstream press, who shied away from reporting dissent or questioning the costs of the war.[2] Then VFP invited Sheehan to speak at its convention in Dallas while President George W. Bush was vacationing at his ranch in Crawford. Sheehan called MFSO's Nancy Lessin in Boston to ask if Crawford was anywhere near Dallas, and what would become the most effective protest against the war was born. It would also mark the emergence of IVAW on the national scene.

At the VFP convention, Sheehan spoke like an old-timey preacher, her lack of polish part of her charm. Her speech wandered, repeated, looped back on itself, and fell into clichés and half-considered ideas: the war is for oil and oilmen; Camilo Mejia, another speaker at the convention, emerged from prison a stronger person; and—a big applause line—Bush must get Israel out of Palestine. But for all her digressions, her message and determination were clear: she was going to keep vigil at Bush's ranch until he moseyed down the road to give her a good reason for her son's death. Like him, she had the whole month of August off from work, and she was prepared to wait.

Sheehan was an ungainly six feet, but her height, the tattoo on her left ankle reading "Casey '79–'04," and her tendency to call the president names were the only things about her that stood out. Her face was slightly elongated, her nose slightly prominent, her short blond hair often tucked behind her ears. She had been married to the same man for eighteen years, raised four children to adulthood, and worked as a youth minister at a local church before moving to an administrative job with the city's program for at-risk kids. She was given to saying slightly goofy things like, "Right on," and, "This is really sad because I have a really cute dress I was going to wear to the banquet tomorrow night, but I'm either gonna be in jail or in a tent in Crawford, waiting until that jerk comes out and tells me why my son died."

Fourteen marines from Ohio had been killed by a roadside bomb just days before, and Sheehan was particularly outraged that Bush had assured their families that they had died "for a noble cause." It was a phrase he used often, she noted, along with the claim that American troops had to stay in Iraq to honor the sacrifice of the soldiers who had already died there. That one really drove her crazy. "Somebody's gotta stop those lying bastards. Somebody has to stop them," she repeated. That someone would be she—and "people from as far away as Dayton, Ohio," because her plans had "kind of mushroomed."

Mushroom they did, somewhat to the dismay of the convention organizers, who were not happy at the prospect of participants decamping en masse to Crawford. Negotiations ensued and a compromise was reached: a caravan of vets would accompany Sheehan to Crawford and stay for a few hours, then return to Dallas for the banquet. So Sheehan left the stage to resounding applause and, with her sister, Dede Miller, and a convoy of about seventy supporters, she drove a couple of hours south to Crawford, Texas, a town of 789 residents, four Baptist churches, one bank, no hospital—and the Western White House.[3]

The group gathered at the Crawford Peace House, an unassuming cottage next to the railroad tracks in the center of town, and began their march down Prairie Chapel Road, which ended at the Bush ranch.[4] They got only about five hundred yards before sheriff's deputies and Secret Service agents stopped them and told them to turn back. The protesters stayed put, sitting down by the side of the road in snake-infested ditches and over one-hundred-degree heat, growing increasingly hot, thirsty, and irritated. That was when VFP's Tony Flaherty stripped off his sweat-soaked shirt and, waving it back and forth like a flag, began reciting the Lord's Prayer. Everyone joined in and the tension ebbed. "I don't know why, but it was the right thing to do at that moment," said Paul Saint Amand, a Vietnam-era veteran and VFP member.

Ann Wright, a retired army colonel and career diplomat, was part of the group negotiating with the police. She reported that the discussion went nowhere until "Cindy just said, 'Well screw it. I'm staying.' We all went, Oh, God. There's not one lick of preparation for this." They pulled some lawn chairs from the trunk of someone's car, hung banners in a tree, and left Sheehan and a handful of women to camp out for the night. Charlie Anderson, a former navy medic and a regional coordinator for IVAW, added this perspective. "The sheriff was just, in my opinion, being a jerk. He said [the protesters] couldn't obstruct the road, had to march in a ditch with cacti and snakes. There were several places that were just impassable, and the third time they stepped out on the road, he shut them down. I think he thought they were going to get on the bus and leave, but of course they didn't. Instead, when they said, 'Okay, fine, we're going to camp here,' he tasked one of his two negotiators with finding a suitable spot, which is how they ended up where they were"—a large triangle of land a couple of miles from the Western White House—"which was perfect." A Secret Service agent, who warned Sheehan about camping on that isolated stretch of road, offered his condolences on the "loss" of her son. Saint Amand recalled her replying, "I didn't lose my son. He was killed in Iraq. If I had lost him, I would go to Iraq and find him." Then Sheehan and company settled in, pulled out their cell phones and began hustling the media.

Anderson was at the banquet the next evening when Sheehan phoned to report. She sounded ill from the heat and frightened by warnings from the Secret Service about danger to the protesters. "She wanted to know if any of her boys could come up," he said. His flight home was the latest, so it was decided that he would go. Someone offered him a ride; they loaded up camping gear, stocked up on supplies at a Walmart, and arrived at Crawford about two in the morning. "There were kids on an ACAV [Armored Calvary Assault Vehicle] riding up and down the street. Honestly, it was surreal," he reported, "surreal" being a favorite word in his descriptions of events that month. Not much else was happening, and the next morning, he flew home to Virginia and his wife and young daughter. About a week later, he got a call from IVAW founding member Tim Goodrich, who was coordinating that organization's presence at what had grown into Camp Casey, named for Sheehan's son. Goodrich needed to return to California and asked Anderson to take over for him. Anderson had gone into Iraq as "the tip of the spear" with the marine 2nd Tank Battalion. (He says this tongue-in-cheek, since everyone in the initial invasion claims to have been on the front lines.) He spent a few months in the Euphrates Valley city of Diwaniya, got back to the States in May 2003, and by the time of Camp Casey, had retired from the military on medical disability and returned to school on the GI bill. When Goodrich called, Anderson was reluctant to leave his daughter again but, as one of a handful of paid staff at Iraq Veterans Against the War, he felt responsible. Besides, the place was exploding.

He was met at the airport by Hal Muskat, a member of Veterans For Peace, and Hart Viges, another IVAW member, who had served as a specialist with the army's 82nd Airborne in Samara, Fallujah, and Baghdad before returning to the States and becoming a conscientious objector. The three drove down Prairie Chapel Road, passing a steady line of cars, buses, vans, and tents, until they reached the triangle lined with booths promoting an array of causes. Anderson was amazed. "The last thing I remember is that there had been two cars, about six people, a couple of lawn chairs, and a cooler. When I came back, there were fourteen or fifteen festival-like stalls set up, banners, chairs, all kinds of signs."

The next day, he got another signal that Camp Casey's message was spreading. His luggage had gone astray en route to Texas and arrived at Crawford with an official notice enclosed, saying that the bag had been searched. On the back was a handwritten note, which Anderson assumed was from the Transportation Security Administration agent at the Virginia airport, a retired gunnery sergeant, whom he had told he was going off to support Sheehan. It read, "Give 'em hell, doc."

Nancy Lessin liked to say that Cindy Sheehan found the ditch with the best acoustics in the country. She certainly found one within shouting distance of a press corps stuck in rural Texas for the month and thirsty for a story. What they found was a middle-aged woman with a little-girl voice and vivid grief, soon joined by more and more relatives and friends of soldiers, all opposing the war and all refusing to shut up and go home. "You never knew who would show up," said Wright, tearing up as she talked about the encampment five years later. "In the middle of the night, we'd see headlights coming up this long, deserted road. Here would be a car full of grandmothers coming from San Diego. You'd ask why they were there and they'd say, 'We heard on the radio or on TV that Cindy's here. And we just had to be here.'"

The military-connected groups who had nurtured Sheehan and conferred with her about the protest now rallied to her side. Gold Star parents were joined by MFSO stalwarts. Scores of Vietnam veterans arrived, first from the convention in Dallas, then from across the country. Civilian antiwar activists streamed in, bringing media savvy, connections, and money. Newly returned Iraq veterans and even some active-duty soldiers from nearby Fort Hood joined the protest and then joined IVAW. The number of protesters on a single day reached a high of about two thousand, but with the steady flow in and out, it was hard to determine how many took part over the course of the month. Camp Casey gave people who wanted the war to stop the opportunity to speak to the hearts of Americans—and everyone from the president on down recognized that as a critical front in the conflict.

By now, claims that the Iraqis had amassed weapons of mass destruction had been discredited, damning photographs of prisoner abuse at

Abu Ghraib prison had been widely circulated, and the reviled Coalition Provisional Authority had fled with its tail between its legs. The army was missing its recruiting goals, and when a soldier asked about inadequate protective armor for vehicles in Iraq, Defense Secretary Donald Rumsfeld had replied, "As you know, you go to war with the army you have. They're not the army you might want or wish to have at a later time." (Met with sweeping derision and dismay, this surprisingly candid statement was not inaccurate; the problem for the Camp Casey groups was the war that Rumsfeld and company had chosen to go to.) Amid this public relations debacle, the number of American and Iraqi casualties ticked unremittingly upward. Sheehan and other Camp Casey protesters stood as sobering reminders that those numbers were somebody's brother, somebody's wife, and somebody's son.

Soldiers fight, families worry, survivors mourn, and everyone is marked, must be marked, by the experience of war. Losing a friend or a child in battle doesn't automatically bestow wisdom or policy expertise, but it does seem to make you think hard about war and its consequences. In language as straightforward as their circumstances, as if their reality neither required nor allowed for embellishment, mothers, wives, children, and battle buddies dredged up awful memories and fears, choked back tears, offered up details of their everyday lives and ambitions, and bore witness to the sacrifice of what was precious to them in the name of justifications that had been discredited or abandoned. You could see them struggling to find the words that would change minds, change history, and they told their stories with such urgency that you began to hope it was possible to talk a foe to death and end the war that way. What kept their ritual storytelling from devolving into a grief-fest was their wonderfully American faith in the power of collective voices. It was a faith the public shared. By the end of August, polls found that three-quarters of Americans had read or heard about Sheehan, and more than half thought that Bush should meet with her.

Dot Halvorsen lives on a hill not far from the center of Bennington, Vermont, in a ranch house set among other well-maintained houses and lawns. Halvorsen too is carefully put together: small, manicured, tanned, a stylish woman who moves quickly, drives fast, and laughs often, but with little joy. Although her voice can fade into uncertainty and distraction, you get the impression that she has always rolled up her sleeves and done what she had to do: get a teaching degree to support her four children when their father didn't, take up real estate in retirement, join Gold Star Families for Peace after her son was killed in Iraq. "Granted there are some mothers who say, I don't want to talk about that, he was patriotic and he died for a cause," she tells me as Camp Casey is coalescing. "That's nice to think that way, but in all honesty, you look at the details and you can't find what the cause is."

On 2 April 2003, two weeks after U.S. troops entered Iraq, a Black Hawk helicopter carrying Chief Warrant Officer Erik Halvorsen and five other soldiers crashed on the banks of the Karbala River. His mother still isn't clear on what happened, since Eric and his friend at the controls were outstanding pilots. "I have a big white binder with lots of papers in it. It's a little suspicious, but nobody really wants to explain. We just don't know." She and her son had disagreed about the war. She saw no point in rushing into it, but he felt that there was unfinished business from the First Gulf War, which he had participated in. Still, she had detected misgivings when she saw him for the last time at Christmas, even if he didn't talk about it much, except to worry about the age of the aircraft he would be flying. Erik was, Halvorsen says with a sharp intake of breath, "a good kid, my best one."

The night before we meet, the first item she heard on the news as she drove home was that Sheehan was still waiting to talk with the president. Of Sheehan, whom she has met recently, she says, "When I see her face on AOL or in the newspaper, what I see is her grief. I wrote an e-mail last night to all the Gold Stars and I said, 'She's not just one mother, she's symbolic of the 1,800 mothers who are looking and feeling the same way' . . . because we feel as grieved and [we're] wondering why we're in this senseless war."

In winter when the trees are bare, Halvorsen can see the hillside where Erik is buried from her picture window. "I wanted him . . ." She stops, begins again. "I thought he would have liked to be in Vermont. I don't know if I made the right choice." She gives me directions to Erik's grave, then decides to lead me there. Cupped in the green hills of southwestern Vermont, the cemetery is lovely and empty and sad. When we arrive, she jumps out of her car to pull up a leggy weed blocking the headstone, a shiny slab of granite with a helicopter etched on its face. Around its base, people have placed flowerpots, flags, carvings of angels, a papier-mâché cow, a small tin with rusted quarters inside, and a plaque saying,

"Love grows here." I add a stone to mark my visit. "I'm not antimilitary," Halvorsen says, firmly, quietly. "I'm patriotic. I just don't think we should be in this war."

"What do you imagine it's like?" Anne Sapp asks when we talk by phone a few days after she and her daughters return from Crawford. "Wood-stock?" I confess. "I wasn't there," she answers, laughing. "What have you heard?" What I've heard is that when the sun is out, Crawford is very hot, and when it rains, it's very muddy, and in any weather, the land is flat and the sky is big and the ditch is crawling with fire ants and nobody is get-ting much sleep. So maybe I imagine a shantytown with a media trailer, or some combination of a carnival, summer camp, and shrine. What I know is that it is *the* place to be if you want to earn your activist stripes.

The task of organizing this ballooning phenomenon fell largely to Ann Wright, who was then in her late fifties. With short, white-blond hair, wire-rim glasses, and a trim body, she speaks with the residue of a languid Arkansas accent but moves quickly, as if there is just too much that has to get done. She joined the army, she told me, "to get the hell out of Arkansas." She rose to the rank of colonel, with thirteen years on ac-tive duty, sixteen years in the reserves, and an overlapping sixteen years in the diplomatic corps. She resigned from the State Department to pro-test the start of the Iraq War and has dedicated herself to peace work ever since.

When she told an interviewer that organizing Camp Casey was harder than reopening the U.S. mission in Kabul in December 2001, she was joking, but only a little.[5] Her experience had been with hierarchical orga-nizations, where her orders were obeyed, but she knew that wouldn't go down well with what she described as "this very antiauthoritarian, no-body-tells-me-what-to-do group." So she joined forces with Lisa Fithian, a seasoned political activist from Austin. Wright says Fithian honored the traditions of the activist community—"lots of buy-in, lots of meet-ings, everybody's voice being heard"—while she dealt with the military segment, who, to her continuing amusement, addressed her as "colonel." Colonels are rare in the peace movement, and Wright is much admired and loved, but there was also the military mindset that kicks right in. "Once it's in you," she commented, "it's in you."

It didn't take long for the campers to be kicked off their first campsite by the owners of the land. "Where's the nearest public property?" they asked the police, who directed them to the ditch, shallow and about six feet wide, along the side of the road. They devised a rudimentary sanitation system, used the Peace House for everything else, wrote up rules of behavior (no violence, confrontation, alcohol, or drugs), created orientation groups, often of people who had arrived only a few hours ahead of those they were orienting, and devoured sandwiches by the hundreds, sent from a Subway ten miles away by supporters calling orders in from California.

Charlie Anderson's return coincided with a meeting of the ad hoc committee that had designated itself Sheehan's representative to, and protector from, the public. The lead was taken by Code Pink, which bills itself as "a women-initiated grassroots peace and social justice movement," creating campaigns "with an emphasis on joy and humor." (The name is a play on the color-coded homeland security alerts in effect at that time.) Code Pink, led by the piquantly named Medea Benjamin, was assisted by True Majority, a grassroots education and advocacy project founded and funded by Ben Cohen of Ben and Jerry's Ice Cream. Code Pink was skilled at staging attention-grabbing protests, and True Majority brought PR know-how, but from Anderson's perspective, the meetings devolved into stultifying battles over the "message of the day." "I've been to boxing matches that were not quite as intense," he said wryly.

His first meeting took place inside a tent, where the heat was terrible, and, like most of the strategy meetings, it sprawled past two hours. As it wound down, someone burst in to announce, "Somebody just ran over Arlington Southwest!" Arlington Southwest, like Arlington West, which had first motivated Sheehan, was a makeshift memorial of 846 small, white crosses, each bearing the name of an American serviceperson killed in Iraq, which had been erected along Prairie Chapel Road. A pickup truck dragging a pipe and chains had driven through the crosses, knocking down more than half, along with several American flags.[6]

"Cell phones start going off all over the room. Women from True Majority were coordinating media, which had shown up en masse," Anderson recalled. "The next thing was, we gotta get some vets out there. So it's me and Hart [Viges]. We get out there and the media's swarming around, crosses are all messed up, and Hart bent down and picked up the first one and it was one of his best friends. He completely fell apart, as he should have. So it's me and [VFP president] Dave Cline, we basically collected up Hart and talked to him for a while." Reporters were uncharacteristically gentle in their questioning, apparently realizing that there was more at stake than just a good story.

At the request of the police, the toppled crosses were left untouched, but when Anderson arrived at sun-up the next day, a woman was already there, resurrecting crosses over the loud protests of veterans and Gold Star families. He volunteered to help her, and as they worked, the woman asked if he supported the president and the troops. They're mutually exclusive, he replied, referring to the president as "George." When the woman scolded that it was "President Bush," he answered heatedly, "When someone uses you as a murder weapon and tries to get you killed and betrays everything you stand for, then they've kind of lost the right to any respect and I'll call him George, just as he called me by my last name." They went back and forth like that, until the woman asked if he had been to Iraq. "Yeah, I saw it, I fought it, and I'm not doing it again," he told her. "Well, that's fair," she said, and nothing else.

It should have been a slam-dunk, picture-perfect, mud-proof protest: all those veterans mourning lost buddies teaming up with all those parents mourning lost kids to take on the president of the United States and finally break through the officialspeak to something that felt genuine. This was family, after all; politics doesn't get more personal than that.

Back in Boston, Lessin and Richardson cancelled their vacation plans to work full time on getting members to Crawford, raising money, and dealing with the ever-more-demanding publicity. In a hurried phone call, Lessin told me that a foundation approached them to offer a $5,000 grant, and the widow of a World War II vet phoned from San Francisco to say that she wanted to sponsor an MFSO member to go to Crawford in her stead, then called back to sponsor another. MFSO's message— backed up by the fifty Gold Star and military family members who went to Camp Casey—was one of immediacy. "Every second counts," Lessin repeated. "Every day can turn a family into a Gold Star family."

MFSO sought to broaden the focus of the protest beyond a single individual, but that struggle was probably lost before it began. The press was already comparing Sheehan to the Rosa Parks of history books: an old woman with sore feet, who just wanted to find a seat on a segregated bus. Parks was, in fact, a trained activist, part of the civil rights movement, as Sheehan too was part of a resistance movement. The news media, however, preferred the image of a lone, distraught survivor—an easily digested sound bite—and so the protest became "Cindy's protest" and the protesters were "Cindy's supporters." (She was, by now, simply "Cindy" to everyone.) What the press didn't make much of, although it was hard to miss, was that most of those supporters were women.

"Oh, yes," Wright agreed, when I mentioned the obvious: Camp Casey was run by strong-willed, tough-minded, big-hearted women who liked being in charge. "The guys that came into the mix, if they didn't have the sensitivity to see what was going on, it didn't take long for us to set 'em straight," she said with a laugh. "Males were welcome and greatly appreciated, but, stand back, don't try to assert any authority." She described a sort of vetting process—men who could shelve their egos and pitch in as needed were given increased responsibility—but women were clearly running the show.

"Your emotions were all over the place," Wright said, tracing peaks and troughs with her arm. Many people came because they had been hurt by the war, and feelings were constantly being scratched raw by the heartbreaking stories told day and night. Veterans and family members did help and support each other, but arguments festered and erupted over who got invited to what and who got to speak to and for whom and who had the real authority. What threatened to turn into the beatification of Sheehan rankled other parents and veterans who were also dedicating their lives to ending the war. Anderson, who had been doing antiwar work for months, recalls being asked by a reporter, "What about Cindy turned you against the war?"

Celeste Zappala, who had been in the strategizing loop since Sheehan first broached the idea of a vigil, also put her vacation on hold, staying in Philadelphia to gin up support for what she thought was to be named "Camp Gold Star." When she and her son Dante arrived in Crawford the second week of the protest, "Camp Casey" was emblazoned across a banner, and she was informed that she could stand in line to meet with Sheehan. "Everybody was trying to make this work," she said, "but Code Pink took over. It's unfortunate how quickly we got pushed out."

American journalists tend to frame their stories around three I's: individuals, institutions, or ideas. Institutions are usually filtered through figureheads, and ideas come by way of experts or spokespeople, so, if a story has legs, sooner or later, it centers on an individual. Some of this is practical: it's easier to interview a person than a group. Some of it is the tendency to confuse celebrity with leadership, some is the double standard applied to protest or outsider politics, some is leeriness of the mob mentality, and some is a consequence of the news media pack mentality.[7] If the *New York Times* had a Cindy Sheehan story, then everyone had to have a Cindy Sheehan story. And so we learned that Sheehan had always opposed the war in Iraq, but hadn't done much about it until after her son was killed; that she was among a group of parents who met with Bush at Fort Lewis a couple of months after Casey died, but had been too distraught to demand answers; that two presidential advisers had met with her briefly at the start of the vigil, but she had rebuffed them; that her husband was divorcing her and her in-laws were denouncing her; and that she stood in the sun a lot and lit candles a lot and cried a lot.

We learned that clergy led marches, Code Pink tried to deliver letters from military mothers to Laura Bush, more than 1,600 vigils of support were held around the country in one night, and a television ad featuring Sheehan cost $15,000. That the day after the president expressed sympathy for Sheehan but refused to meet with her, his motorcade whooshed past Camp Casey on its way to a GOP fundraiser. That neighbors complained about the traffic, one fired his shotgun in the air, and his cousin offered his property for a second, more commodious campsite.[8] That Joan Baez and Steve Earle entertained and that Martin Sheen, Viggo Mortensen, and Margot Kidder of Hollywood; Dennis Banks and Russell Means of the American Indian Movement; Rev. Joseph Lowery of the Southern Christian Leadership Council; and Maxine Waters and Barbara Jackson Lee of the U.S. Congress all dropped by. And that every group from PETA, represented by a young woman in a bikini adorned with lettuce leaves, to the International Socialists posed beside the crosses, set up tables, and sold T-shirts. (Dante Zappala sent the PETA poser packing and dumped the socialist literature down a latrine.) And because journalists like nothing better than to report on themselves, we learned that Sheehan was kept to a strict media schedule whose rigidity and overprotectiveness they resented and mocked.

Americans like their politics wrapped in stories of individual struggle and overcoming, and so, Sheehan was first lionized, then vilified. With head-spinning speed, she went from Everymom to "crackpot,"[9] "an hysterical paranoid ideologist" at "camp fruitbag and nutbag,"[10] document forger and exploiter of death,[11] and, that old standby, encourager of America's enemies.[12] Her vigil, the *Washington Post* reported, "has quickly taken on the full trappings of a political campaign," and the *Boston Globe*, in a mostly sympathetic column, suggested that "she may be just the latest example of a military family member being turned into a prop."[13] For all the stories streaming out of Crawford, the message of the day that rarely came through was that Casey Sheehan, who had enlisted before 9/11 out of a sense of duty to his country, was killed in an ambush two weeks after he was sent to Iraq by his government for a cause that kept shimmering away like the smile of a Cheshire cat. Attacking his mother's character and authenticity neatly changed the subject.[14]

The complaints came, not only from those who disagreed with Sheehan or stood to benefit from discrediting her, but also from her likely allies. It may be the nature of political movements to fracture, but the Left seems to have a special talent for picking fights with itself. Sheehan soon became a Rorschach blot for the peace movement. Everyone honored her suffering, few doubted her sincerity, and most gave her credit for coming up with the idea of a vigil and having the courage to carry it out. But as August wore on, many began to append a reservation or apology to their observations, so that a cumulative assessment could be titled, "Why Cindy Sheehan Bugs Me and Why I Feel Bad about It."

To some veterans and military families, Code Pink was the villain of the piece, commandeering Sheehan and the protest for its own purposes and pushing its style of in-your-face actions. Fernando Suarez del Solar, whose stepson, Jesus, was killed seven days into the Iraq War, was an early member of Gold Star Families for Peace and claims to have introduced Sheehan around in the peace movement, but he said he later warned her not to get caught in other people's agendas. "I have a beautiful relationship," he told me, "but I never integrate." The veterans, who thought they too should be at the center of the protest, complained that Code Pink pushed them to the background. Charlie Anderson ticked off a list of resentments. When Anderson Cooper broadcast from Camp Casey, he snubbed the veterans but made sure they held up their banner behind him as a backdrop. When a group of clergy came for lunch, the veterans were told they couldn't attend because the ministers had come to see the families. Anderson replied, "My guys have given as much as the families have and in some ways more, but it's not a competitive event." (They attended anyway.) "I'm being brutally honest," he told me later. "Code Pink had decided that they were Cindy's mouthpiece. The vast majority of people who had driven, in some cases, days to get here were not represented. MFSO and IVAW were touted at all the press conferences, but the most powerful voices in the room by sheer number were not veterans and not military families, but were people who had clambered onto the bandwagon."

Someone I spoke with at the time suggested that Sheehan had a lot of "undigested opinions," which she hadn't had time to think through before everyone started quoting her. Sheehan as dupe was a popular trope, and when she wandered from her core message, she could get herself in trouble. (One dust-up concerned an e-mail that she may or may not have written connecting Casey's death to the "Neo-Con agenda to benefit Israel"—a position shared by many antiwar activists and, bizarrely, by David Duke of Ku Klux Klan fame.[15]) No doubt she was misquoted or edited down to vacuousness at times, but the inability of Sheehan and other protest leaders to stick to the big idea and stop squabbling over little ones undermined Camp Casey's longer-term impact.

Four years after the event, Nick Jehlen, an adviser to IVAW, wrote in an e-mail: "I think Cindy is a big disappointment, but she was also thrust into a position where she was under a huge amount of pressure and just reacted badly. . . . I think she bought into the cult of personality that Code Pink (among others) tried to build around her, and turned from a really effective action—asking Bush to meet with her—to increasingly absurd actions that made her and the rest of the peace movement look foolish."

Elaine Johnson, an African American woman, whose son, Darius Jennings, had died in Iraq five months before Casey Sheehan, added another perspective. She and Sheehan had campaigned together since 2004, and she too came to Crawford. "The media just focused on Cindy, Cindy. Cindy is not the only Gold Star mother," she said emphatically. "I don't want to be a racist, but we were together and the media focused on Cindy."

Celeste Zappala was even blunter. She believed that what started as an opportunity to bring the anguish of military families to the American public got hijacked by the toxic combination of "a drama queen"—Sheehan—and a press who insisted on an individual heroine and refused to see the whole of the message. Zappala and Sheehan no longer speak.

Amid this cacophony, the Bush administration countered with its own PR blitz, sending the president to Salt Lake City to address the Veterans of Foreign Wars and coordinating home-towner interviews with supportive soldiers. Much was made of who got to speak for the dead, particularly in news stories about the smaller counterprotests.[16] Fort Qualls, named in honor of Louis Wayne Qualls, a twenty-year-old marine killed in Fallujah the previous November, was set up in Crawford, and other Bush supporters settled across the road from the antiwar encampment. The two sets of protesters usually were antagonistic, but Jeff Key, a member of IVAW, told me a slightly different story.

He was raised in Alabama, so felt he understood the counterdemonstrators. "They are operating on the information they have been given, and I know what information they have been given"—he slapped his hand at each word for emphasis—"because I grew up in that culture. So their signs saying, 'Support the troops, Support the president.' . . . Actually, I *do* support the office of the presidency, so much so that if someone's besmirching it, I feel obliged as an American citizen to speak out about it." Often, during his time in Crawford, he talked and prayed with the war's supporters, trying to explain, he said, "based on what I knew their beliefs to be [that] they were on the wrong side of history." Each evening, Key played taps at a prayer vigil honoring those who had died. One day he invited a man whose son had been killed in Iraq to come with him. No political speeches, Key promised, just prayer. "He said, 'I'll only come if I can bring my flag.' He had one of those telescoping flag poles. I said, 'Only if I can carry it for you.' So I took his flag, carried it across [the road], and they came.'"

On 18 August, Sheehan and her sister flew to Los Angeles to attend to their mother, who had suffered a stroke. Her departure sparked hand-wringing debate over whether Camp Casey could continue without her. After it was decided the protest could indeed survive her absence, the atmosphere became less charged, and the press conferences became more inclusive. A second encampment—recognizable from afar by its multi-peaked, startlingly white tent—arose on an acre of private property nearer to the Bush ranch and Secret Service checkpoint, and buses shuttled protesters between the lower and upper camps. Sheehan's departure seemed to create not a vacuum, but breathing space.

It was into this nexus of uncertainty and possibility that Jeff Key had arrived. A strapping charmer of a marine, Key had spent a couple of months in Iraq before being sent home for medical reasons. He was in Los Angeles, performing his one-man play, *The Eyes of Babylon*, when

Tim Goodrich approached him about joining IVAW. "I had completely awakened to all the deceptive things that took us [to Iraq]," Key said, "but I was in the, well, we-broke-it, we-have-to-fix-it camp." When Goodrich called to recruit him for Crawford, Key demurred, pleading busyness and penury, but Goodrich wouldn't be put off. "He says, 'Well, you *have* to. There are other Iraq vets down there.' I said, 'I'll go for three days.'"

Key was driving from the airport with another Iraq veteran when they heard on the radio that Sheehan had left. "When we got there, I guess several hundred people were there. They were kind of lost without their leader. Having been to Iraq and opposed to the occupation, we [the veterans] kind of filled a vacuum there in the middle. It became about the veterans and our speaking about our stories and other military families who had lost children or had children who were still serving." About a dozen IVAW members were in residence, and others passed through or joined during the vigil. As Key talked with them, his ideas about the occupation changed. "It was really about the golden rule," he explained. "What would I want for America if the tables turned? How long would I want the Iraqi military to occupy my country? The Iraqis, look what incredible courage they have. Those who oppose the occupation will do so with sticks and stones against a military budget that is greater than all the rest of the military budgets of the world combined. Don't tell me that we're needed there to squelch violence, we have to be their police force."

Key, still at the encampment a week later when Sheehan returned, joined a group greeting her at the Waco airport. "It was kind of like a gagglefuck in there," he reported. "One of the rent-a-cops came up and said, 'Who's in charge here?' I'm still, you know, six-five, a marine. Thirty people pointed at me and said, 'Him.' So I kind of did what I learned in the marines about how to organize a crowd of people." He was subsequently recruited by Code Pink to be Sheehan's bodyguard on her whistle-stop national tour that grew out of Camp Casey. That put them in close quarters, and, like many others, he is ambivalent in his assessment of her. "I mean, the thing was, Cindy's incredible courage was that she was just not going to give up. Americans self-congratulate so much about our willingness to stand up for freedom and democracy, but really when the rubber meets the road, I don't know how many people are willing to put themselves at great risk, and Cindy certainly was. And I admire that. She drove me crazy and I drove her crazy part of the time, I'm sure." But, he added, "I thought if I had been killed in Iraq and my mother had been trying to end the occupation, bring attention to war crimes, then I would hope that Casey would have done the same for my mom. I don't regret it. It was very exciting. I felt like I was part of history." As for the effectiveness of the Camp Casey protest, Key remained philosophical. "Over and over I'm reminded you do what you do because it's right to do, not because you're attached to any outcomes."

Five days after Sheehan returned to Texas, Hurricane Katrina hit New Orleans, and the national gaze shifted eastward. So did a segment of Camp Casey, as veterans and other activists, by now well-trained in emergency logistics, rushed to help victims along the Gulf Coast. They packed up ten thousand pounds of food and equipment, loaded it into five pickup trucks and a U-Haul, and drove to Covington, Louisiana, where Veterans For Peace helped organize a relief effort. The vigil was breaking up anyway: Bush was ending his vacation and returning to Washington, and the protesters were embarking on a Bring Them Home Now bus tour of veterans and military families, who would visit more than forty cities in more than half the states before converging in Washington for an antiwar march, which they predicted would dwarf any since the war began.[17]

At the very end of August, as U.S. combat deaths in Iraq approached two thousand, American disapproval of the situation there approached 60 percent, and Defense Department spending on that war approached $175 billion, the president finally gave an answer to Sheehan's question about her son's death.[18] Speaking at a commemoration of the Allied victory over Japan in World War II, Bush said that the U.S. military was in Iraq to deny terrorists access to oil fields, which would "fund their ambitions."[19] In other words, it was all about oil, as the veterans had been saying all along.

Depending on your perspective, Sheehan's media-savvy move was intended either to hold Bush accountable or to embarrass him, but, either way, his refusal to accommodate the former made the latter inevitable. Her straightforward, unequivocal, easily grasped demand—end the war to keep other mothers' children from harm—surprised an administration that had previously dismissed the peace movement, and pushed that movement into the public consciousness as no action had before. It changed the story of the war from a military one, the province of experts, to a family one, where everybody's an expert. Most important, it nudged the debate from when victory might come to how quickly the troops might come home.

For the fledgling Iraq Veterans Against the War, the Camp Casey protest had specific benefits, providing them with a national stage, a slogan to rally around, and the kind of intense discussion and camaraderie that clarified the thinking of veterans, such as Key, about the occupation. The most immediate consequence, however, was that the Iraq veterans began to claim their place at the table. Antiwar protests had been respectful of soldiers, but now IVAW insisted that they be inclusive. No longer content to be displayed as victims, these veterans were ready to be leaders, so on 24 September 2005, when hundreds of members of the Bring Them Home Now coalition joined with hundreds of thousands of antiwar marchers in Washington, it was the newly returned veterans carrying the IVAW banner who walked at the lead with Sheehan.

The march, which far surpassed organizers' projections, snaked through Washington's Saturday-deserted streets with determination, a pretty good rhythm section, and occasional flashes of wit.[20] One placard read, "Bush Has Iraqtile Dysfunction," another, referring to Hurricane Katrina, demanded, "Make Levees, Not War," and a post on the ever-irreverent Smedley Butler forum inquired, "Did it occur to anyone else that the biggest difference between this antiwar rally and those of the sixties was that there were more women in bras and less weed?"

The white crosses of Arlington Southwest were arranged in neat rows along the National Mall, and Gold Star parents added pairs of empty combat boots with dog-tags tying their tongues, as if to secure the silence of the dead. As I waited nearby for the march to begin, I struck up a conversation with Jack Amoureux, a graduate student in political science, whose kid brother was in Iraq with the marines. Our talk inevitably turned to Sheehan and Camp Casey, and with apparent amusement at being a good student, Amoureux recited, "In politics, contingency matters." "Contingency" is academese for "stuff happens in relation to other stuff," and Amoureux's point was that Sheehan, the antiwar groups, and the people who had flocked to support them, first to Texas, then in cities and towns all over the country, had altered the political climate. Whatever else Sheehan had accomplished, she had sent the message that change was possible.

It's a surprisingly swampy day for September, and a healthy-size group has gathered on the Common in Cambridge, Massachusetts, to see Cindy Sheehan. She's the headliner of the Bring Them Home Now tour, and the buses are late. People mill around, greet friends, test microphones, jiggle handmade signs bearing earnest messages. The crowd tends toward middle age, perhaps because, as some wag suggests, kids make websites, not war. One woman waves an American flag, two local politicians work the crowd, three police officers watch impassively from the sidelines. Near the makeshift stage, a group of women begins to sing, and "Ain't gonna study war no more" floats in sweet, close harmony into the early autumn sky.

Suddenly, a murmur slithers through the gathering, as a white RV pulls up and about a dozen people spill out. A few clamber to the vehicle's roof to attach a red, white, and blue banner proclaiming, "From Camp Casey, Crawford to Washington, D.C.," while the rest of the entourage, representing the four military-related groups who formed the core of Camp Casey, mounts the stage. After they tell their stories once again, Sheehan will arrive to rock-star acclaim. She'll graciously acknowledge the groups in the coalition, along with the twelve thousand people she'll claim showed up, as key to Camp Casey's success. Then she'll say, "George Bush wouldn't meet with me, but I went over his head. I went to the American people," and her audience will go wild, wanting desperately for that to be true.

By this time, Sheehan is a more polished speaker, but so are the others, who have been addressing similar rallies across the country. So when Jeff Key in a bright red "Peace is Patriotic" T-shirt, takes his turn, he is a magnetic closing act. With a marine's crisp bearing, he takes the microphone to explain that he doesn't know if he's still in the Corps, since he recently outed himself in front of five million people on CNN's *Paula Zahn Now* show. Or, as he puts it to laughter and applause, "I'm kind of C-O-ing my queer ass out of the military." As he talks, a fire engine wails toward Harvard Square, its siren taking him back to the day shortly after 9/11 when he donned his dress blues and went to Ground Zero to pay his respects. "Marine," he quotes the firefighters doing clean-up there as saying, "Promise you won't let this happen again."

"And I'm keeping that promise," he tells the crowd. "Three years later, I'm standing here and I am."

∼ *Derry, New Hampshire, 1 September 2005* ∼

Joseph Turcotte, a baby-faced, twenty-three-year-old lance corporal in the marines, had been cooling his heels in Kuwait for a month when his commanding officer instructed him to write a final letter home, as warriors do before they go into battle. "That night, one of the chaplains went out in the desert and started playing 'Amazing Grace' with bagpipes," he reports. "The next day we loaded up on the trucks and headed out. I didn't know where I was headed."

Entering Iraq through a hole in the wall, they lumbered north in a convoy of twenty-five-foot-long trucks pulling howitzers, exchanging the desert of Kuwait for the green, rolling hills of southern Iraq. Farther north, the countryside grew even more beautiful, "Like what you expect pictures of Old Testament scenery to be," Joseph marvels. Before the marines, he had traveled only as far away as Canada, once, when he was a kid.

Five years earlier, he was a high school graduate in southern New Hampshire with a dead-end job and no money for college, when a military recruiter phoned, looking for his roommate. The roommate was "arthritic, asthmatic, manic-depressive, a laundry list of -isms." The recruiter, no fool he, signed up Joseph instead. "I chose combat support because I wanted all the ribbons," he says. His mother wanted to sic the family dog on the recruiter.

Turns out Joseph is one of the lucky ones. Back home by the Fourth of July. In one piece. Relatively sane. He moved into a tiny apartment in Derry with his girlfriend, got another dead-end job, collected baseball caps and history books, and joined IVAW.

Joseph asks me, "Have you ever read *Henry V*? There's a part where he's talking to someone about a just or unjust war and he says, 'Every man's duty is to his king, but every man's soul is his own.' But what if the

105

king's just cause is unjust, if the whole war is a mistake in the first place? Well, that's on the king's soul. That's how it is."

He thinks for a minute. "I don't blame the individual soldiers. As far as they can't help or control where they are, I think that their souls are safe. But for the men who sent them and the men who created the lies for this, I think they're finding out that there's going to be hell to pay."

6

ONE PARAGRAPH IN

Veterans wax eloquent about bonds born of battle, and for IVAW members, it was almost a mantra that when they found the group, they felt less alone. The group filled their need to be around people who mirrored their views and understood what they were going through without having to spell it out. Andy Sapp likened it to the reason a black student teacher once gave him for preferring to talk about her work with others of her race. It allows you, she explained, to start one paragraph in.

If IVAW was to have an impact, however, it needed to offer more than camaraderie or shorthand. Camp Casey may have put the group on the map, expanded its membership, and created cool T-shirts, but as Amadee Braxton, who was the de facto executive director, observed, "We pretty quickly came to see that we needed to find meaningful ways for members to participate."

Michael Hoffman, who had been on the road promoting IVAW nearly nonstop, wasn't at Crawford, but he was much in evidence on the northern leg of the bus tour, until they got to New York and he had something of a breakdown. An older vet advised him to step away from IVAW for a while. Letting go was hard, but, as Hoffman noted wryly, "It helped that I was losing my mind." It was the right move. "This is a movement, not a person," he said a few years later. "Movements can grow beyond people, and that's what we really had to focus on. It's not just me, it's hundreds of us."

In the fall of 2005, IVAW was only a couple of hundred, and the organization still functioned primarily as a rent-a-vet service for rallies, marches, meetings, panels, anywhere the antiwar movement needed a little battle cred. Members were primed to do something more, but they were scattered around the country, fed up with regimentation, and wary, if not contemptuous, of what they saw as a tired "protest culture." They had big ambitions but minimal resources and little experience in any organization, save for the military—and they had mixed feelings, to say the least, about how that was organized. That was when the interim board, guided by Braxton and Stan Goff, a Vietnam War veteran, began working on IVAW's bylaws and points of unity.[1] They hired four regional coordinators to welcome new members and represent IVAW nationally, and in January 2006, about fifteen members with leadership potential met in Philadelphia to consider overall structure and direction for the organization.

As Hoffman pulled back, others emerged to fill the gap. Camilo Mejia was out of prison; Kelly Dougherty was finishing her college degree; Jose Vasquez was studying in New York while awaiting approval of his conscientious objector petition; Geoff Millard was just out of the National Guard and eager to start a Washington, DC, chapter; Garett Reppenhagen was ready to use the organizational training he had gotten from Bobby Mueller at Veterans for America; and Anita Foster, a CO who had been in military intelligence, brought experience in nonprofit management and fundraising. "[These people were] leaders in that they were vocal, they were persuasive, they were charismatic and they had a high level of commitment to something that was in the process of defining itself," said Braxton. "They were very dedicated to whatever that was, and they were at that point in their lives where they had the time to devote to it."

Their first big action was Walkin' to New Orleans, a six-day, 130-mile march from Mobile to New Orleans in March 2006. Named after the Fats Domino song, Walkin' was organized by Goff to mark the third anniversary of the invasion of Iraq and demonstrate how the war was draining resources from rebuilding the Gulf Coast, which was still reeling from Hurricane Katrina. About thirty IVAWs, including Dougherty, Millard, and Reppenhagen, marched along with members of Veterans For Peace, Military Families Speak Out, and Gold Star Families for Peace. All day they walked, with their banner aloft, while evenings brought poetry, music, frenzied drumming, and a speech comparing not speaking out to holding in farts.[2] This was the first time IVAW had led an antiwar protest. Some members had marched with Cindy Sheehan in Washington the previous fall, and over the past year, they had asked various protest organizers to place them at the head of the marchers, but "they would say, no, that they wanted celebrities in the front—for publicity reasons,"

Braxton reported. "Some of IVAW's leaders were feeling like, why do we keep going and being a part of other people's stuff? This war's about us most directly."

Braxton described the week as "transformative." The younger veterans enjoyed marching together, this time for something they believed in, but while they recognized that such protests had their purpose, they began searching for a fresh approach of their own. Organizing local chapters seemed a good place to start, because smaller groups could recreate the unit cohesion that had once kept the veterans loyal to the military. The first chapter was formed in February 2006 in Colorado Springs, home to seven military installations, a booming defense industry, a macho outdoor culture, and more evangelical churches than you could count. In other words, not a hotbed of antimilitarism. Yet, the dissident veterans found themselves drawn to the city by its heart-stopping beauty and the challenge of organizing in such a conservative community. "It gives me traction," said Reppenhagen, who had spent his teens there. "It reminds me what I'm trying to change about America."

It was also the hometown of Dougherty, who was then IVAW's southwest regional coordinator. When she learned that the board was considering organizing chapters, her competitive spirit kicked in. "I wanted to build membership," she recalled. "And I wanted to be the first." Members were recruited through friendships, military connections, and the philosophy club at Pikes Peak Community College, where several veterans were studying under the GI bill. Eventually, about a third of the chapter was active-duty soldiers from Fort Collins. They met up at bars, hosted poetry readings, erected a ten-foot-tall "tower guard" in a central park to keep watch over the city, as they had in Iraq, and got Rusted Root's front man, Michael Glabicki, to do a benefit concert. Music got their message across, Reppenhagen told me with a knowing grin. "Gotta look sexy, appeal to our generation."[3]

The chapter in Colorado Springs was followed quickly by others in New York City; central New York; Atlanta; Toronto; Madison, Wisconsin; Seattle; Washington, DC; and California's Bay Area. It wasn't exactly decentralization—a chapter didn't initiate and carry out an action all on its own until March 2007—but it was an effective way to absorb and engage new members. Braxton, however, had a larger vision. When we talked a few years later, she explained, "If the organization just continued on building chapters with no clear direction . . . the organization would just go by the way of a lot of national membership organizations, where you just had chapters doing their own thing, but there's no coordinated effort that makes an impact on the national scene. And the war is a national issue. Certainly it had an impact on local communities, but in order to bring the war to an end, there had to be a national approach to that."

A national approach didn't seem so far-fetched. "Weapons of mass destruction" may once have tripped off the tongues of most Americans and nearly all service members, but as it became increasingly clear that victory, by anyone's definition, wasn't at hand, you could almost hear support hissing out like a deflating balloon.[4] In November 2005, Democratic congressman John Murtha, a Vietnam vet with a reputation as a hawk, issued a press release calling for immediate withdrawal of all U.S. forces from Iraq. "It is evident," he asserted, "that continued military action in Iraq is not in the best interest of the United States of America, the Iraqi people, or the Persian Gulf Region." Those fighting the war seemed to agree; a poll taken a few months later found that 72 percent of the troops in Iraq thought they should be out of there within the year.[5]

The midterm elections of 2006 were widely read as a repudiation of the Iraq policy, but by that year's end, the occupation of Iraq had lasted longer than America's involvement in World War II and had cost more than $300 billion, the sectarian struggle in Iraq had intensified into a civil war in all but name, the three thousandth American soldier had died, and the first somewhat reliable estimates of Iraqi civilian deaths put that number between twenty thousand and thirty-four thousand, with around one and a half million more Iraqis in exile.[6] The region was increasingly unstable, America's diplomatic capital was in arrears, and any suggestion about getting out of Iraq addressed only logistical failures, but never the legal or moral ones. In other words, all the resisters' worst predictions had come to pass, and all the traditional ways of challenging the politics and policies that bolstered the war had failed.

This was the climate in which IVAW held its first national meeting. Veterans For Peace hosted it at their annual convention in Seattle that August, and after the Camp Casey hoopla the year before, expectations were mild—until the younger veterans, fifty-six of them, broke the routine. It began on Friday, when Sergeant Ricky Clousing emerged from fourteen months on the lam and called a press conference to announce that he would turn himself in to authorities at nearby Fort Lewis. Clousing, then twenty, had joined the army after 9/11. A born-again Christian since high school, he said he had enlisted to serve his country and his God. He had worked as an interrogator in Iraq for five months and then returned to Fort Bragg, where he decided that he could no longer be party to "the abuse of power that goes without accountability" that he had seen in Iraq.[7] He sought guidance from a chaplain, a psychologist, and a GI rights counselor and, after months of soul searching, he fled.

At the press conference, Clousing, his neatly trimmed hair spiking up from his forehead, was dressed in slouchy pants, a white, long-sleeved shirt unbuttoned at the collar, and sandals. To his left, crosses representing the war dead stretched into the distance; behind him, veterans stared solemnly ahead. Kelly Dougherty, Camilo Mejia, and Hart Viges made brief comments of support, as did Joshua Casteel, an IVAW member who had attended interrogator school with Clousing. Then Clousing took the microphone to read his statement in a slightly reedy tenor: "I stand here before you today about to surrender myself, which was always my intention. . . . I stand here before you sharing the same idea as Henry David Thoreau: as a soldier, as an American, and as a human being, we mustn't lend ourselves to that same evil which we condemn." Clousing then talked to reporters, had a last meal with his family, and, with IVAW members at his side, turned himself in. At his trial in October, the army prosecutor argued that a message had to be sent to the "thousands of soldiers who may disagree with this particular war, but who stay and fight."[8] Clousing was sentenced to eleven months in prison and served three under a pretrial agreement.

The day after Clousing's dramatic surrender, Lieutenant Ehren Watada addressed the convention. Watada had recently become the first commissioned officer to refuse orders to deploy to Iraq, and now he explained his reasons for resisting carefully and clearly. "I have broken no law but the code of silence and unquestioning loyalty. . . . If I am to be punished, it should be for not acting sooner." Apparently he wasn't careful enough; when he was later charged with conduct unbecoming an officer, it stemmed in part from what he said that day.

The third noteworthy event was IVAW's first election of a permanent board of directors, a big step forward for the group. Dougherty was chosen as chair and Jose Vasquez as co-chair. Other board members were Tim Goodrich, Charlie Anderson, Garett Reppenhagen, Joshua Casteel, Patrick Resta, Joe Hatcher, and Tomas Young. In November, when Braxton had raised enough money to hire an executive director, Dougherty took the job, Reppenhagen took over the chairmanship, and, with that, a solid leadership team was in place.

"The soldiers understand their own predicament," observed Tod Ensign, a civilian lawyer who had supported dissident GIs for years. Among the things the antiwar troops were beginning to understand was that they needed to organize at the unit level. So when Jonathan Hutto Sr., a twenty-five-year-old naval petty officer stuck on an aircraft carrier off the coast of Iraq, came across a book that documented hundreds of incidents of GI resistance during the Vietnam War, he was captivated. The book was *Soldiers in Revolt*, written in 1973 by David Cortright, a scholar of peace studies at Notre Dame and a Vietnam-era antiwar activist. Cortright had written the book after his three years of service, combing government documents, unit records, news stories, and more than 250 GI newspapers to compile a review of the incidents and arc of resistance from about 1969 to 1973. The book had just been reissued when Hutto came across it.

Cortright was the product of a conservative, Catholic, working-class upbringing. He had volunteered in 1968 to play the horn in the army band to avoid being drafted into the infantry, but ended up devoting most of his time to organizing active-duty soldiers, first at Fort Hamilton in Brooklyn, then at Fort Bliss in El Paso, where he was transferred in retaliation for his dissident activities. In his book, he documents a movement that grew from individual troublemaking into coordinated resistance and took many forms: desertion, refusal of orders and combat, equipment sabotage, race riots, mutiny, and, one year, a mass refusal of a Thanksgiving turkey dinner to protest the war.[9]

Predictably, such pervasive resistance was met by harsh countermeasures, but one of the most effective deterrents to dissent turned out to be plain old peer group pressure. During Vietnam, soldiers rotated in and out of units on individual schedules, so the makeup of a combat group was in constant flux, and cohesion was tenuous. After Vietnam, the army switched to training, deploying, and bringing soldiers home as a unit. The stated purpose of the change was to foster unit cohesion; the tacit one was to undermine dissent. During Vietnam, "ringleaders," such as Cortright, were frequently transferred away from their support group.[10] IVAW would experience a similar breaking up of that old gang of mine when, in the fall of 2008, five members of its active-duty chapter at Fort Hood, Texas, were all honorably discharged within a few weeks of each other after months of inaction. Ronn Cantu, one of the chapter's most active members, was told that the order for his discharge came all the way down from the division commander. In the span of a couple of weeks, the chapter was effectively destroyed.

In a combat zone, where the primary goal is getting everyone home safely, political protest can seem irrelevant, so it wasn't until grunts returned from Vietnam in large numbers that GI resistance to that war got organized—or as organized as a bunch of young men with antiauthoritarian instincts and a year of guerrilla warfare under their belts would tolerate. Even then, Cortright writes, coordinated actions could succeed "only if supported by an elaborate network of activists in every barracks and small unit—a level of organization seldom if ever achieved within the G.I. movement."[11] The antiwar institutions that had legs were GI coffeehouses, which sprang up near military bases, and GI newspapers, which were published in profusion between 1968 and 1974, some regularly selling out print runs as large as three thousand copies.[12]

It was this level of activity that caught Hutto's eye, and after he returned to base in Norfolk, Virginia, he arranged for Cortright to speak at the local YMCA in May 2006. Among the dozen active-duty service members who showed up to the packed event was Liam Madden, a twenty-two-year-old marine sergeant stationed about three hours away at Quantico, Virginia. Madden had spent seven months in Iraq as a communications specialist, and he too had been reading, although he had kept his misgivings to himself. "Boot camp is not a place of debate," he said succinctly. A couple of Madden's high school friends, who were stationed near Norfolk, had seen a flyer for Cortright's talk, and when he visited that weekend, they decided to attend. It was Madden's first direct connection with antiwar activists.

In contrast, Hutto was an old hand at protest. With a lot of his native Georgia in his talk, he explained that his first involvement in a social justice campaign took place when he was nine and he marched for racial integration in Atlanta. He graduated from Howard University, where he had been a student leader, worked for Amnesty International, and then, incongruously—at least on the face of it—joined the navy in late 2003. He had spent a brief, frustrating period teaching elementary school, and with a young son to raise and loans to pay off, he was looking for a way to "revitalize his life." The navy gave him the opportunity to do some of that—and lose weight, he added with a laugh—but he also encountered racism and disdain for the things he valued. "The military is not a culture that supports thinking. You study for regurgitation," he said in an echo of Madden. In the navy, Hutto, who is black, undertook a protracted fight to lessen racial discrimination at his work center, which earned him a label of troublemaker and, on one occasion, a hangman's noose dangling in his face, all of which he documents in his book, *Antiwar Soldier*.

After Cortright's talk, several soldiers, marines, and sailors gathered at a civilian's home, where Hutto led a discussion about protesting the war from inside the military. In his book, Cortright describes antiwar petitions that circulated around barracks and sometimes ran in newspapers or were sent to politicians.[13] Someone suggested doing that now, but Cortright advised them that petitions were expressly prohibited by an anti-union bill enacted in the late 1970s. According to Madden, "We needed to come up with something patriotic with a tone that wasn't divisive." He and Hutto began researching the possibilities. Through websites for organizations advising resisters, Hutto found that military personnel are allowed direct and unrestricted communication with their congressional representatives without reprisal. This right, first codified in an obscure amendment to a military bill in 1951, became law in 1988 under the Military Whistleblower Protection Act, which has since been expanded to offer service members considerable protection—at least on paper.

Next, he found Defense Department directive 1325.6, "Political Activities by Members of the Armed Forces on Active Duty," a Vietnam-era measure that allows members of the military to distribute material critical of the government when they are off-base and in the United States. They may also participate in peaceful demonstrations, with several restrictions, including not criticizing the president or military command.[14] The directive is ambiguous and the speech of soldiers has much less protection than the speech of civilians, but Hutto took heart from the section that speaks of preserving the right of expression of members of the military as much as possible.[15] He felt confident that they could find a form of protest permitted by these regulations.

Cortright recalled in an e-mail, "It was only some days [after my appearance in Norfolk], as I was talking with Jonathan one evening, that the specific idea of the Appeal crystallized. I can't recall which of us first proposed it. I remember clearly that Jonathan was the one who mentioned the Whistleblower Protection Act, and the fact that service members are protected in their right to contact members of Congress. He was already experienced and sophisticated in using the law to exercise his rights, as he had done in the racial case he describes in his book. When he mentioned the Whistleblower Act, that was the bingo moment." They decided that the collective protest from service members would take the form of a simple, straightforward appeal to their elected representatives, a strategy both legal and powerful. Cortright and Hutto talked over basic language, sent drafts back and forth, ran them by lawyers, and settled on a three-sentence statement: "As a patriotic American proud to serve the nation in uniform, I respectfully urge my political leaders in Congress to support the prompt withdrawal of all American military forces and bases from Iraq. Staying in Iraq will not work and is not worth the price. It is time for U.S. troops to come home." They called it an Appeal for Redress.

In an e-mail, Hutto credited Cortright with the "genius" of the language. "I say the genius because it was David's position the Appeal should be patriotic and respectful in tone. I agreed with David tactically and strategically, less so on principle. However, as we began to engage the public, I realized just how much of a genius principle it was to write the Appeal in such a way. Our opposition was limited in some ways from attack based on how the Appeal was written and pushed to the public."

They set up a task force of the usual confederates—IVAW, VFP, and MFSO—plus the Center on Conscience and War, a Quaker organization. Cortright connected them with Fenton Communications, the PR firm that had guided publicity for Camp Casey. Then Hutto, Madden, and a friend tested the Appeal on three military bases. When they got more than thirty signatures in one weekend, they decided they were ready to roll. They went public on 23 October 2006, a couple of weeks before the midterm elections. Hutto wrote a commentary for *Navy Times* and they unveiled an easily navigated website, which explained the Appeal, laid out legal protections, and listed lawyers and counselors who would help if signers ran into trouble.

The response was immediate and huge. Within a month, they had 624 signatures; three months later when they unveiled the document, there were 1,028. The last time dissent within the military had been as organized and public was in 1969, when 1,366 service people signed a full-page ad in the *New York Times* calling for an end to the Vietnam War.

On 15 January 2007—Martin Luther King Day and a little more than a week after the president proposed a "surge" of 21,500 additional troops in Iraq—Hutto, Madden, and Cortright, accompanied by about twenty other signers and one hundred supporters, held a press conference at the Unitarian Universalist Church of Norfolk, where they read King's speech denouncing the Vietnam War. The next day, Madden; Jabbar Magruder, a sergeant with the California National Guard; and Kent Gneiting, a lieutenant in the Colorado National Guard, all in mufti, gathered outside the Capitol to present the Appeal to Congress. Dennis Kucinich, a congressman from Ohio and prominent opponent of the war, was supposed to accept it and enter it into the *Congressional Record*, but bad weather delayed his plane, so the trio was greeted by Massachusetts congressman Jim McGovern and a bank of news cameras and microphones.

In a scene out of a Frank Capra movie, Madden stood at the podium—clean-cut, smartly dressed in coat and tie, his nose turning pink in the brisk wind—and demanded that Congress stop funding the Iraq War because "troops are dying while our politicians are squabbling." When Kucinich arrived an hour later, he accepted the document on behalf of Congress and offered to bring it to Speaker of the House Nancy Pelosi. Preferring to present it in person, the Appeal contingent made a grand display of marching to Pelosi's office, but no one had bothered to alert her staff that they were coming, and she was nowhere to be found. They left the Appeal with a staff member and later sent a copy to the congressional representatives of each signatory.

The Bush administration was predictably dismissive ("It's not unusual for soldiers in a time of war to have some misgivings," a White House spokesman told the press)[16] and a counterpetition called Appeal for Courage popped up, urging Congress "to actively oppose media efforts which embolden my enemy by demoralizing American support at home," but the Appeal continued to resonate.[17] After thirteen active-duty signers appeared on *60 Minutes* in February, it gained hundreds of new signatures, topping off at 2,100. The signers' names were not made public, but organizers calculated that about 70 percent were active duty, 60 percent had served in Iraq, and 15 percent were officers. This was about three and a half times the proportion of active duty troops who had signed the Vietnam ad.

A month after the Appeal was presented to Congress, Hutto emphasized that its significance was in educating both the American public and the military. "Military members are not perceived as active in the political process, but they're the people directly affected and know the issues," he told me. "My hope is that we have an effect on policy. My blue-sky is to revitalize and rebuild a GI culture."

Hutto never joined IVAW, but Madden did, becoming a kind of Zelig of the organization. Madden is broad-chested and medium height, with dark hair and thick eyelashes sweeping over sleepy eyes. A mix of diffidence and determination, he seems to move forward by refusing to retreat. Madden is a confident speaker, as if born to take the microphone, and once he found a like-minded group of veterans, he became impatient with politics as usual. "We're realizing that Congress won't vote to end the war, and if they do, it won't be because they believe it's wrong, but because of the political climate," he told me over coffee in Boston's North End the summer after he worked on the Appeal. "It needs to get volatile, not lobbying or asking politely."

Madden grew up in Bellows Falls, Vermont, a small mill town which had seen better days. Six months out of high school and unready for college, he enlisted. "I thought the marines were a stepping stone to the rest of your life," he said. He got to boot camp in January 2003, just in time for the Iraq invasion, but that didn't alarm him. "I didn't buy the propaganda, but I had a little more faith in our country. Also, the only other military engagement in my lifetime was the First Gulf War and that was over in a couple of months." He wanted to be an Arabic linguist, but, he said with the mild irony that seemed the most he could muster, "They didn't think they needed that." Instead, he trained as a communications electronics specialist and was stationed at Okinawa, Japan, until his unit became the first sent from that country to Iraq. Madden spent six months in bloody Anbar Province, then finished his term at Quantico in an Honor Platoon for the almost daily funerals. He was honorably discharged a few days after he presented the Appeal for Redress to Congress.

Madden was deeply involved in IVAW activities by the following May, when he appeared as the lead-in to an article in the *Atlantic Monthly* that challenged the impetus for the Appeal. The article was written by Andrew Bacevich, a retired army colonel, professor of international relations at Boston University, and father of a soldier who would soon die in Iraq. The Appeal, Bacevich wrote, "herald[ed] the appearance of something new to the American political landscape: a soldiers' lobby." This kind of movement, he argued was "short-sighted and dangerous" because it implied that "national-security policies somehow require the consent of those in uniform." Moreover, it would "sow confusion about the soldier's proper role, which centers on service and must preclude partisanship." Observing trenchantly that Americans who choose not to serve in the armed forces assuage their guilty consciences by valorizing those who do, Bacevich concluded his piece with a warning: "What is unforgivable is that elected officials and activists have indulged and nourished that desire [for political influence], while the problems that are producing an increasingly politicized military establishment continue to be ignored."[18]

Madden fired off a response, asking which presented the greater danger: "soldiers engaging in political discourse or a generation that stands by silently as the military is recklessly committed to unwinnable and illegal war?"[19] The *Atlantic* edited that out when it ran Madden's letter to the editor, but retained his rousing finish: "All people, especially soldiers, are bound to their consciences before their commander in chief. Accordingly, when I served in Iraq, I was a human being first and an American second. Further, troops are bound to serve their Constitution before their orders. Accordingly, I was an American first and a marine second. This philosophy is what protects humanity from militaries in the wrong hands."[20]

Bacevich's critique may have stung sharply because it indirectly challenged IVAW's reason for being. IVAW wanted soldiers to act politically. They didn't think of themselves as a soldiers' lobby; in fact, they rejected lobbying as a tactic and saw little difference between Republicans and Democrats when it came to ending the occupation of Iraq. But IVAW's opposition to that conflict did imply that if you chose to join the military—the premise of an all-volunteer force—you also got to choose which wars to fight. As Bacevich has continued to point out in his writing, that doesn't work very well.[21]

A well-functioning democracy requires that its citizens be politically aware and informed. Once citizens reach awareness, though, they often want to act on it, and, as heartwarming as it may be to watch young men and women in uniform grow into political consciousness, there remains the question of just how political a military ought to be. The answer usually depends on what it's politicized for, but here Americans are ambivalent. History abounds with examples of the dangers of unrestrained armies, yet we thrill to displays of martial might and seldom define patriotism without it. We teach children to come up with better ways than hitting to resolve disputes, yet embrace warfare as a form of play. Think Capture the Flag and chess, or such family fun as a Veterans Day event at Old Sturbridge Village where "children can join the Sturbridge Militia and learn drilling exercises." We believe maturity involves weighing the consequences of our actions, yet shun and punish soldiers who question orders, particularly when they cite moral repugnance at violence or bullying.

The shift to a volunteer military in 1973 successfully promoted fidelity in the ranks, but it couldn't stamp out dissent entirely. Now, as soldiers were sent back to Iraq for third and fourth tours of increasing length in a conflict that was getting bogged down in an increasingly volatile civil war, they were pissed off. Being pissed off is a common motivation for political activism, yet the Appeal for Redress was hardly a Praetorian revolt or call to subvert democracy. As Madden wrote in his response to Bacevich, as long as soldiers were used by both political parties "as political human shields in the debate over war funding," they didn't have the option of sitting out the debate.[22] The Appeal gave soldiers a chance to claim their right as citizens to ask something of their elected representatives, and what they asked for was peace.

It was in this climate of frustration and possibility that IVAW embarked on an ambitious planning process. The planning was led by Nick Jehlen and Jethro Heiko, a team of civilians who created direct actions for social and political change under the name of Action Mill. Their philosophy: "You give people skills, then encourage them to use them." Amadee Braxton had met Jehlen and Heiko through an action they initiated at George W. Bush's second inaugural parade, called "Turn Your Back on Bush," where some five thousand people simultaneously turned their backs in protest as the president's motorcade rolled by. Action Mill had broached the idea online; it quickly went viral and unfolded with volunteer organizers in forty-seven states, no permit, and only the slightest of prearranged signals. The press ate it up.

Heiko and Jehlen, then in their mid-thirties, made a high-energy pair, bursting with ideas, examples, impatience with traditional training techniques, and a talent for locating the best sushi restaurant wherever they happened to find themselves. Heiko was solidly built, with a quick, half-smile and a forceful way of speaking, which he reinforced by jabbing a finger up and down rhythmically. An artist and a community organizer, he was living in Philadelphia, where IVAW was based. Jehlen was slender and sported an earring, wire-rim glasses and oversized sideburns shaped like quotation marks. He was a writer, graphic designer, and the art director for *The Progressive.* Heiko became IVAW's organizing guru, and Jehlen took on the role of web master.

One evening as we ferried some videotapes from Washington to suburban Virginia for remastering, I sat in the back seat of a car with Heiko while Jehlen drove and carried on an intense conversation on his cell phone. "If we can't do it, we won't, that's okay," he said at last to whomever was on the other end, and hung up.

"This is how Action Mill works," Heiko instructed me. "No panic."

"Do you worry beforehand?" I asked.

He considered this for a minute. "No, I don't think so."

Later, when I repeated this exchange to Jehlen, he laughed loudly, but added, "I'm pretty sure we've never panicked at the same time."

Action Mill guided the first of IVAW's four strategy sessions in Philadelphia in January 2007, along with Doyle Canning, a grassroots community strategist. Three more meetings followed in Los Angeles, Chicago, and suburban Maryland and involved about a quarter of the membership. Each session unfolded with minimal ground rules ("Don't take our work too seriously, but take our work seriously"), as the veterans reviewed the history and future of U.S. military involvement in the greater Middle East, learned about theories of power and campaigns of resistance, considered different political philosophies, brainstormed actions they could undertake, analyzed who could help and who would hinder them, and debated what it meant if IVAW was in it for the long haul.

At first, the members' instincts were mostly about what they didn't want to do. They were mistrustful of other people's prescriptions for their movement and impatient with traditional methods of protest—lobbying, political endorsements, rallies, marches—which the government scorned and the public greeted with a collective national shrug. "At the end of the day, you want to have risked something more than just being tired from marching," Jehlen observed. Leery of civilian groups, who tended to take over, they gravitated to other veterans organizations, whom they respected, even when their goals or strategies diverged.

Heiko and Jehlen introduced IVAW to the consent theory of power, an idea advanced most fully in modern times by Gene Sharp. An obscure but influential theorist of nonviolent resistance (and, coincidentally, a military resister during the Korean War), Sharp has offered pragmatic ideas about peaceful protest, which have been picked up by popular liberation movements from Burma to Zimbabwe, Cairo's Tahrir Square to New York's Zuccotti Park. According to Sharp, "The rulers of governments and political systems are not omnipotent, nor do they possess self-generating power." Instead, their power depends on the cooperation and obedience of those they govern, which means that the governed can undermine the power of the governors by withdrawing their consent. They can do this peacefully through symbolic protests and persuasion; through noncooperation, such as calling strikes or refusing orders; or through interventions aimed at changing or disrupting a situation: occupying a public space is an example. While such challenges to power include individual resistance, Sharp argues that "if the rulers' power is to be controlled by withdrawing help and obedience, the noncooperation and disobedience must be widespread." In other words, what is needed is a nonviolent insurgency.

Of course, power seldom gives itself up gladly, and rulers usually respond harshly to challenges from below, but Sharp believes that protesters can turn this to their advantage by continuing to struggle nonviolently—he calls it "political jiu-jitsu"—which can end up increasing sympathy and support for their cause.[23] The veterans particularly liked this idea, citing examples of hostile responses to Camp Casey, such as knocking down the memorial crosses, which elicited support for their protest from people who might otherwise have ignored it.

The consent to power theory is not new—it dates from the sixteenth century and was used by theorists and agitators, including Rousseau, Tolstoy, and Gandhi—but it was heady stuff for these men and women who had left school behind, often with relief, and had spent most of their lives playing by someone else's rules. Besides, it made sense. Hadn't the Vietnam War ended in large part because enough GIs had withdrawn their obedience from their commanders? Starting from the premise that they too could withdraw their consent, the IVAWs envisioned the Iraq War as an inverted triangle, balanced precariously on its tip. They determined that the counterbalancing forces, or "pillars," which kept the triangle from toppling over were military support, public opinion, war profiteers, schools, the oil industry, the president, Congress, and the media. After debating how to destabilize some of the pillars, they focused on weakening consent within the military. After all, they reasoned, you can't wage a war without the bodies to fight it. Members would continue to tell their stories, support individual resisters, and take part in protests, but organizing within the military became their central strategy and set them apart from other veteran and antiwar groups. By design or default, IVAW was creating an outsider movement, a kind of do-it-yourself operation, which sought not to argue with the military establishment so much as to challenge it at its core.

The second significant take-away from the planning process was Action Mill's axiom that the action is the message, an activist take on the adage that writers should show, not tell. Heiko and Jehlen showed a film about sit-ins at southern lunch counters to protest racial segregation as an illustration of an action that required no explanation or interpretation to make its message clear. Professional trainers whom IVAW had brought in before tended to baby the vets and put them through empty exercises, but Acton Mill challenged them to plan real and specific activities or campaigns that would be self-explanatory and would alter the way the war was perceived. At that, Jehlen said, "They went nuts."

To counter recruitment, they figured they needed to make it look cool *not* to join the military, so someone proposed "Befriend a Recruiter," which would entail bombarding a recruiter with questions to monopolize his time and prevent him from working on more promising targets. Someone else came up with "Not This Soldier," in which IVAWs would form a human barrier around a resister about to be activated, thereby forcing military authorities to scuffle with veterans protecting one of their own. To mobilize soldiers and encourage them to reconsider reenlisting, they would organize a bus tour to active-duty bases with lots of music and barbeque, and when it was too hard to organize on-base, they would create safe, independent spaces, such as GI coffeehouses, where soldiers could gather. Some of these tactics came to fruition, others never made it past the idea stage, and others proceeded in starts and stops, as the veterans discovered that often the most interesting stuff is done on the fly.

By the end of the planning process, IVAW had begun to see itself as the vanguard of a new kind of movement. Its members might borrow from earlier activists, but they would do things their way, even—especially—if that meant reinventing the wheel for the sheer pleasure of self-discovery. Impatient, action-oriented, angry at the betrayals that had taken them to

Iraq, guilty over what they had done there, and guilty again over being safely home, the veterans needed to see results quickly. If they didn't, Jehlen worried, they would feel betrayed yet again. "They want to get back to believing in this country, get back to the point they were at when they were recruited," he fretted months after the planning ended. "They want to end the war now."

IVAW's insistence on "now" was gut-level, but it was also strategic: in staking out an uncompromising position, they made room for others to negotiate a middle ground. Jehlen cited Kelly Dougherty's frustration when someone—a supporter, a reporter, he doesn't recall—phoned and asked, "What do you mean by 'now'?" Her eloquent reply: "Just bring them frackin' home."

The strategic planning gave the veterans a blueprint for moving forward, a vocabulary for their ambitions, and an historical basis for challenging what they had come to see as the big lie about America's international intentions. It was an ambitious program, but want of ambition was never IVAW's problem. "It was nice to finally say, okay, this is what we're going to do," said Dougherty. "At the same time, it was just hard to maximize the effect of coming up with this strategy because there was so much afterward." As executive director, she, along with her growing staff, were constantly bowing to the tyranny of the immediate, which left little space to refine or implement the plan.

It is hardly unusual for small, loosely organized, underfunded, and undertrained groups to lurch from action to reaction or opportunity to crisis, but IVAW had an added problem: its members may have planned to destabilize the military, but their military experience had destabilized them. Mark Wilkerson, then president of the Colorado Springs chapter, told me, "A lot of times when you're a part of an organization like IVAW, you're speaking to soldiers, telling sometimes really depressing stuff, and it takes you back there. We have members who, a week or two at a time, won't answer their phone, won't answer their e-mails, then come right back in after a few days." What brought them back was that old standby, loyalty. If you screw up, he explained, "You're not just letting down your boss, you're letting down your friends, your family."

Friends and families can have disagreements, however, and it wasn't long before IVAW started slogging through a host of them: personality clashes, questions of ideological purity, conflicts over respect or disdain for the military, and tension between those who fought in Iraq and those who stayed stateside. It was hardly surprising that the habits and hierarchies of the military spilled over. "It would be interesting to work out a graphic of points that doing things earns you," Michael Hoffman once mused and offered a ranking of his own: the marines, his branch, at the top, then the army, navy, air force, and finally the coast guard. More often, status was unspoken, but no less understood. You got points for deploying to Iraq (Afghanistan, too, though for a long time that tended to come as an afterthought), points for pulling combat duty, and points for being a sniper. Regular army looked down on the reserves and National Guard, women had a hard time whatever they did, and Special Forces trumped all.[24]

Pete Sullivan never deployed to Iraq, instead spending fourteen months at Fort Polk's Joint Readiness Training Center, a kind of military Disneyland where elaborate explosions and battles were staged in mock Iraqi villages. (Universal Studios supplied some of the special effects.) After leaving the army, Sullivan considered joining IVAW, but felt slightly fraudulent because he hadn't been to war. A college class assignment gave him the impetus to join, and he found that his posting mattered less than he had thought. "As it happens," he reported, "they've really helped me to see that, despite the fact that I haven't been into combat, that doesn't mean that I don't have something valid to say."

Having something to say and saying it without other people's filters became a cornerstone of IVAW's work. A messaging document advised, "Everything that an IVAW member says is predicated on their personal experience. That is our ultimate weapon and our greatest tool." The telling and retelling came from a need to make sense of the ways the members' lives had been altered by this war they had fought but didn't support; speaking for themselves was a way to regain control of their lives. As they constantly reminded each other, the one thing that could not be taken away from them was their story.

Early IVAW members tended to be in their twenties, and their stories tended to begin like the stories of other young enlistees. They joined up because they were bored or unmoored or headed for trouble, because their girlfriend or boyfriend dumped them, because they were stuck in a dinky town and were ready for something new, because they needed a job or money for school, and almost always because they didn't have any better option. And they joined because they wanted to do something good in the world, that too. The details of the IVAW stories vary, but their arc is remarkably consistent—right up to the metaphorical tossing away of crutches and embrace of a righteous cause.

IVAW members believed their stories were instructive and important precisely because they had been in the military—a parallel to the more popular idea that all soldiers become heroes the moment they enlist. Yet artful narrative is selective, and we tell the stories we want to tell in the way we want to tell them, which is why we're outraged and confused when our story gets spun beyond our control. These veterans had been somewhere civilians don't go, and that experience had made them hope like hell for a nugget of truth in what they had been through. As Dougherty said in a 2007 speech, "There's nothing like actually being an occupier in a foreign country to make you finally realize that foreign policy affects you directly." Yet, when stories about the follies of war are piled on, they numb listeners to their country's broader military intentions and to the reality that soldiers do bad things, often for bad reasons.

Jehlen and Heiko, who stayed on as consultants after the planning process, pushed for a slightly different take on storytelling. "You want to talk about the battle of the story, not the story of the battle," Jehlen explained, meaning that IVAW needed to stick to its core message of ending the war, rather than waste time recounting its run-ins with the powers-that-be, as antiestablishment groups tend to do.[25] Action Mill encouraged the veterans to analyze how the story of the war in Iraq was framed by the various players: Who were the good and bad guys, the sympathetic characters and the victims? What assumptions underpinned each story, and how could opposing stories be challenged? (One useful, if disheartening, insight was that the American public wasn't necessarily antiwar, but rather, anti-loser.) How do you convince without brow-beating or getting on a soapbox? How, Jehlen asked, do you let members speak for themselves and still "manage the meme"? This was before "meme" had entered the vernacular, so the concept of a cultural element that gets passed along like an inherited gene felt fresh. A central IVAW meme went: I signed up to protect and defend the Constitution, but what I did in Iraq had nothing to do with that, so I have the right and duty to refuse to fight an illegal war, which is screwing up the military, our families, our heads, and most of Iraq. "What we're saying is not radical," member Steve Mortillo insisted. "It's conservative."

Memes were useful also in dealing with the news media. Deploying troops were given "media awareness training," where they're advised to keep their comments positive and not much deeper than "Hi, Mom." Andy Sapp said that, in his experience, the process was managed so that reporters met the soldiers officers wanted them to interview. He was made available to the press, but he added with a laugh, "The kid who took on Rumsfeld? You can be positive that kid will never speak to the press again if anyone in the military has any say about it." Eli Wright was serving in Ramadi when "the kid"—thirty-one-year-old Thomas Wilson, an airplane mechanic with the Tennessee National Guard—asked Defense Secretary Donald Rumsfeld publicly why they had to scavenge in dumps for metal to armor their vehicles. "We were all so stoked that that kid did that," Wright said. "The military shut him up and punished him for it, but he helped us." (It's unclear if or how Wilson was punished, but follow-up news stories suggested that a reporter had put him up to it, implying that he couldn't think up the question on his own.[26])

As a kind of man-bites-dog story—soldiers against war, say what?—IVAWs got more media attention than their numbers warranted, but it wasn't necessarily the kind of attention they wanted. They expected to manipulate journalists to win the battle of the story, but the news media, applying their own filters and battle stories, usually glossed over the message of resistance to focus on the vets-as-victims angle. Interview requests from the mainstream media were nearly all for veterans dealing with PTSD, rotten medical care, family problems, or other reacclimation woes. When the more sympathetic alternative press came calling, they usually compared the Iraq veterans' resistance to Vietnam veterans' resistance—and found the new resisters wanting.

In Iraq, service members got their news mostly from the Armed Forces Network and Fox News, playing endlessly in chow halls. To keep in touch with family and friends and to document their deployments, they used Myspace and Facebook and, when they became available, YouTube and milblogs.[27] Antiwar material wasn't likely to show up any of those places, so if IVAW was to recruit within the military, it had to have a presence on the websites and blogs active-duty soldiers visited—or, better yet, create its own sites. Garett Reppenhagen, IVAW's first active-duty member, helped pave the way.

Reppenhagen, fit, attractive, and charismatic, is a veteran out of Central Casting. An army brat, he moved around the country until he was thirteen, when his father, a Vietnam veteran, died of Agent Orange–related cancer and his family settled in Colorado Springs. Reppenhagen swore he would never enlist, but in the end, it was the usual story: he was a high school dropout with a kid to support and no better job prospects. He joined the army a month shy of 9/11, served as a peacekeeper in Kosovo, then got stop-lossed and sent to Iraq in February 2004, where he was a sniper and cavalry scout. He was based near Baquba, which put him in the Sunni Triangle when the insurgency heated up, or, in his recounting, "when the shit really broke loose."

Reppenhagen had his doubts about the war before he went, but they were more about strategy than politics. "I didn't really understand how morally it was wrong until I was operating there," he told me. "It was just kind of like every day there was a little bit of evidence and a little bit of evidence that convinced me that the war was wrong." In frustration, he joined with Jeff Englehart and Joe Hatcher, buddies from basic training, to create the first antiwar blog by active-duty forces in Iraq. They called it Fight to Survive, or sometimes, just FTS, letting others decide what that stood for.

The seeds had been planted back in Germany when the three went drinking one night with the Bouncing Souls, one of their favorite bands, after a concert. Keep in touch, said the musicians, let us know how it's going when you get to Iraq. "So I'm in Iraq," Reppenhagen continued, "and I decide I'm gonna go ahead and write the Bouncing Souls. So I sent them a letter and I get a short reply back. I send them another letter and soon Bryan [Kienlen], the bassist, writes me back. He's just like, 'We've been on tour, we haven't been able to really reply to you, but I finally got to sit down and read your letters carefully and they're amazing.'" (The band later based a song, "Letter from Iraq," on a poem by Reppenhagen.) Kienlen proposed posting the letters on the band's website, so Reppenhagen enlisted friends to write, and they began to get fan mail. "All these guys saying, 'I thought all soldiers loved George Bush and loved the war and bled red, white, and blue, and you guys are really different.' All of a sudden we felt like there was more of a reason for us to be there because we could be the eyes and ears for Americans who weren't getting the news."

Blogs were still a novelty then, so the FTSers had to learn how to make theirs work, but by April 2004, they were up and running. "We were an antiwar milblog," Reppenhagen announced with pride, adding, "We didn't know how close to the edge we were really walking. Ever. None of us could find any rules on posting." Their one caution was to take *noms de blog*. Reppenhagen chose "the heretic" because, he explained, "I sort of felt that I was outside the norm, going against the regular institution." Englehart became hEkLe, Hatcher was Joe Public. At first, it was a hassle to get online. Reppenhagen's battalion of one thousand had all of six personal computers, and those were housed in repurposed shower stalls. You signed up for a fifteen-minute slot, pulled a shower curtain shut behind you, and worked maniacally until your time was up, then went to the back of the line for another fifteen-minute opening. Later, he roomed with someone working in supplies who rigged up an Internet connection in their living quarters, and that provided slow, but sufficient time online.

Fight to Survive announced itself as "the mouthpiece for a group of soldiers who are fighting in a war they oppose for a president they didn't elect while the petrochemical complex turns the blood of their fallen comrades into oil." Entries were long, there were almost no visuals, and the white lettering dropped out against a black background was hard to read. With a smattering of slang and a spate of profanity, the three bloggers offered precise description, irreverent posturing, pithy summation, high-flown rhetoric, angry and increasingly informed political commentary, and bad spelling and punctuation, which Reppenhagen later found slightly embarrassing. "By the time I wrote that, I had probably read five novels in my life," he explained. "That's how I wrote." In fact, how he wrote was vivid, edifying, and very effective. Take his post from September 2004 about being in a bar while on home leave when footage of the aftermath of a car bomb in Iraq came on the news, followed immediately by a report of the birth of a baby rhino. The latter, he blogged, drew more attention. "I felt recentment to all the free people that get the privileges of freedom and have the right to ignore the issues. In the end I look at my reflection in the glass of stout and understand that I am the retard that signed the contract. If there is anyone out there foolish enough to consider joining the Armed Forces, please don't."

It felt good to tell people what was going on in Iraq, what it looked and smelled and sounded like. It made him feel less guilty and provided an alternative to the mind-numbing pointlessness of his days. Maybe if he had known of other soldiers who had refused to deploy or fight, he would have done that instead, he said, long after he stopped blogging, but it never occurred to him that it was possible to resist. Besides, he liked sticking it to the army. "We knew we were kinda doing something that the army didn't want us to do. That definitely fueled something inside of me that I didn't know was there: this want to rebel against something I thought was unjust." He almost got away with it.

Technology regularly outpaces efforts to regulate it, so it took the army a while to figure out how to respond to blogs and even longer to harness social media for its own purposes.[28] Electronic communication is more immediate, unfiltered, and harder to censor than the letters and dispatches from earlier wars, and although milblogs mostly ignore politics or stick to the flag-waving kind, they can raise concerns, some valid, some kneejerk. Blogs can be graphic, in-your-face, satirical, and disturbing. They can cause pain to families of dead or injured soldiers, and they can breach operational security.[29] After FTS's debut, sporadic reports filtered out of blogs being shut down and soldier-bloggers being punished; security was usually the excuse, but bloggers maintained that censorship was the intent. In April 2005, the Pentagon issued its first policy memo on blogs, ordering that all blogs maintained by service members in Iraq had to be registered with their chain of command by that July. It was up to unit commanders to enforce the policy, so responses varied widely, but the message that someone was watching came through clearly.[30]

Apparently someone was watching FTS, because about eight months after its launch, Reppenhagen got taken to the woodshed. It began, he told me, when the sergeant of his sniper team "came into my hooch and he started a conversation. 'Rep, you haven't been writing anything stupid on the Internet, have you?'" Reppenhagen laughed. "I replied, 'Well, I don't think anything I write on the Internet is stupid.'" He was ordered to report to his commander, who asked about the blog and personal e-mails, informed Reppenhagen that there would be an investigation, and ordered him to stop writing. "He basically said that if I was found to break operational security or had committed treason that I was going to go to jail for a long time." He then met with his command sergeant major, who said that if anyone had the right to free speech, it was Reppenhagen, because he was there defending it. Meetings with other officers went less well—"My captain is a Texan, and he basically told me that if he had his way, he'd take me out to the desert and shoot me"—while reactions from his fellow soldiers ranged from hostility to quiet signals of support.

It was a lonely time for Reppenhagen. He was pulled off sniper duty to spend the last two months of his deployment on base, doing boring and demeaning work. "I never once slacked in my duty," he said of his combat missions. "Even when it resulted in killing innocent civilians, I still went out of the gate every single day and did my job to the best of my ability. I think I was less trigger-happy than a lot of the other soldiers, and I was a little more cautious and friendly with the Iraqi people, but I still kept everybody safe in my unit. So being pulled away from them and put on this other duty was kind of a blow to the pride and ego." His fellow FTS-ers fared better. Englehart was a gunner for a senior officer, and although his command probably knew he was one of the bloggers, friends in high places helped him hide the extent of his involvement. No one identified Hatcher, which Reppenhagen found ironic, because he had been the most openly antiwar of the three. In the end, Reppenhagen got off too. The investigation found nothing actionable, and he was honorably discharged in May 2005.

War has always taken young men—and more recently, young women—far from where they began. It jars them from the expectations of their lives, shows them larger worlds, and teaches them to look beyond the soothing lies that hold countries together. (The lies vary; the reliance on them does not.) Some are sent searching for a greater truth, and through their search, they become someone new.

That's the stuff of stories, but there are some stories that can't be told. In his final post on Fight to Survive, Reppenhagen wrote that, as he left Iraq for home, he filled two duffle bags: the first held his gear, the second his guilt. He continued: "The ritual a soldier goes through to fill a duffle with the maximum amount of gear is a wrestling match. It took every trick in the book to fit all my soul debt into the long green bag. So when you see a soldier returning home with a duffle bag at a bus stop . . . think about what is inside the bag. It might be rolled clothing of browns and tans. Or, it could be dark secrets that he will never reveal to his family."

∼ *Different Drummer Cafe, October 2007* ∼

Eli Wright sits at a card table in the Different Drummer, dismantling and reassembling a ballpoint pen as he talks, probably not noticing what he's doing. The Drummer is an Internet café, aka GI coffeehouse, in Watertown, New York, which is next to Fort Drum, where Eli is stationed. He's twenty-six, fair-haired, slight of build, and his arms are mosaics of elaborate tattoos. A sergeant and medic, Eli joined up just after 9/11, not out of patriotism, he's quick to add, but because he believed he had a duty to help humanity. Medics carry guns, a contradiction Eli never resolved in his head, and sometimes they're specifically targeted by combatants, because if you take out the medic, you debilitate the entire squad.

For a year starting in the fall of 2003, Eli worked at an aid station in Ramadi, treating minor injuries. Nights, his unit went out to stop Iraqis from planting IEDs; days, they patrolled the streets in a show of force to stop Iraqis from even thinking of planting IEDs. He learned a little Arabic, joked with Iraqi kids, and always carried extra Band-Aids. People called him "doctor" and he liked that. Things got a lot bloodier during his time there, but, he says, "I still believed my job was to help, not hurt."

One day, he saw an Iraqi man injured in a motorcycle accident. He wanted at least to stop the bleeding or splint the leg, but his fellow soldiers pulled him away. "Why?" I ask, the obvious question. "Our rules of engagement pretty much said that if we didn't hurt 'em, we can't help 'em," he answers, still frustrated by the memory. "Everything we're doing in this country was harming them. Just our presence there was harming them."

Eli says he also treated Iraqis who were being interrogated, or—what he doesn't say—tortured. "Under the Geneva Conventions, we have to provide medical care," he explains. He's reluctant to say more—he's still in uniform—but I can't quite let it go.

"That means fixing up a prisoner so he can be interrogated again?"

"Yeah," he answers after a long pause, exhaling the word. "The fact is that if they're your prisoner, you gotta keep them alive. A lot of prisoners have died under our care, our containment, our interrogation, whatever. So our job is to provide aid to keep them stable, to keep them healthy, I guess."

Another IVAW member once told me, "I would be surprised if anybody has a short story when you ask, 'What made you join IVAW?'" Eli has already said that it's never one thing that changes your mind about war, but all the many things piling up. That's when your worldview—his word—shatters—also his word.

"Then all of a sudden," he says, "it's like, welcome to the truth."

7

WE'LL BRING 'EM ON

"Iraq veterans against the war? Well, fuck! That's me," Adam Kokesh exclaimed when he stumbled across the IVAW website a few months after he left the marines. He joined immediately. Kokesh hadn't been active politically before he went to Iraq. He disdained antiwar protesters as perpetually stoned, unwashed hippies who didn't appeal to his libertarian beliefs, but IVAW, with its big-tent philosophy, was something different, and soon he was at the forefront of its actions.

It was in the spring of 2007, when he was twenty-five, a graduate student in political science at George Washington University, and ready to move on with his life, that he received a letter from a Major Whyte of the Marine Corps Mobilization Command in Kansas City, Missouri.[1] He was surprised, in part because it was so ham-fisted. Whyte wrote that he was assigned to investigate Kokesh's possible violation of military regulations, since he appeared to have worn a military uniform for political activities, which was prohibited. Whyte reminded Kokesh that he was a member of the Individual Ready Reserve, or IRR, until 18 June of that year and was, therefore, still subject to marine rules. Kokesh disagreed. "I thought I got out in November 2006," he told me with a laugh.

He had joined the marine reserves in 1999 and had volunteered to deploy to Iraq, thinking he would help rebuild the country. Also, as he wrote in *SIT-REP*, the IVAW newsletter, he didn't want to miss "the party." Kokesh spent seven months in the Fallujah area with a civil affairs team. They were attached to infantry units, who didn't seem particularly interested in rebuilding anything, so in response, his team came up with the slogan, "We care, so that you don't have to." Kokesh was a good marine: he made sergeant, taught himself Arabic to communicate with Iraqis, and received a Combat Action Ribbon and Navy

Commendation Medal. Later, however, he was bumped down to corporal for bringing home a gun he claimed he bought from an Iraqi policeman and the marines claimed he took as a war trophy.

Kokesh, a firebrand with a flair for political theater, hardly kept a low profile. (A video of him unfurling an antiwar banner during John McCain's acceptance speech at the 2008 Republican National Convention—along with McCain's momentary discombobulation—was a YouTube hit.[2]) But it was his involvement in an action on the fourth anniversary of the invasion of Iraq that caught the marines' attention. That March, he and a dozen other IVAW members had staged the first Operation First Casualty (OFC), a piece of spooky street theater in which veterans, wearing desert camouflage and miming guns at the ready, prowled the rush-hour streets of Washington, DC, to reenact an urban military patrol. He had stripped his uniform of his name tags and military emblems, but the marines identified him from a photograph in the *Washington Post*, and they were not happy.[3]

Kokesh apparently wasn't the only one for whom clothes make—or break—the marine. Liam Madden had also gotten a letter. After his work on the Appeal for Redress, Madden started popping up at all of IVAW's big actions and many of its smaller ones. A week after his discharge from the marines in January 2007, he spoke at an antiwar demonstration in Washington, wearing his combat blouse over an IVAW T-shirt. The protest, and IVAW's role in it, was tracked by the Department of Homeland Security, which included another *Washington Post* story in a compilation of intelligence reports.[4] Madden spoke again the next month in New York at the Emergency Summit to Impeach Bush for War Crimes, a grandly named stop on a grandly named campus tour, "Mission of a Generation: Stop the War Now! Drive Out the Bush Administration." Dressed in a dark jacket layered over a white shirt and a T-shirt, he urged students to reframe the discussion about the Iraq war, saying, "Betraying the American service members is surely a crime." The implication was that the president had committed a criminal act by invading Iraq, but Madden never stated that directly.

Madden too had participated in Operation First Casualty and shortly afterward got his warning letter from the marines, who cited his antiwar activities and charged him with violating regulations by wearing a uniform for political activities and making disloyal statements.[5] At first, he was alarmed, but his research led him to believe that the rules he was charged under didn't apply to him, since he was no longer under the marines' command. Then he got a second letter, this one threatening to recommend him for a less-than-honorable discharge. When he learned that Kokesh and Cloy Richards, another IVAW member, had also received letters, he realized the marines were serious.

Typically, a military contract includes four years of active duty, then four years on the Individual Ready Reserve roster. IRRs are essentially civilians; they are not paid, do not wear uniforms, and do not drill or report for duty. However, an army website notes that they may be subject to involuntary mobilization.[6] In June 2004, the army announced its first major call-back of 5,600 ready reservists to help fill its ranks, and that number remained in the thousands in subsequent years.[7] IRRs may or may not be subject to the Uniform Code of Military Justice (as a legal point, it remains unresolved), but, as Kokesh and Madden learned, they are expected to abide by some regulations.

Louis Font, a 1968 West Point graduate, who has practiced military law for more than three decades, explained, "In very small print, [the enlistment contract] says, essentially, IRR means whatever we want it to mean." Still, he found Kokesh's and Madden's cases highly unusual. "IRR was always just a dormant list and you got taken off as your calendar date came up. This is the first war I've encountered where they're trying to discharge someone in IRR." Font has defended many military resisters, including Camilo Mejia, and when we spoke in December 2007, he had worked on two cases of soldiers who were called back after they had completed both the active and inactive parts of their contracts. Font assumed the army saw the call-backs as a statistical game in which they would catch some people who didn't know they could challenge the order.

He described multiple phone calls to the Human Resources Command in St. Louis, which was in charge of IRR call-backs: after a long wait, accompanied by martial music, someone would come on the line to announce that he would not talk to a lawyer, only the soldier. "He's a civilian," Font would reply, to which the army repeated, "We'll only talk to a soldier," and would then would put him on hold again. He suspected, though had no evidence, that there had been soldiers called up without basis through IRR who had died in Iraq. Font had also worked on several, more common IRR challenges in which a soldier was called back while his IRR calendar was still running. There too he found it difficult to get even the most basic information, such as why a challenge was denied or who sat on the board making the determination. He argued that this amounted to a denial of due process, and usually when he challenged the decision on the basis of law, the board backed down.

Most soldiers, however, lacked knowledgeable legal counsel like Font or other resources to challenge an involuntary recall, so many simply ignored the order. They refused to sign for certified letters, got rid of landline phones, and never answered a call from a number they didn't recognize. That usually worked: the army acknowledged that only about a fifth of IRR "no shows" between 2004 and 2009 faced repercussions.[8] But soldiers probably didn't know that then, so the threat of being recalled from IRR was used as an inducement, and sometimes an ultimatum, for soldiers to reenlist.[9]

The IRR bluff was not the first time the army used contractual sleight-of-hand to make up for recruitment shortfalls. Three days after 9/11, President George W. Bush signed an executive order authorizing a stop-loss policy, which allowed all branches of the military to extend terms of enlistment involuntarily and keep service members in uniform after they fulfilled their contracts. Under the policy, the military could suspend discharges, transfers, and retirements and retain members of units that had been deployed or alerted for deployment. Stop-loss orders had been authorized by Congress after the Vietnam War and used during the First Gulf War, but this was the first large-scale implementation, and those caught by it were not pleased. They and whatever lawyers they could find to argue their cases characterized the policy as everything from involuntary servitude to a "backdoor draft." MFSO's Charley Richardson observed, "We don't have a draft—except for people who have volunteered."

The first, full legal challenge was filed in October 2004 by a California National Guardsman identified as John Doe.[10] Doe was a combat veteran who had completed active duty, then enlisted in the National Guard under Try One, a one-year program for veterans, but his unit was deployed for an eighteen-month tour of duty, which included time in Iraq. Michael Sorgen, one of Doe's lawyers, argued that stop-loss violated the soldier's right to due process, then added the novel twist that the policy involved excessive presidential authority, so, without a declaration of war by Congress, the involuntary extension of service was a breach of contract. It was a creative argument, but the courts were unimpressed and refused to prevent Doe's deployment.

That December, the Center for Constitutional Rights (CCR) tried again, bringing a class-action lawsuit against the policy on behalf of all affected soldiers.[11] The plaintiffs were eight soldiers who had found their way to CCR through GI counselors, Internet searches, MFSO, and a widely circulated call to "Beat the Back-Door Draft!" Seven of the plaintiffs were serving overseas and, fearing retribution, they signed on as John Does. The only named plaintiff was David W. Qualls, a thirty-five-year-old specialist in the Arkansas National Guard, who was home on leave when the suit was filed. Qualls was not against the war, but felt stop-loss was unfair. "They [the plaintiffs] were fraudulently induced to sign up," argued one of his attorneys.[12] The army argued back that stop-loss was essential for unit cohesion, the military's holy grail since Vietnam. The court declined to prevent Qualls from being sent back to Iraq while the case was being heard and, a couple of months later, he reenlisted with a $15,000 signing bonus. He told reporters that he needed the money.[13] The suit went forward, but when the government filed a motion to obtain the identities of the seven pseudonymous John Does, all but one dropped out. The court subsequently decided that the case was moot and dismissed it in January 2006, demonstrating, once again, how supine the courts can be when dealing with the military.

The number of soldiers affected by stop-loss varied with the number of troops deployed. By the time the army began to phase it out in March 2009, about 145,000 service members had been affected.[14] That October, Congress approved retroactive bonuses of $500 for each month a service member had been stop-lossed. Anyone who had accepted a bonus for reenlisting, however, was ineligible.

No doubt the army likes the ambiguity of policies such as stop-loss and IRR call-backs because they are perceived as orders, which soldiers have been trained to obey. Decades earlier, Font was a young, outstanding first lieutenant when he decided that he could not obey orders to take part in the Vietnam War, a decision that earned him the distinction of being the first West Point graduate to refuse to serve in war on moral grounds. He reminded me that the military is a separate society with complete control of soldiers' lives while they are in uniform, and that "throughout history, there has been a difference between military justice and military discipline." How a soldier is treated, he said, depends on whether a commander uses intimidation and fear or respect and loyalty to get obedience, but whatever the command climate, "The military cannot let an idea destroy it."

If intimidation was the marines' intent when they went after Adam Kokesh, they chose their target unwisely. In his reply to the e-mail from Whyte, he cited his record, questioned wasting the marine corps's time on such folly, and concluded, "So, no I am not replying to your e-mail in order to acknowledge my understanding of my obligations and responsibilities, but rather to ask you to please, kindly, go fuck yourself." He signed this missive, "Adam Kokesh, PFC, Proud Fucking Civilian." The marines responded by adding "disrespecting a superior officer" to the charge of failing to obey an order and recommended that his discharge be downgraded to other-than-honorable.

Kokesh found a civilian attorney well-versed in military law and challenged the charges. By this time, IVAW was sufficiently organized to rally behind its embattled members.[15] Word went out on the IVAW website and supporters' blogs, and the mainstream press covered the conflict at length. A CBS News blog wondered, "Is Adam Kokesh the New Cindy Sheehan?"[16] And when Kokesh, Madden, and Richards appeared on *Good Morning America* early in June, they came across as sympathetic victims. Even the national commander of the Veterans of Foreign Wars got involved in the case, issuing a statement titled, "VFW to Corps: Don't Stifle Freedom of Speech," and suggesting that the marines "exercise a little common sense."

Still insisting that the Uniform Code of Military Justice did not apply to members of the inactive reserves, Kokesh appeared before an Administrative Separation Board in Kansas City, Missouri, on 4 June 2007. The written record of the proceedings is a marvel of opacity. It lists board members, attorneys, witnesses, and titles of the written evidence presented and states that so-and-so discussed such-and-such, but it includes almost nothing of what was said. The record does note that Kokesh "agrees that he is above average in intelligence" and that he believed he had the right to be disrespectful. The hearing lasted a full day. Kokesh's attorney argued free speech, the marines argued violating orders, and the board split the difference, recommending a general discharge, which was a lesser punishment than he had been threatened with. Kokesh assumes that decision was predetermined as a face-saving measure. He vowed to appeal.[17]

"Adam's case blew up in their face," Madden said. "It was a PR night-mare. My case, they were like"—he threw his hands up in mock alarm—"Hot potato!" Particularly disturbing from a civil liberties perspective was that his New York talk was included in the evidence against him. A videotape shows that he was out of uniform that day, so that charge had to be based on his speech. It can't be pleasant to have the marine corps tracking your words and wardrobe, but Madden wasn't entirely displeased. For one thing, the harassment gave him a platform for his ideas and brought some wavering supporters into his camp. For another, it meant that someone was paying attention to those ideas and considered them consequential enough to try to suppress.

After Kokesh's slap on the wrist, Madden tried to provoke the marines into continuing his case. He wrote a letter to the *Marine Corps Times*, reiterating his point that it was dangerous to stifle the voices of the troops fighting in Iraq. Shortly afterward, he got a call from his military lawyer, offering him a deal: the Corps would drop the charges against him if he refrained from wearing his uniform while engaging in political protest for the three years left in his IRR contract. He wrote in reply, "I will orally agree to not wear my military uniforms while engaged in any political protest, hell, I'll have it carved in stone if you'd like, upon receiving a signed, written statement on official USMC letterhead acknowledging that my statements in question were neither disloyal nor inaccurate." The marines did not reply. Instead, they dropped the charges and announced, inaccurately, that he had agreed to their terms. Their version got wide circulation in the press, which irked Madden considerably.

Madden and Kokesh were far from chastened by their ordeals. By the time the charges against them were dropped, they were barreling down the east coast on the Yellow Rose of Texas Peace Bus on a two-week tour of military bases. IVAW had identified organizing active-duty personnel as its primary focus, and this was the next major project. As with many of the veterans' undertakings, it unfolded as a kind of freewheeling, mul-tipronged, seemingly spontaneous action, which sometimes went by the name of "swarm."

The term comes from a late 2001 RAND Corporation monograph, which identified a new kind of political activity it called "swarming at-tacks."[18] The idea is that small, flexible groups of civil-society activists, ter-rorists, or extremists learn of other like-minded groups, usually through social media, and converge for a direct political action, which spurs another action, and so on, until a movement emerges. Swarm is based on the principle that the whole is greater and more dynamic than the sum of its local and self-regulating parts. (Even events that seem to arise spontaneously usually require some planning and forethought.) The concept got picked up by anticapitalist activists, who slathered on metaphors about bees and ant colonies and applied it to resistance movements around the world.[19] About a decade later, it would emerge on a national scale in the popular uprisings in North Africa, the American Occupy Movement, and transnational campaigns using social networks to thwart banks from imposing new fees on consumers or corporations from seizing control of the Internet. RAND monographs weren't on the reading list of your average antiwar veteran, and, like most of the groups the term applied to, IVAW didn't talk about swarm, but it was an apt description of what the group hoped to accomplish on its first active-duty organizing tour.[20]

Jim Goodnow, an older veteran with a ponytail and a sharp sense of outrage, donated the Yellow Rose for the trip and stuck around to drive it. The size of a city bus, it was hard to miss, what with an IVAW sticker emblazoned along its side and an "Impeach Bush" banner slung across its rump.[21] The veterans' aim was to raise IVAW's profile, especially within the lower ranks, where few even knew it existed, and to recruit active-duty members and connect them to antiwar veterans in their area. The peace riders planned to get on base whenever possible. When it wasn't possible, they would visit GI hangouts, such as Walmarts, dollar stores, and fast food joints, where they would leaflet, strike up conversations, and, on the assumption that free food and music were an irresistible combination, invite everyone to a cookout and concert at a nearby public park. They hoped to engage soldiers through a combination of emotional appeals (I'm pissed off that contractors are making so much more than soldiers, aren't you?) and discussions, for instance, of the role oil played in the war. And they intended to clarify that IVAW was not against the military, but against the war because it was morally wrong.

The tour kicked off on 23 June with a concert featuring Tom Morello of Rage Against the Machine at Jammin' Java, a music club in Vienna, Virginia. (If every movement needs a good soundtrack, Morello topped the charts for IVAW.) Then, Madden, Kokesh, Geoff Millard, Michael Blake, Steve Mortillo, Nate Lewis, and Sholom Keller, all of IVAW, set off for Maryland to visit Andrews Air Force base and Fort Meade, the home of the National Security Agency. From there, the crew stopped at the naval base at Norfolk, Virginia, where they were met by Jonathan Hutto, and then pulled into Fayetteville, North Carolina, where Jimmy Massey, an IVAW founder, joined the tour. The target here was the marines' Camp Lejeune, one of several military installations strung out along North Carolina's coast. Lejeune is huge, with 56,000 acres of manicured lawns, riverbanks, swamps, and beaches, and a culture of crisp politeness raised nearly to a fetish. It was the easiest base for the veterans to enter, apparently because no one was expecting them.[22] They soon ran into hostility, however. On a blog dedicated to the trip, Kokesh quoted a marine, who recognized him from his appearance on CNN, saying, "Damn, you've got some big balls comin' to Camp Lejeune!" "Yes, I do," Kokesh claimed to have replied.

The next stop was Fort Jackson in South Carolina, where more than half of all army recruits are trained. (Jackson also hosts the Army Chaplain Center and the Defense Academy for Credibility Assessment, which apparently trains soldiers to administer lie detector tests.) The veterans checked in as civilians at the visitors' entrance and went on base to meet an IVAW member stationed there. The base police had warned them not to hand out IVAW literature, a prohibition they got around by writing information about their cookout on the back of business cards. Still, they were surprised when, just as they sat down to lunch, the police pulled five of them outside, lined them up against a row of vending machines, and made a show of checking their IDs.

Although the veterans must have anticipated some official opposition, they seemed not to have planned a response. Kokesh reported on the blog: "Sholom [Keller] happened to have a copy of the Constitution on him and began quoting some craziness about rights, like 'to be informed of the nature and cause of the accusation.' One of the officers went to give him back his ID card. 'Is this your ID card, brother?' 'Yes it is, and I'm not your brother. Dr. King was a brother, Malcolm was a brother, Huey P. Newton was a brother. You are a traitor and a sellout.'" Keller, a former army sergeant, who is white, habitually carried a copy of the Constitution in the back pocket of his jeans, an unnecessary precaution since he had memorized it word-for-word. The veterans were handcuffed and brought to the police station briefly for questioning, then returned to their car, escorted off base, and informed that they would be arrested if they were seen around the front gate again.

They didn't even get that far at Fort Benning, Georgia. Benning is home to the Western Hemisphere Institute for Security Cooperation, formerly known as the School of the Americas, a center for training Latin American soldiers in counterinsurgency and, probably, torture. Benning is an "open post," meaning that all you need to get on base is a valid ID, but as Madden and Nate Lewis, who were wearing IVAW T-shirts, approached the guard at the gate to ask about entering, they were handcuffed and arrested. Kokesh arrived as they were being driven away in a police cruiser and was told they were arrested for protesting. He was warned to stay away, but after changing out of his IVAW shirt to avoid a similar charge, he tried to go on base to find out what had happened to the others—whereupon he too was arrested. The three veterans were detained at the military police station for several hours and charged with criminal trespass on federal property. As several press accounts of the incident noted, the arrests came two days after the marine corps dropped its earlier charges against Madden. They were released, lawyers got involved, the bus tour rolled on, and several months later, Madden received a letter from Fort Benning's commanding general restoring his privilege to visit the base, contingent on good behavior.

From Georgia, the veterans headed back north uneventfully: Philadelphia for the Fourth of July, then the Naval Submarine Base at Groton, Connecticut, and finally, Fort Drum in northern New York State. As anticipated, this last stop was the high point of the tour, because IVAW's first active-duty chapter had just formed there in April and already had fifteen members. The bus crew settled into the Different Drummer, the GI coffeehouse in Watertown, then hit the bars to survey their recruiting prospects. When Kokesh and other IVAWs came to Fort Drum's front gate a couple of days later to pick up soldiers for a cookout, he was greeted by name and told by a soldier there that "we" had been reading his blog. "We" seemed to include army detectives who, unhappy to be called in to work on their day off, told the veterans that they would not be allowed on base. Several active-duty soldiers showed up at the event anyway, along with seventy civilians and veterans. The chapter signed up new members, and everyone took part in a good-humored, can-you-top-this contest to tell the best tale of military incompetence. Competition was stiff.

The tour as a whole was judged a success, bringing twenty-one new members and several other active-duty soldiers and marines who chose not to join, but who could be called on for moral or logistical support. For old members on the bus and at events, the tour yielded a shared experience and sharper organizing skills, both crucial to keeping them involved. It also brought significant attention and credibility to IVAW, which could now point to a concrete accomplishment. Perhaps most important, the bus tour spread awareness that GI resistance existed, making whatever new resistance that followed harder to stifle.

In theory, follow-up with active-duty fell to the chapters located near the bases, but few took it on in earnest. For veterans, organizing soldiers is hard: you have to be in it for the long haul and you have to keep returning to places where you aren't welcome—places where you are, indeed, alone. IVAW members felt awkward striking up conversations about something so controversial, and many found it disconcerting to return to the regimented world they had gladly left behind. Active-duty recruiting seemed to work best when active-duty members formed their own chapters, and in the several months after the tour, chapters began at Fort Meade in Maryland, Fort Sill in Oklahoma, Fort Hood in Texas, Fort Collins in Colorado, and Fort Lewis in Washington. But Drum was the first and, for a time, the most active.

Fort Drum, one of largest army bases in the country, sits on a flat plain several miles east of Watertown, a city of about twenty-seven thousand. Since 1985, it has been home to the 10th Mountain Division, which, in the fall of 2007, when I visited, was among the most-deployed divisions in the army. The base is a self-contained community, with its own water and power plants, ball fields, parade grounds, construction sites, low brick office buildings, rickety-looking World War II–era housing painted in schoolroom pastels, and a section for families with ranch houses and swing sets on barren lawns. Security seemed relaxed, although Eli Wright, my IVAW contact, who was driving, suggested that I put my notebook away when we arrived at the gate to avoid making the guards "nervous."

Wright was then deeply committed to IVAW and active-duty organizing, but it took him a while to get there. After returning from a tour as a medic in Iraq in 2004, he worked in the neuroscience ward at Walter Reed Hospital in Washington, where he had hoped to do rehabilitative care, but his illusions were soon punctured. "It was as bad or worse than Iraq," he said. A series of chance encounters introduced him to IVAW, and he joined late in 2005—with reservations. "At that time there wasn't a lot of public opposition among service members, so I was afraid about speaking out," he admitted. He followed IVAW's website and read to educate himself about the war and the politics behind it, but it was a bad time for him: his PTSD was acting up, he drank too much, he was spiraling into isolation and depression, an all-too-typical story. To top it off, he was sent to Drum, stop-lossed, and ordered to redeploy to Iraq.

Ironically, it was through his chain of command that he found his way back to IVAW. Someone in his unit went AWOL and sought help at the Different Drummer, which brought the coffeehouse publicity. When Wright's mother, an active member of MFSO, came from Denver to help him recover from an operation on his shoulder, she wanted to visit. That was where Wright learned that an IVAW chapter had just formed at his base. "As soon as I found out, I said, okay, it's time to step up and actually do something now," he told me.

Modeled on the GI coffeehouses that sprang up in military towns during the Vietnam War, the Different Drummer was the first of its kind for this generation of soldiers.[23] It was the child of Tod Ensign of the GI rights group Citizen Soldier and local antiwar activists, who sought to create a safe place where soldiers and veterans with misgivings about the army could meet. While the Vietnam-era coffeehouses were counterculture hangouts, the Drummer, appropriate to its time, was more of a lounge with Internet access and no booze. It was a big, open space at the back of a 1950s mall with high ceilings and large windows, a small stage, a scattering of card tables, racks of books and magazines, and a bank of computers, which, significantly, nobody monitored. In a stab at interior decoration, someone had hung posters for the film, *Sir, No Sir*, and for a talk by Camilo Mejia, a photo of Gandhi, and a psychedelic peace poster, which had probably been moldering in some basement for forty years. "It's kind of tacky," Wright said as he showed it off with a mixture of embarrassment and pride. The Different Drummer closed in 2009 for lack of funding, but to this point, it had staged a few well-attended events and, because there wasn't much else going on in Watertown, it attracted townies, who were a prime target for counterrecruiting.

Building an active-duty chapter is a challenge, largely because members are frequently getting deployed or discharged. "It's a double-edged sword," said Nate Lewis, another Drum member. "It's good when guys are getting out of the chapter, because it means they're getting out of the army. But it's bad for the chapter, keeping it going, especially when you've had a core group who have been so dedicated and active." Lewis grew up in rural, western New York State, got recruited his senior year in high school—"I kinda wanted to test myself, to see if I could do it," he said—and arrived at basic training on 28 August 2001. He drove trucks in the initial invasion of Iraq, got home that July, when the situation was still relatively calm, and left the army shortly afterward. When we talked in August 2008, he was studying to be a social studies teacher at SUNY Potsdam, about an hour and a half from Fort Drum. Of his first involvement with IVAW, he said, "It was this sensation, like, damn! I've been studying history this whole time. I never thought I was gonna make history."

For Lewis, active-duty recruitment was "always about building and building." You needed to spend time in the barracks, gain soldiers' trust, help them overcome their apprehension about official reactions, and couch your message in terms that made sense to them, even as you challenged their core beliefs. You also had to stay clear of any infraction of the rules—all the while dealing with what Lewis called "crappy memories" of being in the army. "You feel like you're in the belly of the beast, but you still got to be friendly, coax people in. It's a very unnatural thing for a soldier to do that kind of stuff."

IVAW members at Fort Drum were careful not to recruit or protest while in uniform or while carrying out their military duties, and they avoided flaunting their activities on base. "We don't keep it no secret," Wright explained, "but we've done the research into the military regulations and, as far as political activities of service members go, we are constitutionally and by regulation protected in what we do. While I'm in the military, I'll abide by the laws, even though the military doesn't in many ways." There hadn't been any backlash from his activities, he told me, but shortly after my visit, he was called in for questioning after he spoke to another reporter about "search and avoid missions."[24] The military officials may have thought that was sufficient warning, as there were no further repercussions.

Of course, there is official disapproval, and then there is peer disapproval. Wright, like other Fort Drum chapter members, had no intention of hanging around the army any longer than required, but he still had to live among people who disagreed with him, often vehemently. "Obviously, having any dissenting opinion within the military is looked down upon and usually punished. The whole camaraderie thing, brothers . . ." His voice trailed off. "[The military] builds upon this entire structure of like-mindedness. When that individual breaks ranks and stands up and says something outside the status quo, they're usually removed quickly from the equation and silenced. The military doesn't like that bad apple that can spoil the rest of the bunch." The military doesn't have to clamp down on dissent often, he added, because it's so good at distracting service members and limiting the information they get or even want. "It takes a specific kind of soldier to take that individual interest and step out there and find the information and seek it out. Those become the most effective, dedicated activists."

While the Fort Drum chapter was one of IVAW's fastest growing, it represented barely a blip on a post of about fifteen thousand soldiers, but Wright insisted that you had to look at the context. "We have an economic draft, where the military is made up largely of low-income, uneducated troops. You got maybe 95 percent of this country who has no direct personal connection to this war whatsoever. So to have a small chapter like this, it doesn't say a lot, but it does show that we're breaking ground and we're actually getting somewhere." He shrugged. "We're sort of reinventing the wheel, but we're making it a much nicer wheel, I think."

It's a freakishly warm November evening for upstate New York when Wright and I drive about an hour south from Watertown to North Syracuse. IVAW members Tim Dunlap and Michael Blake are already there, hanging out in the living room of Michelle and Steve Feek. The Feeks' son is stationed at an army base on the other side of the country, and Michelle has become an unofficial den mother for the Fort Drum crew. She has a pineapple upside-down cake in the oven when we arrive, so we kill time before heading out for dinner, half-watching the TV playing in the background.

Dunlap is in his mid-twenties, tall, slender, gap-toothed, a nervous smoker. He dropped out of high school in Farmington, New Mexico, and signed up for the army's infantry because, he explains, he likes to fight. It was supposed to be a three-year stint, but he's now on year seven, having hit a trifecta of bad luck: called back from the Individual Ready Reserves, stop-lossed, and wounded. The last happened in Afghanistan, where he was deployed after having fought in Iraq. Dunlap fell off a Blackhawk helicopter when his team was headed to a battle position and the pilot swerved. He fell about twenty feet and tumbled down a mountain into a pile of logs. "I was pretty messed up," he says dryly. He was medevacked to Germany, then sent to Walter Reed Hospital, where he was turned away for lack of space, and on to Andrews Air Force Base, where he was warehoused for a week. Eventually, he was sent to Fort Drum. There, he hobbled painfully into the medical center, was told to return the next day, and was then informed that the base lacked the capacity to treat him. Oh, and the army wanted him to pay about $1,000 for the equipment he had left on the mountainside when he was flown out. He's now counting the days until his discharge comes through.

"Who was there to help me when I was injured?" he demands. "I got injured doing something for them, even though I didn't want to be there." At the Fort Drum medical facility, he met Wright and other IVAW members, who took up his case. "Without them I probably would not be able to walk now," he says. "With them, I got what I deserved."

It's a common refrain: dismissive, deficient, turn-a-blind-eye medical care. Things began to budge after the *Washington Post* exposed the shockingly inadequate conditions at Walter Reed's outpatient facilities in February 2007,[25] but veterans, including IVAW members, continued to run into roadblocks for something as basic as a diagnosis.[26] The situation was supposed to improve when the military instituted a new system, changing how and when soldiers are evaluated for disability and what benefits they receive, but as of mid-2011, it was still taking more than three years on average from the time of injury to the completion of a disability discharge.[27] Wright, for example, will not get proper treatment for his PTSD and possible traumatic brain injury until months after we meet, and then only because he has been quoted in the *New York Times* about the long wait and bad medical care at Fort Drum.[28]

Michael Blake, twenty-four, guesses that he may have had PTSD when he returned from his eleven months in Iraq in 2004, but no one talked about it much then, even though the Defense Department was estimating that more than 9 percent of army personnel suffered from it.[29] All Blake knew was that he was drinking too much and was desperate to get out of the army. He filed for conscientious objection, the process went surprisingly smoothly, and he was discharged in February 2005. He joined

IVAW, served on its board, rode the bus on the base tour, and is now studying political science at SUNY Cortland. "Once you get immersed in the peace movement, you become radicalized quickly," he says. "I'm completely against the entire establishment."

Blake tells me he enlisted from a "misguided sense of idealism," though it sounds as if there was also a desire to stick it to his parents, who were politically antimilitary. He was in basic training when 9/11 occurred. "We're going to war," a fellow recruit said. "Against who?" he asked. "It doesn't matter," came the reply. "Somebody." That turned out to be accurate, at least as far as Blake could tell. In Iraq, he says he found a constant cycle of violence with no purpose beyond perpetuating the occupation. "We'd go on patrol and wait to get shot at," he complains with the understatement that seems to be his dominant mode.

Blake watches the Feeks' TV with a blend of wariness, irony, and paranoia, repeating portentously, "Be afraid, be very afraid." He thumbs through a science magazine and shows Wright a story, which gets them talking about implanting chips in human brains, which leads to more paranoia. It's jokey-serious-safe stuff in front of me. He shows me the tattoos on his arms: one records the dates of his tour in Iraq; the other is a quotation about dust in the air, a commemoration of a good friend who was blown into such small pieces by a bomb that there wasn't enough of him left to bury.

We go out to dinner, and when the guys order beers, the waitress examines their IDs carefully. They tell her they're combat vets and kid back and forth, but when she leaves to place our order and takes the IDs with her, Blake seems upset and follows her to find out what's going on. She's just teasing, she says, then tells them about her brother who was in the army. He may have killed himself—it's not clear, though it's definitely not a happy story. "Does the army treat you well?" she asks. The three give an emphatic, no, but she misses how angry they are, and when we leave, thanks them for their sacrifice. They brush it off. They've heard it before.

"You can't count on veterans to do anything," Blake tells me, but, in fact, these veterans count heavily on the others to do what IVAW does remarkably well: take care of each other. They know when to step in and when to stand back, and they know it without having to be told. In the parking lot, as Dunlap strolls to the car, talking on his cell phone, a German shepherd in the SUV next to us suddenly lunges at the window, barking savagely. Dunlap lurches to a stop, even though the window is closed and the dog can't get at him. With a shaky laugh, he turns and walks the long way around to avoid passing the dog again. Wright and Blake laugh too, but you can tell they recognize how freaked out he is and their laughter dies abruptly.

∼ *Mass Art, 17 August 2009* ∼

The two Drews are in Boston, setting up for a Combat Paper workshop at the Massachusetts Institute of Art and Design, better known as Mass Art. This one's for a middle school summer program, so instead of readying old military uniforms for transformation into handmade paper, as they usually do with veterans, they heap old T-shirts and other scraps of fabric onto the wooden tables. Drew Cameron and Drew Matott have driven down from Vermont early this morning in Cameron's '73 VW bug, which appears to be another of his reclamation projects, and by 10:00 a.m. it's already nearing ninety degrees with 90 percent humidity. In a small room off to the side, two Hollander beaters, the machines that turn fibers into pulp, clatter so loudly you have to wear earmuffs. Plus, someone has nailed the windows shut in the third-floor papermaking studio, where we'll be working for the next few days.

Cameron, however, is cool behind reflecting sunglasses as he organizes the sullen kids and sets them to cutting the mounds of cloth into pieces the size of postage stamps. Plugged into iPods and chattering on cell phones, they seem to cut according to their natures: neat, geometric patterns for one, random shapes for another, quick, fierce slices for a third with the cutting wheel that works like a pizza slicer. While Matott attends to the mechanics, Cameron leans on the table where the boys have gathered, quietly answering their questions about the army, the war, Iraq. He pulls out a *National Geographic* map from 2002 with notations about weapons of mass destruction. He shows them what Iraq looks like and where he was stationed and tells them what he did when he deployed there. It's a subtle counterrecruiting tactic, so mild that no one notices.

Unlike the kids, I'm given an army shirt of winter camouflage to work on—heavy fabric, long-sleeved, probably warm. I cut around the name tapes and Cameron lets me keep the one saying "U.S. Army." The other, someone's name, gets added to the batch of pulp, which seems to perpetuate itself endlessly, like a yogurt culture. I rip the uniform into strips and pass them to the kids to cut up. It's keenly satisfying.

The next day, we "pull" sheets of paper. We begin by stirring the pulp into a slurry, which feels like soggy mattress batting. (In a video of an earlier workshop, a vet dips his hand into a flow of pulped uniforms and says, "That's North Carolina, that's Germany, that's Iraq.") Then holding a wooden frame called a deckle against a fine-mesh screen, we dip them into the bath and scoop the captured pulp upward to let the water drip out. Next, we upend our sheets onto a plastic mat, where they will dry into fine-quality paper. The kids catch on much quicker than I and play around with adding a hand print or a second color. As the day ends, they peel their sheets one-by-one from the pressing boards and place them onto the drying boards with such gentleness and care.

Late that afternoon, some IVAWs show up for an after-hours Combat Paper session where they'll pull oversized sheets and hang them to dry, like laundry flapping in the night breeze. They wait for the school kids to finish up, clustering in the back of the room and talking among themselves, while the kids ignore them in return.

Ian LaVallee, who spent four months in Iraq at the beginning of the occupation, pores over the map Cameron used the day before. It shows the country as almost all desert, and I realize that in my mental picture, Iraq is monochrome and dust. "Is Iraq really brown?" I ask.

The veterans all laugh. "Yeah, it's mostly brown," LaVallee says ruefully and turns back to the map.

8

ART HEART DREAM PEACE

"Hi ho, rock 'n' roll, grab your weapon, get ready to roll," sings Drew Cameron as he loosens the tie on his army dress uniform. "'Cuz you will be going to war," he continues in a steady tenor as he pulls dog-tags from under his shirt. "Too early, too early, too early in the morning." He jerks the chain from his neck, holds the tags at arm's length and drops them to the floor with a clink, then strides out through the audience sitting in stunned silence at the Green Door Studio in Burlington, Vermont.

Cameron is followed by Aaron Hughes, who performs a poem he has written in response to a prompt to use one of the phrases: "I am," or "Who served," or "Forgive me." Hughes fractures and rearranges all three in an increasingly agitated performance. Shedding words as Cameron has shed clothing, Hughes repeats, "I am who survived." Then, "I am who?" And finally the extended cry, "I I I I I," before, grim-faced, he too stomps off stage.

Cameron and Hughes are key players in a growing group of veteran-artists who use their experiences in Iraq and Afghanistan to explore the interrelation of war, politics, and art.[1] This early performance came in April 2007 at the culmination of a Warrior Writers workshop, where a group of young veterans studied the writing of older veterans, then got down to work creating their own poems, sketches, reminiscences, and spoken-word performances.

Soldiers have long written about—and against—war, but the art coming out of this GI resistance movement feels different. In the style of the day, it is confessional, provisional, profane, and YouTube-anointed, but this is dissident art: it's meant to shake things up. It is also meant to convey what it's like to inhabit the skin of people who fought wars that stopped making sense to them about ten minutes in and left them feeling betrayed, bewildered, and abandoned. Some of the veteran-artists began writing, performing, or making images as a form of therapy, buying into that very American faith in the healing power of self-revelation. But chronicling their war times forced them to relive what they wanted to move beyond, so it wasn't all that therapeutic, at least not in the usual sense of curing a disease. That's probably why they have preferred to talk about "healing"—for themselves, other veterans, their country, the countries they invaded—as they seek, not just to bandage their wounds, but to confront why those wounds fester. So what sets this art apart is its direct challenge to the national myths, political pieties, and adulation of the military, which time and again have led the country into misbegotten fights. When it works, it is a translation from what the veteran knows to what the civilian audience can know or, more accurately, can be brought to understand.

The Vermont Warrior Writers workshop was the second led by Lovella Calica, a civilian, then in her mid-twenties, who was IVAW's membership coordinator. The first had taken place in New York City in February, when the project didn't yet have a name. She and several veterans had been sharing their poetry when, she says, "It hit me that these poems have to be heard by other people. I can't be the only one." For the vets, suffering from PTSD, and Calica, who had been abused when she was young, writing was both creative and healing. "There was this depth to them," she said of the veterans' poems. "Stuff they had gone through and come out on the other side. I wanted to help them deal with this shit, as I had done." She had also been taking photos of members at events, wanting to capture them at this point in their lives and, as she came to realize, to give her generation images of veterans who were their own age.

Calica launched Warrior Writers in 2006 with Cameron and Hughes, modeling the project on writing workshops Maxine Hong Kingston had initiated for Vietnam veterans. The idea, honed over time, was to build a creative community where recent veterans could document and transcend their experiences of war. Since Warrior Writers grew out of IVAW, its participants tended to share an antiwar sentiment, but workshops were open to veterans of all philosophies, with Calica insisting, "There is absolutely no censorship."

From the first, what emerged was such a richness of writing, drawings, and photographs that it felt as if someone had pulled a stopper and

memories and metaphors poured out. IVAW members had already ze-
roed in on storytelling as a core tactic to move their audiences to action,
and the Warrior Writers recognized a similar power inherent in their
writing. But there is a difference between telling a story—a direct, public transaction between teller and listener—and writing a story, which is
essentially a private, creative act, which may never be shared. The stories
IVAW offered at rallies and meetings were polemical and didn't shrink
from naming the enemy. The stories coming out of the workshops had
some of the same sharp anger, but it wasn't usually directed at anyone—
except at the writers themselves.

Warrior Writers gatherings were meant to be healing, nourishing, an
occasion for bonding and contemplation. Calica called them "a sacred
time," and testimonials tended toward the New Age utterances that emotionally intense group experiences engender. For the many veterans who
felt robbed of their voices, protective of their unwanted knowledge, and
unable to communicate with anyone who hadn't been to war, the workshops helped them find the means to say what they couldn't say any other
way. (They may also have provided a slightly passive-aggressive response
to the prurience of civilians: You want to know what it was like? I'll tell
you what it was like. I'll tell you more than you ever want to know or
know what to do with.) These were not your typical war stories: they had
little swashbuckling or war porn, and if they wallowed in anything, it was
a kind of moral imperative to revisit moments of misery.

As the writers struggled to make their jumble of feelings and ideas in-
telligible—first to themselves and then to others—some discovered that
they needed not just the community of people with similar experiences
and sentiments, but also a community of artists who could help them
master their craft. Over the next several years, Warrior Writers would
publish anthologies—the first were *Move, Shoot, and Communicate; Re-
Making Sense*; and *After Action Review*—hold workshops and retreats for
about one thousand veterans, stage readings and performances, create a
large mural in West Philadelphia, and encourage at least a dozen veterans in their careers as artists and art teachers.

Writing about World War I in *The Great War and Modern Memory*,
Paul Fussell observes that the horror of war is so commonplace that it is
the small, ironic details that stick in the soldier's memory.[2] Details, ironic
and horrific, are what make the work published in the Warrior Writers
anthologies vivid. Kelly Dougherty, working from a journal she kept in

Iraq, notes that everything "looks half-dead, hot, and starved," including the camels plodding across the desert "knock-kneed with dreadlocks of fur" and the kids with "too-big heads," who know just enough English to beg for food.

In "Ghost Limb," Garett Reppenhagen concludes his ode of sensual longing for "oh the comfortable caress of my cradle rifle," with the observation, "some amputees say they can still feel their missing limbs." And Drew Cameron requires only a terse caption of a photo of himself grasping two weapons: "Rifles taken from young men strapped with ammunition and given to more young men strapped with ammunition." Many of the writers seem to be on a quest, trying to figure out not just what they're against but what they are for. Maggie Martin was a sergeant in the army signal corps with two Iraq tours under her belt. In her poem, "Daydream Legacy," she invokes GI Joe, Joan of Arc, Forrest Gump, and "words, oaths, and codes we are dying to believe," then comes, uneasily, to this end: "I was looking for something more than reality TV. / A chance at redemption."

American civilians turn away from images of war, occasionally peeking at the reality between their fingers, but preferring not to be reminded of the brutality, or to be reminded only with the reassurance of jingoism. We get a frisson of derring-do from war movies and war reportage, but we're spectators, getting our hits of danger and destruction from a safe remove and seldom breaking through the taboos of what cannot be said or seen.

American soldiers in the thick of the recent wars, like soldiers everywhere since cameras democratized image-making, did break those taboos, taking photographs of dead Iraqis and Afghans as war trophies and posting them on blogs and websites.[3] A particularly graphic one was nowthatsfuckedup.com, aka NTFU.com. It was launched in the spring of 2004, originally as a place for amateur pornographers to post their work. After the site administrator offered free access to U.S. service members stationed abroad, NFTU.com also became host to an active thread of graphic photos and mocking commentary about Iraqis and Afghans killed in the war. This was not a site for the squeamish, especially the section labeled "gory," which featured crude snapshots of bloody, mutilated, dismembered, and shattered corpses and body parts. (The soldiers didn't usually appear in the frame with their "kills," so maybe there was some squeamishness after all.) NTFU also included a forum in which debate, largely among soldiers, took place over the U.S. role in Iraq, making it one of the few well-trafficked sites where soldiers felt free to say the unsayable.[4]

The media scholar Kari Andén-Papadopoulos looked carefully at the photos, which she called "representations of distant suffering," and proposed several reason why the American soldiers took them and publicized them online: to relive, authenticate, or erase a painful experience; to create a group identity separate from the civilian world; to prove the soldiers' power to the enemy and their survival to themselves; to distance themselves from their actions through "documentary neutrality"; to force civilians to bear witness; and to counter the official, sanitized view of the hostilities.[5]

The veterans working with Warrior Writers would undoubtedly resent equating their images with those on NTFU, and with good reason. The images they contributed to the anthologies, while not prettied up, were hardly ever of dead or suffering Iraqis or Afghans. Still, their reasons for creating the images were similar to those on Andén-Papadopoulos's list. They might add the all-important caveat that they were working for peace, but they were also working for peace of mind, as, in an awful way, the contributors to NTFU.com may have been too. Soldiers' re-creations of what they saw in Iraq and Afghanistan, be they beastly or benign, are part of that basic human impulse to say, "I was here."

When Cameron hosted the Warrior Writers weekend in Vermont, he was already remaking his Iraq war experiences into art. A visual artist and papermaker, he had arranged for workshop participants to make paper with him. "It was beautiful," he said, especially the way it dovetailed with the writing. "It really shaped my connection with paper." I first met Cameron the following year, when he was twenty-five years old. Slender and boyish, with an elongated, almost-elfin face, a soul patch that continued under his chin, and a hairline already receding, he looked younger and less solemn than in the video of his performance. Cameron had joined the army after high school in Iowa City, enticed by a recruiter's pitch. "I wanted to do it my own way," he told me, "kind of disappear, get out of town. How could I say no?" He worked hard at being a good soldier, made sergeant, even considered an army career, but after a couple of years, he had had enough and was ready for college. Then orders came down in January 2003, and he was sent to Iraq. He was with 75th Artil-

lery Brigade, assigned as a gunner for rocket launchers, but the launchers got left behind in Kuwait, so for eight months, he drove Humvees
and trucks, mostly near Balad, and collected piles of munitions from the
Iraqis to store or detonate. "Part of it was exciting," he acknowledged.
"Standing in the hatch of a truck with my sunglasses and my finger on
the trigger, feeling on the edge."

Cameron's family was military—his father had been in the air force—
but they opposed the invasion of Iraq. He, however, was a believer. "I
thought if my country sent me to war, I would walk in the steps of others.
I thought I'd be doing charity, but it wasn't that at all. It was sort of the
antithesis of charity." He let his misgivings slide, though, especially when
he got back to the States. "It was Drew time. I was going to start using
that GI bill." He followed a girl to Vermont, enrolled in the community
college in Burlington, and joined the National Guard for the educational
benefits, managing to ignore his growing doubt about the military, until,
one day, he came across a notice in the paper for an antiwar protest in
Montpelier. He went, saw a bunch of guys marching under a Veterans
For Peace banner, and said, "I'm a vet. Can I walk with you?" He joined
IVAW soon after and began to put his Iraq experience in context.

It was 2004, when, on a whim, he took a papermaking workshop
with Drew Matott, a papermaker and performance artist who became
his mentor, friend, and collaborator. Cameron had first learned Japanese
papermaking as a teenager from his father, but now it became central to
his life. "I obsessively made blank paper. It was cathartic," he said. One
day, also on a whim, he donned his army uniform for the first time since
he left the military and began to lop it off in pieces, his heart beating faster and faster. "It felt both wrong and liberating," he reported. "I started
ripping it off. The purpose was to make a complete transformation." A
friend took photographs, which Cameron and Matott used for a series
of prints, titled "Breaking Rank." Later, it occurred to them to turn the
uniform into paper, and in May 2007, Combat Paper was born.

That Veterans Day, Cameron gathered seven other disaffected veterans at St. Lawrence University in Canton, New York, near Fort Drum.
They cut up a uniform that had been worn in Iraq, boiled the pieces, beat
them into pulp, and formed that into art-quality paper. Some sheets were
creamy, some speckled, some swirled with the muddy colors of desert
camouflage. Some were used for printmaking, some for books or journals, while others were put aside to create sculptures. All were meant

to honor the men and women fighting the war these veterans could no longer support.

Transforming a discarded battle uniform into a pristine sheet of paper is almost too perfect a metaphor, but it's also an incredibly cool process, tactile and sensual, with all the mucky pleasure of playing in the mud. Cameron and Matott were soon leading workshops around the country for veterans of wars from World War II to the present, who brought their old uniforms, some of which had been packed away for decades—another apt metaphor. (Soldiers buy their uniforms, so can do what they like with them once they leave the military.) The workshops were small, eight to ten vets, very emotional—"brutal" was Cameron's word. They were designed as a time for veterans to reflect, talk, and create, and, inevitably, a lot came out in the wash. "Combat Paper can be healing, cathartic," Cameron acknowledges, "but it's also a craft and a fine art."

Cameron went on to get a degree in forestry from the University of Vermont, and in the early days of the project, he told me, "In my studies in forestry, I'm interested in reclamation ecology, if you will. This project is like that for individuals. It's a chance for them to redefine or remake their relationship with their stories, their history, their experiences. For me it definitely has been an empowering and healing experience, but it also is very much my method of sharing my sentiment as a veteran that's against the war. I'm taking something that's very sacred and that holds a lot of symbolism of service and duty—and then transforming it."

Tara Tappert, Combat Paper's curator of exhibits and archives, noted that in the past, the military itself had shown an interest in the therapeutic potential of arts and crafts. During World War I, military hospitals used them for rehabilitation and vocational training. After World War II, the emphasis shifted slightly to art as a means of promoting well-being. That's when the Red Cross and major museums got into the act: the Smithsonian exhibiting veterans' art and New York's Museum of Modern Art housing a War Veterans Art Center, which offered "recreational and prevocational classes." Tappert pointed out that none of this is happening now, so recent veterans created their own grassroots movement of what she called "witness art" to take up the slack. She suggested that this generation of veterans had seen how difficult it was for many Vietnam vets to move beyond their war experiences and had resolved not to get mired in the same swamp. "They don't want that crap to be stuck in their heads," she said. "They want to write it out. They want to dance it out. They want to make paper."

The two Drews, ardent advocates of papermaking, eagerly trained other veterans, who started experimenting in turn, not just with making paper, but with what could be made with it: masks, sculptures, including a couple of life-size rifles. Eli Wright, who regularly drove from Fort Drum to their studio in Burlington to make paper, took his childhood teddy bear to a shooting range, shot it with an assault rifle, cut it open, and refilled it with Combat Paper, bullet casings, and buttons from uniforms. Then he closed it back up with surgical sutures and strung a noose around its neck to create a sculpture stuffed with symbolism and suppurating wounds.

Wright went on to set up a Combat Paper mill at the Printmaking Center of New Jersey. By 2012, affiliated workshops were also operating in Ithaca, New York; Reno, Nevada; and San Francisco, where Cameron had relocated, and Matott had spun off Peace Paper, a sister organization based in Madison, Wisconsin. Combat Paper art had been acquired by the Library of Congress, the Boston Athenaeum, and numerous university libraries and had been exhibited at venues as disparate as the Seminole Nation Museum in Oklahoma, St. Paul's School in New Hampshire, and the Holland Paper Biennial in the Netherlands.

"I qualify everything in the States as a spectacle and everything in Iraq as real," said Aaron Hughes a few years after he returned from a tour in Iraq with the Illinois National Guard. Hughes, then a graduate student in art theory and practice at Northwestern University and an active IVAW member, was also using his art to reimagine the myths, images, and ideas that had brought him into war. His method was to pose questions, his media were drawing, painting, and simple but arresting events he staged in public places.

When I struggled to define those performances, Hughes directed me to the work of Stephen Duncombe, an activist and media scholar at New York University, who, in 2007, published *Dream*, a manifesto of sorts aimed at reclaiming the much-maligned term "spectacle" for progressive political activities. American life is full of spectacles: Disneyland, fireworks, Super Bowls, political conventions, video war games, just to start the list. Spectacles can delight, surprise, and entertain us, but they seldom make us think. In fact, their purpose is quite the opposite. Duncombe has something else in mind. He takes off from, among others, the radical Situationist movement, a group of avant-garde artists, intellectuals, and political theorists who differentiated passive, soporific, and manipulative "spectacles" from interactive, open-ended "situations," and issues a call for political action that he names "ethical spectacle."

Ethical spectacle, as Duncombe defines it, is participatory and egalitarian in both planning and execution; transparent in that it doesn't pretend to be real or a stand-in for reality; and firmly rooted in reality, while using dramatic tools, such as exaggeration or illusion, to amplify, reinterpret, and reveal reality. Most important, if ethical spectacle is to do something truly different, it must represent a dream or aspiration; that is, the artist-activist needs to imagine and aim for a better world. "Instead of a dream's replacement," he writes, "the ethical spectacle is a dream put on display."[6] Ethical spectacle, it seems, is a sister to swarm, with more stirring language and artistry added in.

Ethical spectacle also turns out to be a wonderfully protean boost to the imagination. You can imprint a haunting image on a place, as several Veterans For Peace did weekend after weekend, resurrecting a transient cemetery for the war dead at Arlington West. You can amuse and titillate, as IVAW's San Francisco chapter did in its Make Drag Not War fundraisers, featuring "San Francisco's fiercest drag queens."[7] Or you can take a page from PTAs and other civic groups, who are paid better in lip service than funding, and create Bake Sales for Body Armor, a project that did pretty much what it sounds like.[8] The limits seem to be only one's vision and taste for the unpredictable.

Hughes sometimes played the role of IVAW's theorist, so it's not surprising that Duncombe's ideas appealed to him and informed his work, even as he remained leery of the term "spectacle" with its overtones of hucksterism and phony experience. He preferred "situations" to describe his art and the actions he helped create for IVAW. In a discussion of situations or actions the group could undertake, he urged the veterans to think about how to disrupt conventional interpretations of the symbols they dealt with—for instance, political protest = cops versus protesters. What emerged was Operation First Casualty (OFC), the urban guerrilla theater that got Adam Kokesh and Liam Madden in trouble with the marines. The title came from the adage that truth is the first casualty of war. (Nuance, irony, and justice are also in the running for that distinction.) OFC debuted in Washington, DC, in March 2007, as a dozen young veterans in uniforms patrolled the city's streets from Union Station to Capitol Hill. With imaginary guns swinging erratically at imaginary targets, they accosted volunteers in civilian dress, threw them to the ground, frisked and zip-cuffed them, and pulled sandbags over their heads, all the while screaming at them to shut the fuck up.

OFC was intended to give Americans a taste of life in an occupied city, "to rupture the everyday," as Hughes put it, and, in case anyone missed the point, volunteers passed out explanatory flyers. The mock patrol ended at Arlington National Cemetery, where the veterans set up a memorial with boots, dog-tags, and a rifle, as it was done on a base when someone was killed in Iraq. Then they took off their military blouses in a symbolic shedding of their military skin and dropped them in a heap on the ground. The patrols were unsettling to witness, especially because, from a distance, it was hard to tell that the actors weren't really armed. The performance was even more stressful for the veterans, as all the truisms about war rushed back: that everyone beyond the buddy on your left and right is a dangerous blur; that unfamiliar landscapes look uniformly hostile; that when you feel threatened, you stop seeing people as human beings; and that the trained response to perceived threats is a ready finger on the trigger. By the end of the day, they were shaken, but they felt that they had completed a rite of passage.

Geoff Millard, who had spent a year in Iraq with the New York National Guard, helped organize the event, along with Hughes and Garett Reppenhagen. "A few of us were talking one night and I cited Operation RAW. It was one of the coolest actions, and no one knows about it," he explained. Operation RAW was the mock search-and-destroy mission carried out under the auspices of Vietnam Veterans Against the War in 1970. Then, some two hundred Vietnam War veterans and a few active-duty GIs marched along the route George Washington's Continental Army had taken two centuries earlier. The culminating rally featured Jane Fonda, an eloquent John Kerry, and Louis Font, the lawyer, who was then a first lieutenant, but the spectacle's highlight came when the veterans responded to the command, "Break arms!" by cracking their fake guns across their knees and stomping them to pieces.[9]

Operation First Casualty was meant to be an evanescent jab in the ribs and perhaps more indelible for that. It was also designed to be nimbler than RAW. "The beauty of IVAW [is we] can learn from mistakes," Millard said optimistically. "So we did it [OFC] in DC and wanted to make

it small enough to be able to duplicate it other places, make it a model."
They had checked with lawyers to make sure they stayed within the law
and trained participants to avoid antagonizing the police, whom they
assumed (correctly) would show up. "We made sure not to engage civilians," he said. "We didn't want them to like what they see, didn't want
them to be comfortable, but we wanted to show a tiny sliver of the occupation."

Over the next few years, IVAW staged OFCs in New York, Chicago,
Denver, Hartford, Seattle, San Francisco, Santa Monica, and Denver
again at the 2008 Democratic National Convention. Each time, it elicited
an array of responses from passers-by, including some who thought it
really was the National Guard, called in to police an American city. News
outlets, recognizing a good photo op, featured Operation First Casualty
prominently, videos popped up on YouTube in the days before everything popped up on YouTube, and for at least a few minutes on their way
to work or school or Starbucks, spectators found it hard to remain oblivi-
ous to the war. For IVAW, Operation First Casualty accomplished what
Action Mill had urged the veterans to do: use their experiences to give
their audience an encounter that alters its perceptions of war. Artists too
alter their audience's perception of reality, creating something that takes
on its own reality. Art may be one of the few arenas where the doing can
be reconciled on a deep level with the image.

Meanwhile, Hughes was creating his own artwork, which is not easily
categorized or encased in the white box of a gallery. Unexpected encounters seem to suit him best. In the fall of 2006, a couple of years after he
returned from Iraq, he walked to the middle of a busy intersection in
Champaign, Illinois, and propped up a signboard that read: "I am an
Iraq War Veteran. I am guilty. I am alone. I am drawing for peace." Moving crablike over the tarmac, he chalked a picture of a bird perched on
barbed wire, forcing pedestrians and vehicles to stop or navigate around
him. In a video, the only remnant of the piece, people walk past, giving at
most a glance over their shoulder, as if unsure what—or whether—they
should be noticing. As he is finishing up, a police officer arrives on a
motorcycle and tells him to get out of the road or go to jail. "I assumed
stopping traffic without a permit was illegal. I was willing to be arrested
if I couldn't finish the drawing," Hughes told me later. So he persists,
silently returning to complete his drawing. When he is done, he shrugs,

folds up his sign, and walks away. He had achieved what he set out to do.

Hughes's situation/spectacle/drawing/performance/obstacle course was an attempt to claim a respite from the everyday and its constant motion. "If there's a moment that doesn't fit in [people's] daily comprehension, it's something that will recycle in their heads," he said. "Hopefully they will work through this and begin to try to construct their own understanding." The problem with the usual tools of antiwar activism, such as marches or reading the names of war dead, he explained, is that they're predictable; they fit too neatly into a category in our minds labeled "protest." Instead, actions are most effective when they surprise us out of our assumptions and create a kind of mental itch, which can only be scratched by digging deeper. "People respond to thoughts they can actually own," he concluded.

Hughes is tall and rangy, his face is a map of sincerity, his walk a purposeful lope, and his voice a steady hum, though it can tighten with frustration. He joined the National Guard out of high school in 2000 and rose to the rank of sergeant. Like so many IVAWs, he enlisted for reasons ranging from the practical to the idealistic, but never imagining that he would end up spending one year, three months, and seven days hauling supplies all over Iraq. "At first it seemed like liberation, then occupation," he said. His story echoes a familiar refrain of lives derailed by war. "I went to college set to be a designer. I wanted to design the coolest stuff and make lots of money. Then I got deployed and I lived with my sleeping bag and rucksack and a couple of books." He hated that he had no control over his life, that he couldn't help the people he thought he was sent to help. And there was the guilt. "Maybe I can find ways to . . . forgive myself," he said, his voice halting for the first time in our conversation. The only alternative to cynicism, he eventually concluded, was art, or what he called "creative processes." Hughes was ultimately interested in nothing less than transforming the whole culture. "We're disconnected," he said, "Not only from the war—we're disconnected from each other. We've built up all these cultural barriers and somehow we've got to poke through them. That's what I'm trying to do."

Hughes's imagination is fertile, his energy seemingly inexhaustible. He spearheaded IVAW's Winter Soldier hearings, worked for the organization for four years as a field organizer, and led Operation Recovery, a multiyear campaign to stop the deployment of traumatized soldiers. In 2012, he organized a protest in Chicago reminiscent of Dewey Canyon III, in which more than forty veterans of the recent wars tore their medals from their chests and hurled them toward the building where NATO representatives were meeting—and ignoring the continuing war in Afghanistan. He also made new artwork, such as the "Tea Project," an installation-performance meant as homage to the countless cups of tea he was offered in Iraq, the drawings prisoners in Guantanamo etched into Styrofoam cups as their sole creative outlet, and the remarkable endurance of gestures of shared humanity in the midst of war.

All this activity caused Hughes to revisit the long-term efficacy of spectacle. "Using spectacle to rupture the everyday doesn't change the cultural narrative, which is what I'm interested in now," he told me in the fall of 2012, as he was about to leave IVAW to travel and study the interaction of art and social justice. Now he was asking a larger, probably unanswerable question: "How do we create meaning in a world where meaning has been shattered, where your own identity has been shattered to the core?"

As Hughes and other veterans were exploring the intersection of art and protest, a more basic argument over which is which, and what expression gets legal protection, was playing out in the prosecution of Army Specialist Marc Hall after his commanding officers learned of his rap song, "Stop Lossed," which he composed in protest at being kept in the army after his contract ended. Hall, aka hip-hop artist Marc Watercus, had served in Baghdad from October 2007 to December 2008 and was stationed at Fort Stewart the following July, when he learned that his unit was being sent back to Iraq before the end of the year. Under stop-loss, he would be required to deploy with them. Hall poured his frustration into a profanity-laced, in-your-face rap—hardcore, but not unlike a lot of the music GIs listen to. "Those who do understand hip-hop didn't take it as a threat. Those who don't understand hip-hop run the military," Hall commented dryly. A CD of the song got mailed to the Pentagon (Hall insisted he didn't know who sent it) and eventually made its way to Colonel Thomas Beane, chief of the army's Enlisted System Division, who sent it on to Hall's commanders at Fort Stewart. Among Beane's reasons for doing so, he later testified, was to get Hall the psychological attention he needed.

Hall agreed that he wasn't in good shape. He felt burned out, probably suffered from PTSD, and was scared that he couldn't trust himself to carry out his duties as a soldier. "The very thought of holding and being around a loaded weapon again gave me the chills. I did not know who my enemies were anymore," he wrote his supporters. He tried explaining this to his officers and chaplains in the few counseling sessions he attended and in a grievance he filed about the care he received, but the army's cursory mental health evaluation determined that he was fit for redeployment, and he was expected to return to Iraq. A few months after Beane received the CD—and, significantly, just weeks after army psychiatrist Major Nidal Hasan killed thirteen people and wounded thirty-two others at Fort Hood, Texas—Hall was arrested and charged with eleven counts of communicating threats under a catch-all provision covering actions "to the prejudice of good order and discipline in the armed forces." The army imprisoned him, first in the United States, then in Kuwait, where he was put to work filling sandbags for four months while awaiting his court-martial.

As with the marines' attempt to punish Kokesh for taking part in protests, the army's case against Hall was weak. At his Article 32 hearing, the military equivalent of a grand jury proceeding, prosecution witnesses tended to strengthen Hall's position more than the army's, testifying that no one took his song seriously as a threat. The army, meanwhile, maintained that this was never a First Amendment issue. Military officials did seem more interested in punishing Hall for being a troublemaker than in contesting his right to rap or express his anger, but the case ultimately turned on the question of how literally to take the words of a song. Hall had said of his music, "It's how I get my frustrations out, instead of acting on them." And his civilian lawyer, David Gespass, later pointed out, "Not everybody who writes a song about shooting a man in Memphis just to see him die actually shoots somebody in Memphis." It was possible that the lyrics crossed from protected speech to threat. It would certainly have been an interesting argument to have in a military court, but it never got there. By the time his court-martial was scheduled, Hall had had enough. His lawyers made a deal for him to apply for a discharge in lieu of a court-martial and plead guilty to one of the charges against him, as required. He was released from the army in April 2010 with an other-than-honorable discharge and loss of most of his benefits.

The context in which art is presented and the relationship of artist to audience matter in all art, but they were particularly fraught for the artist-veterans drawing on experiences that were so fresh. This was something that preoccupied Joshua Casteel, a playwright and early IVAW member. Casteel spent five months as an interrogator at Abu Ghraib prison shortly after the scandal broke there in 2004 and, soon afterward, left the army as a conscientious objector.

Casteel and I met when we served together on the Truth Commission on Conscience and War in 2010. He testified there about his journey from soldier to pacifist and activist, insisting to his audience that "what you come into the war with will dictate how you come out of war. There is no such thing as a private conscience." Casteel had given this talk, or something like it, dozens of times, including at the Vatican, and he was an impressive and forceful speaker. The following morning, the commissioners—mostly clergy, with a smattering of veterans, artists, and activists—reconvened to review the testimony of the evening before. We broke into the usual small groups to have the usual earnest discussions, then gave the usual rambling reports about what we had discussed. As we finished, Casteel approached my group, upset at what had not been said. We urged him to the microphone, where he gave an impromptu and impassioned speech to the effect that casting the soldier's experience as unfathomable to anyone who has not been to war is not only inaccurate, but also damaging because it leads to the "ghettoization" of veterans and cuts civilians off from things about war that they need to understand. Continuing the conversation with a small group afterward, he added that he never felt so isolated and lonely as when people were afraid to ask about his experiences during the war.

Casteel grew up in Cedar Rapids, Iowa, where he played football, led his school's Young Republicans chapter, and graduated first in his class. Military service was a tradition in his family, so he enlisted in the army reserve at seventeen and enrolled in the military academy at West Point. That's when his all-American mantle began to unravel. Turned off by the rigidity and lack of imagination he found there, Casteel transferred to the University of Iowa, where he studied literature, science, and the arts. When he graduated and the war began in Iraq, the military was still central to his life, but he was uneasy about what his country was doing there. He had been raised in a strong evangelical Christian tradition, and he considered appeasing his conscience by becoming a chaplain, but that didn't go as planned either, because he couldn't justify advising soldiers that they should participate in the war. Instead, he trained in Arabic and methods of interrogation.

"Exploit the greatest amount of intelligence in the least amount of time," says a character in Casteel's one-act play, *Returns*, quoting a textbook definition of interrogation. It was not easy for me to imagine Casteel exploiting anyone. When we met, he was in his early thirties, tall, blond, and handsome, with a wispy mustache and heavy-rimmed, nerd-cool glasses. He was almost alarmingly articulate and confident of his thoughts in a smart grad student way, but his voice occasionally rose at the end of statement, as if to ask if I followed or, maybe, if this idea would be allowed.

Casteel was a rarity among soldiers who turned against the war in that he could pinpoint the exact moment he had a change of heart. In his oft-told story, he was at Abu Ghraib, when a Saudi *jihadist* about his age, whom he was supposed to be questioning, said to him, "If you're Christian, you're not following Christ's teachings." In Casteel's account, "He and I were both idealistic kids, devoted to our people, devoted to our religion"—and both willing to kill. Their conversation went on for a while—about Islam, Jesus, righteousness—until Casteel realized that he had lost all objectivity. "I wanted to talk to him about the things that mattered to him and to me," he said. Recognizing how impossible this was, he ended the interrogation and told his chain of command that they would have to send someone else to finish.

Casteel left the army soon after. He studied at the prestigious Playwrights Workshop at the University of Iowa, won an award at the National MFA Playwrights Festival, published a book of his letters from Iraq, converted to Roman Catholicism, began a doctoral program in religion and literature, and continued writing. Only slightly tongue-in-cheek, he told me, "Actually, I found the idea of becoming a playwright almost a secular version of being a priest, especially from the Catholic perspective. We believe in transubstantiation, you make the word become flesh. That's what a playwright does: through words, you make flesh on stage."

Returns, his most accomplished play, was performed at the University of Iowa, Columbia College in Chicago, and the McCarter Theatre in New Jersey. It is a dreamscape of a narrative that loops and unspools through an interrogation session. Its protagonist is an interrogator, sometimes called "Priest," which was Casteel's nickname in Iraq, and it clearly draws on his interaction with prisoners there. In a "Note from the Playwright," he describes the play as being "first and foremost about young men— about the violation of youth. . . . *Returns* is also a story of post-trauma, which is to say, the very search for a story after one has returned, after the movement and the noise and the lights have become still."

Post-trauma may be another name for the indelible mark war leaves on soldiers, even after they move on, and artists are often motivated by the need to make something of their felt experience. Casteel explained, "When I was in the military opposing the Iraq war, I had a very coherent narrative that I had made for myself that was intensely ideological. I knew exactly what I opposed. I didn't necessarily know who I opposed, but I certainly didn't know what or who I affirmed. And when I left, that's when the real ambiguity and the problems started because I now had to be *for* something and to *be* something."

In the foreword to *I Hacky Sacked in Iraq,* the first book published by Combat Paper Press, Drew Cameron wrote, "When someone says: 'I cannot know what it was like over there,' we want them to. When someone says: 'I can't imagine how it must have been,' we need them to. . . . To know war, to understand conflict, to respond to it is not an individual act, nor one of courage. It is rather a very fair and necessary thing."[10] Summing up his ambitions as an artist and a person, Casteel said, "I want to see my life be a life of charity and generosity and compassion. I want to see my writing be deft and caring and sensitive and . . . ," he paused, searching for the right word, "full-bodied."

It was nearly six years after Casteel left the army when he told me this. Less than two years later, he was diagnosed with stage IV lung cancer, which spread quickly and searingly through his body. He was surprisingly young for such a disease, and he believed that it was directly related to the burn pits in Iraq where toxic waste was incinerated around the clock. He had been reassigned there after he refused to continue interrogating Iraqi prisoners.[11] Joshua Casteel died on 25 August 2012. He was thirty-two years old.

When you perform a play you wrote, you put, not just your words, but your own flesh on stage with few barriers between you and your audience. That's what Jeff Key did for about seven years in his one-man show, *The Eyes of Babylon,* which he based on a journal he kept during his two months in Iraq before he was evacuated for noncombat-related surgery. His solo performance earned him a nomination for a New York Drama Desk Award in 2012. Reviewers made much of the twin tattoos on Key's arms, "warrior" on one, "poet" on the other. *Eyes* embraced both, charting his journey from naive, knee-jerk love of country to knowing, rueful love of humanity.

The play opens with Key standing alone on a darkened stage wearing only his underwear. Addressing the audience directly, he dons his uniform, piece by piece, until he is transformed into the marine he became at the late age of thirty-four. *Eyes* unfolds as a series of monologues, which Key recites in a deceptively soothing drawl, while prowling the stage with the military bearing he can't quite shake—even when enacting a brief flirtation with an Iraqi man (their greatest intimacy is sharing lip balm) or his enchantment with Mehadi, an Iraqi boy who adopted him.[12] After sketching in his backstory (Alabama boyhood, evangelical upbringing, public schooling on the heels of desegregation), Key moves the action to Iraq, where he sort-of deals with being a sort-of closeted gay marine, then back to the States, where he sort-of deals with his growing unease about the military. The two threads come together in a funny clip from the *Paula Zahn Now* show, when he is supposed to be talking about the effect on morale of the killing of four civilian contractors in Fallujah, but instead uses the occasion to announce his homosexuality publicly, while Zahn tries valiantly to stay on script.

For Key, like Casteel, working in theater had religious overtones, although his were more mysticism than catechism. "I don't think of the play as a performance, necessarily. It's this meditation that we do together?" he suggested. The goal for him too was connection. "When they laugh to relieve the pain of what we're having to collectively visit, we laugh together. The tears we shed together. The nature of homosexuality in this culture is such oppression of isolation that to feel that connection and to feel their acceptance. . . ." He trailed off, still moved by the bond his play created.

Performing *Eyes* was more complicated than catharsis or lessons in tolerance. "All the unpleasant emotions associated with the war are represented at some point during that play," he said. "I have to visit that emotionally: that I have been a party to killing hundreds of thousands of people. We all bear responsibility, but depending on where you are in the grand scheme of things, I was pretty fucking close to the trigger. Gratefully, I never pulled it except to test my weapon." He found the curtain call the hardest part of the play and always acknowledged the audience in return. "It's deep gratitude to them for having the courage to sit there. It takes courage to come and sit in that chair and examine their role in what we're talking about."

It was at an early performance of Key's play in Los Angeles that he met Tim Goodrich, who enlisted him in IVAW, and his acting and activism have intertwined ever since. "The effectiveness of activism is based on your ability to connect to the people who disagree with you. Gandhi knew this, Martin Luther King knew this, Thoreau knew this, they all knew this," Key said emphatically. "Activism in that way is just like art, the ability to connect with another heart and express what's in yours. So if you're doing political theater, all the things that empower you as an activist inform the art."

"Every morning brings us the news of the globe, and yet we are poor in noteworthy stories," the German literary critic Walter Benjamin wrote between the world wars. He argued that information, which must be constantly replenished, does not endure, but that stories do.[13] The antiwar veterans knew this at a gut level. For them, stories, military life, healing, and political activism formed a kind of Venn diagram, which overlapped with their efforts to get through to the civilians in whose name they were sent to fight. So add reconnect to the long list of "re-" words—reclaim, redeem, release, renew, even occasionally rejoice—that these veteran-artist-activists invoked. Neither their art, nor their healing was meant to forget what happens in war. They didn't want to, even if they could. Instead, they set to work as artists, using what they remembered as veterans, to make something new.

⌒ *Cambridge, Massachusetts, 16 September 2005* ⌒

Tamara Rosenleaf stands on the Common on a makeshift stage extolling the joys of living in a ditch with Cindy Sheehan at Camp Casey for the past month. She's a solidly built woman from Montana, much pierced and tattooed, with a thick rope of braid hanging down her back. Her husband, an army specialist at Fort Hood, Texas, will soon deploy to Iraq, but she's been on the Bring Them Home Now bus tour for weeks, so it doesn't come as a surprise when she mentions that she feels guilty at leaving him behind.

Guilt. It's a curse echoing through conversation after conversation I have with soldiers, veterans, and the people who love them. Guilt for being lucky enough to survive your combat tour and guilt for what you did on that tour. Guilt at feeling blessed when your child comes home in one piece and guilt at your relief when the knock comes on someone else's door. Paul Rieckhoff's guilt for liking the power he has as a platoon leader in Baghdad. Chris Arendt's guilt at learning that he's going to Guantanamo because it sounds like a cushy posting on a tropical island—until he finds out what he has to do there, which creates a different guilt. Jonas Lara's guilt over not deploying to Iraq with his marine unit after being severely injured in training. Rob Sarra's guilt after shooting at an unarmed Iraqi woman, which becomes so intense that he refuses to fight as his platoon continues on to Baghdad.

Anne Sapp feels guilty when she drops something in the kitchen because it triggers her husband's PTSD, which, feeling guilty, she can do nothing to assuage. Celeste Zappala feels guilty that she didn't stop her son from enlisting, although she offered to drive him to Canada when he (probably feeling guilty) trained for his mission in Iraq by driving over cardboard cut-outs of children. Even Cindy Sheehan, who turned her life

171

upside down to end the war, feels guilty that it took her son's death to bring her to action. In what seems like a rare, unrehearsed moment, she confesses, "I've never felt so alive. It took Casey's death to awaken me." Guilt can be confusing and paralyzing, but apparently it can also be a great motivator.

I come across a list of "existential functions of guilt" compiled by someone who has worked with Holocaust survivors. To deny helplessness. To keep the dead alive in thought. To insist that there is some justice in the world because at least one person feels guilty.

Andrew Bacevich writes about a Fourth of July baseball game where a sailor, flown in from the Afghanistan war as a surprise for her family, strides onto the field to cheers and tears. He notes that this kind of unmerited, feel-good moment is what the theologian Dietrich Bonhoeffer named "cheap grace." If we, as a nation, speak of soldiers with respect and appreciation, it probably makes it easier for them when they get home, but not nearly as easy as it makes it for us to ignore them.

At the Bring Them Home Now rally, Rosenleaf cedes the microphone to Al Zappala, Celeste's former husband, who says that their son's life was an ordinary one—except that he went to war. "Truth be told," he continues, "Most people out there don't send their kids to fight either."

So add this to the list: guilt for the rest of us at having been given a pass on this war.

9

DISGRUNTLED

It's August 2007, Veterans For Peace are convening again, St. Louis this time, and for Iraq Veterans Against the War, it's a declaration of independence. About ninety members are here, at least half of them new to the group, making it their largest gathering to date. They clump and sprawl on overstuffed sofas in the hotel's lobby, swagger and cut their eyes sideways at the long hair, tie-dyed T-shirts, and antiwar ballads of the older vets. Polite, as always in public, they praise the earlier generation of GI resisters as family and forerunners, but they're tired of being told how to do things by an antiwar movement that has been marching and chanting the same phrases for four decades with little change.

In fairness to VFP, many of its members are also fed up with their ineffectuality. Recognizing themselves in the younger veterans, they're eager to figure out how they can be helpful without getting in the way. As if in poignant illustration that the time has come for the older generation to pass the baton, VFP's Dave Cline and MFSO's Charley Richardson show up in fragile health (Richardson has been diagnosed with aggressive cancer, and Cline will die within the month),[1] and Cindy Sheehan, who doesn't attend, has recently announced that she's resigning as "the face of the antiwar movement."

Losing face is not the movement's central problem; the war-without-end is. The older veterans, having butted up against entrenched power for decades, now assume that there will be American troops and bases in the region for years, no matter which party is in power, and predict that if the military or public becomes too restive, the occupation will turn into an air war, as Vietnam did, with increasing reliance on Special Forces, bombing raids, and unmanned drones.[2] Civilian antiwar groups seem to have bought into the futility of this perpetual-war scenario too, distracting themselves with demands for impeachment or buoying their spirits by theorizing some spanking new movement. Newspapers support ending the war—the journalism site Romenesko counts fifty editorial boards calling on the administration to get out of Iraq—but two years after Camp Casey, Congress continues to fund that war at the mind-boggling rate of about a quarter of a million dollars a minute.

Still, for the veterans gathered in St. Louis, there is work to be done. They attend workshops on engaging active-duty personnel, supporting GI resisters, and opening GI coffeehouses. They learn about the military's "don't ask, don't tell" policy and a water project in Iraq, and they fill a room to overflowing to discuss the situation of women in the military—which seems to come down to a choice of two roles: bitch, because you're not sleeping with someone, or slut, because you are. "You forgot dyke," ex-army sergeant Jen Hogg calls from the back of the room. On it goes for four days, reminding everyone of what they already know: this war has gone on too long.

Convention goers gather on Friday night for a "public speak-out" at the Centenary Methodist Church. Amid speeches by veterans, resisters, parents, activists, and Congressman Dennis Kucinich, backed by the finger-snapping rhythms of Raw Earth Drumming, the show stealer is Elaine Johnson, a Gold Star Mother, who had issued a challenge to George W. Bush to meet with her after her son, Darius Jennings, was killed in Iraq. A big, pretty woman with a round face framed by cornrows, she cuts a figure as she arrives on stage, swathed in orange from head to toe, and proceeds to describe her meeting with the president with crack comic timing.

She was in Colorado Springs for Darius's memorial, she tells her audience, when she got a call from Special Agent So-and-So, announcing that the president would like her to come to the White House. Okay, Johnson says she replied, but only if he foots the bill for her trip. Apparently, he did, because the scene switches to a White House security checkpoint, where Johnson is stopped, although she has made a point of not carrying a purse so as not to waste time. "They thought I wanted to shoot the president. I'm not a killer," she says. Waits a beat. "Not like him." Johnson reports that she presented the president with the names and addresses of South Carolina mothers to whom he has not yet written condolence letters, that she refused to participate in a photo op with Bush unless her son's widow was included, and that, when he asked if he could kiss her, replied, "First you want to have your picture taken with me and now you want to kiss me?" Little wonder that, as Charley Richardson has reported, she's known around the White House as "the Elaine Johnson problem."

Amusing as her delivery is, Johnson is deadly serious, ending her talk with the Elaine Johnson Plan for Peace: Gather all the Gold Star Mothers at the White House, let them figure out how to end the war in six months, and when they're finished, turn the government back over to the president. As she'll say later, "The reason I will never give up my struggle is because a coffin came home."

Garett Reppenhagen, who follows Johnson on stage, is equally determined. "If the politicians don't end this war," he announces in what will become IVAW's rally cry, "we will march on Washington, we will take the Capitol, and we will end it for them!" So it is with a mix of hopefulness and fear—hope that individuals banding together can change history, fear that they will not—that Iraq Veterans Against the War embarks on its most ambitious, productive, and questing season. It is probably no coincidence that this is also the year that the U.S. military presence in Iraq peaks, the greatest number of American soldiers are killed, and well over half of the American public comes to see the war as a bad mistake.[3]

"IVAW is on the cusp of literally changing the world."[4] So wrote board members of Vietnam Veterans Against the War to IVAW in 2008 in what could be read as an encouragement or a warning. For the younger organization, struggling to balance its rapid growth from a ragtag band of disgruntled veterans into an alliance of activists with specific goals, it was probably both.

War is often portrayed as a game, a seductive spectator sport, which civilians seem most eager to engage in when they have, as the saying goes, no skin in the game. Video games and drones are only the latest technologies that increase the distance between us and killing. Political movements too have a gamelike quality, with opposing teams, game plans, coaches, fans, and score keeping, though whether or not a movement catches on is probably more a matter of luck, timing, resources, and perseverance than rightness of strategy or cause.

In *Doing Democracy*, a book popular with grassroots activists, Bill Moyer, an organizer and educator (not to be confused with the journalist Bill Moyers), argues that social justice movements run in cycles of progress and retrenchment. He proposes eight not necessarily linear

stages. The first stages involve working for change through official channels—largely to prove that doesn't work—and taking advantage of "trigger events" to dramatize the problem and raise consciousness. Then come
the heady days when the movement takes off, only to be followed by a
slough of despond when results are inadequate and a sense of failure prevails. Moyer argues that this can be a productive time if used to clarify
the implications of actions and to find alternative approaches. Eventually,
if conditions are right, in the penultimate stage, the movement succeeds
in getting policies changed, but there is still another stage: continuing the
struggle. In other words, altering social or political consciousness takes
time, usually measured in years or decades.[5]

IVAW's take-off stage began almost immediately after its national
meeting, as members participated in a flurry of antiwar activities in
Washington, dubbed the National Days of Action. In the group's most
prominent action, an honor guard of about fifty Iraq Veterans Against
the War dressed in fatigues led a large antiwar march on 15 September
2007. Carrying the distress signal of an upside-down American flag and
five black flags with the logos of the major military contractors then in
Iraq, they marched with a security line of Veterans For Peace from Lafay-
ette Park to the Peace Monument, aka the Civil War Sailors Monument,
near the Capitol. "Support the troops! We are the troops!" they chanted,
while members of the prowar Gathering of Eagles chanted back, "Trai-
tors go to hell!"[6]

It was all standard stuff—march, flags, chants—except that the recently returned veterans were in the lead, occupying a moral and strategic
high ground. When the IVAW squad, led by Adam Kokesh, approached
the Gathering of Eagles standing along the parade route, he ordered,
"Column, halt, left face." Turning directly to their hecklers, the antiwar
veterans gave a crisp salute and held it for a long time before moving on.
A reporter from a local television station turned to a fellow bystander
and said, "I have one minute and twenty-seven seconds to cover this."

To cap the march, Kokesh and others from IVAW had worked with
the ANSWER Coalition, a leftist umbrella group, to organize a symbolic
"die-in" at the monument. ANSWER had preregistered participants online, suggesting that each carry the name of an American serviceperson
killed in the war, but when the moment arrived, the plan fell apart. The
march stretched a long distance, diers-in were scattered, the sidewalk
where they were supposed to fall was narrow, and people were splayed

across the neighboring National Mall, making it hard to tell the dying from the merely resting. Still, at the signal—a twenty-one-gun salute blasting from a boom box—as many as five thousand people dropped to the ground and lay there in illustration of the human cost of the war.

That mass action was accompanied by an unadvertised one: those willing to risk arrest continued past the monument and tried to crash through or hurdle over the low, metal barrier erected at the bottom of the Capitol steps. The police, responding with notable restraint, used chemical spray against a few protesters, rebuffed others, and arrested nearly two hundred, among them Adam Kokesh, Garett Reppenhagen, Geoff Millard, and Liam Madden. "Conflict does not steal the spotlight; it owns it," writes Sarah Sobieraj, a sociologist studying political protest.[7] Confirming her point, the die-in got plenty of press, while a teach-in about the war, held the following day, earned almost none.

A couple of days later, veterans from IVAW's Washington, DC, chapter and ANSWER activists launched a truth-in-recruiting project, visiting military recruiting offices in four-person teams to leaflet, picket, and chant, "No justice, no peace / U.S. out of the Middle East." TV cameras whirred, and within an hour, teams at a recruiting station in Northwest Washington called in to report that they were being harassed by the Gathering of Eagles. Kokesh, who helped organize the action, and a couple of older veterans rushed over to offer assistance. They found a dozen police officers lined up between the Eagles and the antiwar crew, trying to separate the groups, who spent the next hour chanting and yelling at each other. Nonetheless, the counterrecruiters deemed the action a success: as Kokesh observed, with a phalanx of police at the door, no one dared cross the threshold to talk with a recruiter that day.

Things had not been going well for military recruiters for some time. Two years earlier, the army had missed its recruiting goal by almost seven thousand. They tried new PR campaigns, such as getting *Cobblestone*, a magazine distributed nationally to middle schools and libraries, to dedicate an entire issue to the army,[8] but the quality of recruits—those with high school diplomas, basic skills, physical fitness, and no criminal record—continued to decline.[9] It would be another year before all branches of the military would meet their goals, and probably then because the sinking economy made war one of the few growth industries around. Meanwhile, legal and ethical violations by recruiters, including sexual harassment, bullying, falsifying documents, and violating guidelines by using class time for recruitment, were increasingly hard to ignore.[10] The situation was so bad by May 2005 that the army ordered an unprecedented "stand down." This was intended as a day to retrain—or restrain—recruiters, but it was hard to know how effective this was or how many violations continued, because the Pentagon had no oversight in place.

Theatrics aside, IVAW's attempts to undermine military recruiting were most effective when members visited high schools targeted by recruiters. These tended to be in poorer neighborhoods, even though all schools are required by the 2002 No Child Left Behind Act to provide military recruiters with the names and contact information of their students.[11] The veterans called their work "truth in recruiting" to differentiate it from counterrecruiting, but the goal was the same: to correct what they believed were deceptive elements in recruiters' sales pitches and to suggest alternatives to enlistment. They knew the recruiters' spiel well, having been on the receiving end, and their own experience had taught them that the most vulnerable kids didn't think they had better options. Often they didn't.

IVAW member Patty McCann worked with the American Friends Service Committee's Truth in Recruitment Program in Chicago after returning from a tour in Iraq with the Illinois National Guard. She had enlisted in 2000, while a junior in high school, having admired the Guard ever since they helped after a flood near her home in Carbondale when she was ten. Several years later, enlisting seemed to offer independence and a way to take care of herself. When you grow up in a small town, she noted, you don't know much about options. Four other students in her high school class enlisted the same year, and she recalled recruiters paying kids $100 a day to wear their uniforms to school and proselytize. "Some people join the military to escape gangs and others to find a way out of their parents' houses," she observed of the students she counseled about alternatives to enlisting. "It's not so different from me trying to escape southern Illinois and some of the social problems of that area."

It wasn't easy for IVAW members to get permission to visit schools, but when they did, they explained to the students that the military is not a social club or a tuition assistance or job training program; it is, they made clear, an organization that fights wars. They explained what soldiers did day-to-day and told students about other jobs or paths to college. Because most of the veterans weren't much older than the students they talked to and because they didn't try to sugarcoat the situation, they could be very persuasive. As Camilo Mejia put it, "We talk about war, combat, what it is like to kill a human being and see your friend get killed in front of you or come home without legs."[12]

By the end of 2007, IVAW had grown to seven hundred members, thirty-eight increasingly active chapters, and a staff of six full-time employees, three organizers, three consultants (including Action Mill's Nick Jehlen and Jethro Heiko), and a fluctuating flock of volunteers. The staff worked out of the national office at the headquarters of the American Friends Service Committee, a complex of brick buildings clustered around a courtyard and charmingly out of scale with the surrounding office towers of downtown Philadelphia. IVAW occupied three rooms crammed with desks, tables, chairs, cartons, computers, posters ("There's wrong . . . And then there's Army wrong"), and a constantly brewing coffeemaker. On a map of the United States pocked with pins to show where members and chapters were located, only Nebraska remained unmarked. From these cramped quarters, staff and volunteers welcomed new members, argued with banks about setting up satellite accounts, fielded calls from reporters, and took a crash course in running a national organization. Things weren't exactly humming along—a supporter told me, "Of course they had all their problems because their main membership is young, male vets, and they're nuts"—but the excitement of building something that felt both epic and unstoppable filled the air.

With many of the troops on their third and fourth deployments, IVAW was confident that antiwar sentiment within the military was ready to be tapped. One member reported seeing IVAW graffiti at a base in Iraq, another pointed out that top generals, albeit retired ones, were taking a public stand against the Iraq War. Anecdotal evidence was backed up by official reports of widespread morale problems. Beginning in the fall of 2003, the army created Mental Health Advisory Teams (MHATs) to conduct yearly studies of the well-being of its troops in Iraq. That year, the war's first, more than half of the soldiers surveyed—mostly male junior enlistees—reported low or very low unit morale. That rate improved over the following years, but reports of high or very high unit morale never topped 12 percent.[13] (In Afghanistan, where MHATs started surveying troops in 2005, nearly half rated unit morale low, and that number got steadily worse.)

In its 2006 survey, MHATs asked about battlefield ethics for the first, and apparently only, time. They may have stopped asking because the answers were so alarming. Fewer than half of the soldiers and marines surveyed agreed that all noncombatants should be treated with dignity and respect, and while the percentage saying they condoned torture under certain circumstances—well over a third—was similar to American public opinion at the time, soldiers in Iraq were more likely to be in a position to use torture than American civilians. Over one-third of respondents reported having insulted or sworn at Iraqi civilians, 5 percent reported hitting or kicking civilians unnecessarily, and 11 percent reported damaging or destroying Iraqi property unnecessarily. These were self-reported rates, so the reality was probably considerably greater. Only a third said they would report a fellow soldier for mistreating or stealing from a noncombatant.[14]

Clearly, soldiers in the field were fed up, exhausted, and shorn of any illusions about the efficacy of the American enterprise in Iraq, but they were still apprehensive about active resistance. They sometimes banded together to advocate for improvement in specific conditions, such as better training and equipment, shorter deployments with longer breaks in between, better health care, and more attention to physical and psychological injuries. But being bone-weary or chafing at rules is different from believing that you're fighting the wrong war for the wrong reasons. "The majority of people are sick of the war," observed IVAW's Ian LaVallee, "but they're not sick of it for the same reason we are."

In a 1970 speech about the women's movement, Jo Freeman, a feminist activist and writer, observed, "Unstructured groups may be very effective in getting women to talk about their lives; they aren't very good for getting things done. . . . It is when people get tired of 'just talking' and want to do something more that the groups flounder, unless they change the nature of their operation."[15] As IVAW moved from the just-talking to the doing stage, it struggled with problems typical of loosely structured, grassroots, outsider groups: deciding which actions are merely symbolic and which will yield the biggest payoff; getting noticed amid all the causes clamoring for attention; dealing with a news media with a double standard for reporting on political protest; and finding the resources required to grow, which usually aren't available until the organization has grown. Despite this last hurdle, money wasn't then a big problem for

IVAW, in part because the group didn't require much. Its 2007 budget was about $250,000, cobbled together from foundation grants, sale of merchandise, and small, individual donations. Salaries were low, but not far out of line with army pay. "They're used to being poor," said Nick Jehlen, who was by then working closely with the group.

To these predictable stumbling blocks, the veterans—always impatient, often fragile, sometimes explosive, mostly inexperienced—added a heap of their own. Stability is not the strong suit of recently returned veterans struggling to establish their place in civilian society, and by the time these veterans got to IVAW, they were usually antiauthoritarian, while the authority they knew best was the military—and their feelings about that were mixed, to say the least. While some members rejected that hierarchical model outright, others found comfort in structure and still others fell back on it by instinct. This range of impulses led to endless loops of discussion and recrimination.

"The problem is that in a grassroots organization, everyone thinks democracy means voting. And then everyone's unhappy," Jehlen complained. He wanted to train the veterans to work by consensus, but their suspicion of rules and rejection of prescribed behavior made that hard. Then there was the group's decentralized structure, which helped attract new members and keep them involved, but also undermined decisions of the staff and board and created conflicts between chapters and the national office. Chapter size and strength fluctuated wildly, especially in chapters with many active-duty members, who got moved around, deployed, or discharged. And while members' high energy, mission orientation, and flexibility allowed them to take advantage of opportunities and respond quickly to changes in the political landscape, that predisposition also led them to overextend themselves or leave projects half-finished. Working as small, guerrilla-style units, IVAW could surprise or disconcert or annoy, but that limited their effectiveness. Gadflies are easily swatted away.

Tension also arose because IVAW fashioned itself a leaderless organization and resisted pressure to put forth a figurehead. The veterans had seen what had happened at Camp Casey when Cindy Sheehan was anointed Mother-of-All-Mothers. They didn't want to repeat the damage that had caused, both to the protest and to her. Inevitably, though, leaders emerged by dint of personality, talent, self-confidence, vision, or persistence. Among those prominent at the time were Camilo Mejia, Garett

Reppenhagen, Adam Kokesh, Liam Madden, Aaron Hughes, and Kelly Dougherty. (Ironically, becoming an official leader made Dougherty feel more vulnerable. "Once I became executive director, it was like, bit by bit, relationships started going south," she said sadly.) These prominent members attracted and inspired other members and helped reinforce the personal ties and trust that kept IVAW going. The organization was increasingly good at creating unit cohesion; it was less skilled at building a brigade.

Even as the veterans drew away from the military, it was impossible to get away from military metaphors. Action Mill's Jethro Heiko, a civilian, who was on contract as director of organizing, came up with a plan to hire a large number of field organizers to act as "force multipliers," the military's term for attributes that increase the potential effectiveness of a combat force. When funding didn't come through, he worked with two veterans to train others in organizing, direct action, and whatever theory had caught his attention.

Heiko loves theories. One afternoon, he drew me a diagram of wedges, each representing a faction or player in a political conflict, which fanned in an arc between opposing positions or goals. His point was that rather than waste time trying to convert your most hardened opponent, you needed to focus your energy on moving the in-betweens closer to your way of thinking. The far end isn't worth your time, he argued persuasively, because, while you may be able to isolate or weaken your enemies, you won't change their minds.

"There's also value in not demonizing the other side," I suggested.

"But do you think there are enemies?" he asked.

"Oh, yes," I said, "I do believe in enemies."

So did the veterans, although they didn't necessarily need external foes to create strife, given their gift for coming up with their own. IVAW's goals were more practical than ideological, which allowed the group to accommodate a spectrum of political views. Sounding like a bad joke, members boasted that their ranks included Republicans, Democrats, socialists, libertarians, anarchists—and a rabbi. The diversity fostered the entrepreneurial spirit and quick reactions important to their kind of activism, but it also encouraged attention-grabbing spectacles, the kind that are more fun than the slog of movement building, but, as Aaron Hughes pointed out, are less productive in the long run.

Bill Moyer describes an activist type he calls the "negative rebel."[16] It is the true-believing, highly quotable rebel with a cause—usually himself—and every antiestablishment movement has its share. Moyer argues that negative rebels make bad revolutionaries, but because they can be clever in their tactics and compelling in their anger or passion to tear down boundaries, they seldom lack for followers—or publicity. IVAW wasn't immune to this kind of showboating, and it wasn't long after the Kumbaya of its 2007 convention that its unity began to fray. That October, everyone in a leadership capacity was called to an emergency meeting in Philadelphia, where an outside facilitator tried to help them sort out the tensions within the organization, but there was a more immediate crisis to attend to. Jehlen described a series of frantic conference calls about the do-your-own-thing proclivity of the Washington, DC, chapter and specifically of Adam Kokesh, who had the awkward habit of getting himself arrested. The first time had been the previous April at a protest at the Senate Office Building, the second at Fort Benning during the summer bus tour, and the most recent, the past September at a rally protesting fines imposed for pasting up posters for an antiwar march.[17] (In 2013, Kokesh, who had become a gun-rights advocate, spent four months in jail after videotaping himself loading what appeared to be live shells into a shotgun not far from the White House.)

As IVAW leaders met, Kokesh was all over the news again, this time for his opposition to something called Islamo-Fascism Awareness Week at George Washington University, where he was a graduate student in political science. He told me that he had seen firsthand what the "belittling of Islamic people" had spawned and he wanted to do something about it, so he and several others students put up posters intended to satirize anti-Muslim racism. Unfortunately, other students perceived the posters as promoting racism, and the action and reaction quickly grew into the kind of tempest in a teapot that flourishes on college campuses. Kokesh argued that he was acting as a student, not on behalf of IVAW, but Dougherty and Action Mill argued back that, as a board member, he was perceived as representing IVAW and its values, whether he intended to or not. Kokesh didn't buy it. "There's a debate over controlling our public image," he said. "There are jealous guardians of it. I'm not one of them. I'm of the opinion that until we're a public name, any publicity is good publicity."

The board was split on how to respond, though this was hardly the first time the organization had had to deal with an errant member. In its early days, IVAW's push to increase its numbers, coupled with an over-extended staff, led to carelessness and screw-ups. In 2006, a young man named Jesse MacBeth approached IVAW, claiming to have fought in Afghanistan and Iraq as a member of the elite U.S. Army Rangers. IVAW wasn't yet checking members' credentials, so MacBeth joined and began speaking on the group's behalf, telling stories of atrocities his unit had routinely committed. Problem was, MacBeth had been nowhere near a battlefield, having spent all of forty-some days in the army before being dismissed as unfit during basic training. He was later imprisoned for getting military benefits under false pretenses. When MacBeth was exposed, IVAW publicly severed ties with him, but not before the group's detractors pounced gleefully on such a good opportunity to discredit the antiwar vets. IVAW instituted a policy of checking members' proof of service (usually a DD 214, the military certificate of release or discharge), but two and a half years later, 29 percent of members still hadn't filed such proof.[18]

IVAW was linked to another high-profile imposter in 2009. Rick Duncan, whose real name was Richard Glen Strandlof, never joined IVAW, but was friendly with members of the Colorado Springs chapter, including Reppenhagen, and he appears to have helped out on the Winter Soldier hearings the year before. Members appreciated his work in behalf of struggling veterans—until they found out that his claims to having been a marine captain, wounded veteran, and Purple Heart recipient were all fabrications. Only when Reppenhagen saw a news story revealing Duncan/Strandlof as an impostor with mental problems and an outstanding arrest warrant did he realize that he had been duped. "You sort of feel like a jerk by even doubting someone," he told the *Denver Post*.[19]

He and IVAW were hardly alone in their credulity. Military.com, a virtual community of veterans and military personnel, which claims to have ten million members (and where MacBeth also misrepresented himself) doesn't verify members' biographies; Iraq and Afghanistan Veterans of America didn't begin requiring proof of service for membership in its Community of Veterans until 2008; and politicians, professors, and other storytellers are frequently caught lying about or exaggerating their military experience.[20] Veterans are often the first to smell a rat in the credential line, but nearly everyone, civilian or military, seems reluctant to challenge such claims. Why this particular biographical item should be sacrosanct is another piece of military mythology, but it resonated enough for Congress to enact the Stolen Valor Act of 2005, making it a federal crime to lie about receiving military awards. The Supreme Court recognized the dangers of criminalizing résumé enhancements and struck the law down on First Amendment grounds in June 2012.

IVAW was particularly vulnerable, however. Many organizations have no litmus test for membership—the ACLU doesn't insist that its members never try to tell someone to shut up, and the NRA doesn't require that its members be armed to the teeth—but IVAW, with its egalitarian structure, organizational naïveté, and willingness to promote any member who volunteered as a spokesperson left itself wide open to such public perception debacles.

Fakers turned out to be easier to manage than loose cannons and the unhinged. IVAW eventually instituted a code of conduct, but it was weakly enforced and the board was hesitant to confront members. Some board members acted out of a creed of inclusiveness, others from a reluctance to be prescriptive or confrontational, and still others from sympathy for fellow veterans who seemed to need help more than chastisement. The reasons varied, but each time, the discussion about disciplining a member was agonizing.

Excommunicating a member was even harder than disciplining one, though it was sometimes necessary. In the week before Winter Soldier, IVAW's largest and most public event, members Evan Knappenberger and Jon DeWald blogged violent threats to right-wing opponents of the organization. On his blog, *Wobblynomad* (since taken down), Knappenberger, who had trained as an army intelligence analyst and spent a year in Iraq, called blogger and columnist Michelle Malkin a "bitch" and a "slut" and wished graphically for her torture by an Iraqi death squad. The seldom-given-to-understatement Malkin responded with due outrage, and IVAW responded with due alarm, admonishing the two men to cut it out. When they didn't, the board hunkered down for damage control. They decided to terminate DeWald's membership and suspend Knappenberger indefinitely, but allow him to appeal the decision.[21]

Clearly, an organization dedicated to nonviolence cannot tolerate members speaking or acting violently, but all IVAW members, by definition, had been trained in violence, and the board and staff often read such noxious outbursts as signs that the speakers or writers were out of control. (In a particularly creative bid for attention, one member absconded with his chapter's cash, gambled it away, then checked himself into a VA hospital.) Along with the punishments they handed down, IVAW usually tried to get the offending members the help they needed.

The problem arose again in late 2009, when the board was forced to consider action against member Carl Webb for apparently advocating violence and for "his stated aims to divide IVAW and force other members to quit."[22] This referred to Casey Porter, another member who had gathered evidence of Webb's factious intentions and led the campaign against him. Webb's statements had been roiling the organization for some time, but it took a while for the board to censure him, in part because they seemed to fear being accused of persecuting him for his radical political views. In an attempt at even-handedness, they kicked Webb out of the organization and gave Porter a lifetime ban on membership for "divisive behavior towards a fellow member." By then, Porter had quit.

Then, on 20 March 2010, IVAW board member Matthis Chiroux burned an American flag at a rally in Washington organized by the ANSWER Coalition, and his provocative action quickly popped up on YouTube and Facebook. In a statement on the IVAW website, Executive Director Jose Vasquez pointed out that burning the flag is constitutionally protected expression, but went on to consider the implications of a member acting on his own versus as a representative of the organization—which brought the issue full circle to the debate over Kokesh's protest two and a half years before. The board considered sending Chiroux a letter of reprimand, but ultimately came to no clear consensus, and the matter went unresolved.[23]

Hard as it was, IVAW usually understood that it needed to sever ties when a member's actions were disruptive and harmful to the organization. Amadee Braxton, who was on staff from the MacBeth kerfuffle onward, said, "Any time we've asked people to leave, we get e-mail from people thanking us for doing that because they don't want to be associated with an organization that doesn't have its shit together, where people can say or do whatever they want with no consequences."

From time to time, suspicions arose about threats from outside: members who were government informants or agents provocateurs. In the summer of 2008, in a memo to his then-feuding fellow board members, Camilo Mejia wrote, "As far as informants . . . it wouldn't surprise me to know that there are a few among us, but rather than getting all paranoid about it, I think we should concentrate on the things that bring us together, and not on those that divide us." That seemed to be the general sense, as members vacillated between self-deprecation (we're not important enough for the feds to bother with) and the jokey paranoia of people acting in opposition to a system they still buy into. There were members whose stories were too hard to verify or too good to be true and lots of members who were unstable or difficult, but there wasn't any real evidence that they were government agents or moles.

Evidence did emerge that the government was spying on peace activists, if less zealously than it had on VVAW or 1980s Central America solidarity groups—as far as we know. (The cover of *Virtual Roll Call*, a digest of intelligence reports compiled for the Department of Homeland Security, featured the quotation, "We Don't Know What We Don't Know" and attributed it to "Unknown"—which raises the intriguing question: Does DHS have a sense of humor?) DHS, which includes the Secret Service, U.S. Coast Guard, Federal Emergency Management Agency, Transportation Security Administration, and immigration agencies, kept records of public protests and other actions where IVAW members took part, including Operation First Casualty.[24] These records were available to an array of government agencies at the local, regional, and national level through a universe of data collection and retention that is huge, intrusive, and very secret.

At the heart of the system are more than one hundred joint terrorism task forces (JTTFs), which are supposed to investigate criminal and terrorist activity, and seventy-two state and local fusion centers, which are supposed to be JTTF intelligence counterparts. The fusion centers grew from the Intelligence and Terrorism Prevention Act of 2004, which mandated an "information sharing environment," and that opened the door to a technofix known as data mining. Data mining, as a national security tool, is based on the theory that if enough bits of disparate information are brought together, mathematical algorithms can be used to identify patterns, which can predict and preempt terrorism and other crimes. It is not a new idea; in the 1980s, the FBI monitored users of technical and science libraries and databases under an "information mosaic" theory, which held that researchers from hostile countries could combine discrete and benign data to create threats to American security and commerce.[25] Since 2004, the same concept, under a different name and enhanced by a national love affair with "big data," has been invoked to justify collecting vast amounts of information about American citizens and making it broadly available to an array of law enforcement entities.

To call this system intricate is an understatement. The hierarchies and lines of communication and reporting are impossible to unravel, and the alphabet soup of acronyms—TIDE, TALON, TOLLS, FAST, FUSE, FIG, SWISS, RISS—reads like Dr. Seuss edited by Kafka. The numbers that were made public are mind-numbing: by 2011, at least eight hundred thousand local and state law enforcement officials were feeding information into fusion centers, and some 1.5 billion records were stored in the FBI's National Security Branch Analysis Center. Bureaucracies, by their nature, bloat and sprawl, but inscrutability seemed to be built into this system, and if anyone understood it in its entirety, no one was telling.

Occasionally, the system could be pried open just a bit. Information discovered through a public records request in 2009 revealed that an anarchist known as John Jacob had infiltrated and spied on antiwar groups near the Fort Lewis army base (later renamed Joint Base Lewis-McChord), including IVAW, which is listed in one document as a "Threat Group."[26] Jacob was really John Towery, a veteran who was working as a civilian intelligence analyst for the Fort Lewis Force Protection Service. His primary target appeared to be Port Militarization Resistance (PMR) in Olympia, Washington, and from at least the spring of 2007 until July 2009, when he was outed, he attended PMR's meetings and maintained its Listserv, which could be used to make members' personal information and contacts available to the army, FBI, local JTTF, state fusion center, and local police and sheriff departments. According to the ACLU, "A document leaked by WikiLeaks outlines how a 'fusion cell' in a military police garrison integrated with local, county, regional, state, and federal law enforcement can avoid the usual constraints on military intelligence by operating 'under the auspice and oversight of the police discipline and standards.'"[27] Towery, who was apparently good at insinuating himself into established networks of friends, tried to befriend members of local IVAW chapters and reported on IVAW's activities, including events at Coffee Strong, a GI coffeehouse closely affiliated with IVAW. An ambiguous but chilling e-mail sent to an intelligence analyst by the director of an intelligence group of the Washington Fusion Center passes on information about a fundraiser at Coffee Strong featuring Camilo Mejía and appends the comment, "I'll let the arson guys know."[28]

So, yes, IVAW did have enemies, known and unknown, but its most intractable problems were internal. Like VVAW years before, IVAW was learning the hard lessons of political activism: commitment wavers, leaders burn out, members crack up, allies disappoint, and factions splinter off. In other words, they faced all the difficulties of keeping a movement going without stifling the energy and creativity that attracts members in the first place—all with an overlay of post-traumatic stress disorder and lives interrupted. And because membership required only past military experience and commitment to three long-term goals, deep and sometimes bitter divisions about strategy and tactics were inevitable.

For instance, was Iraq Veterans Against the War a protest group whose raison d'être would evaporate when what they were against—the wars in Iraq and Afghanistan—finally ended? Maybe they could get rid of the "the" in its name and become an ongoing peace and antimilitarism group? But would that make them just a next-generation Veterans For Peace, and if so, did they need a separate organization? Maybe they should be an identity group, advocating for veterans and their political standing, but if that, what could IVAW do that other groups weren't doing, and often better?

Resolving these issues took time and soul-searching, but members weren't much given to reflection. They thought a lot about the U.S. military, its wars, the destruction war wrought, and their role in all of that. They thought about their future and their friends, especially the ones whose futures had ended abruptly with a bullet or a bomb. They thought of themselves as part of something big, something historic, something that mattered, and they became increasingly sophisticated in their analyses and defense of their ideas. But when it came to figuring out what IVAW could and should do, they usually acted first and dealt with consequences only when that became unavoidable. "They have a saying that it's better to ask for forgiveness than to ask for permission," said Heiko in frustration. "I'd like them to understand that they don't have to do either."

Jehlen, meanwhile, worried that if the dominant image of IVAW was of civil disobedience and arrests, the organization would "be stuck in neutral forever." Embedded in that concern was the overarching question of how radical the group wanted to be. That was hardly a new question for antiwar veterans. Sectarian strife had riven Vietnam Veterans Against the War and seriously undermined the organization by 1972. IVAW also had its internecine conflicts. For VVAW, the radicals had been the Maoists; for IVAW, they were members of the International Socialist Organization (ISO).[29] Early in 2008, the ISO faction organized a

Caucus for Grassroots Democracy within IVAW, and soon accusations flew. Sometimes the opposing members simply didn't like each other, but the conflict was also political and was stoked by the fear that the ISO cadre intended to advance that group's aims and subvert IVAW's. Members may have been sharp and accurate in recalling what they did while in uniform, but when it came to who said what to whom and what purges were under way, it was like walking onto the set of *Rashomon.*

The globalist faction of IVAW argued that the wars were a product of America's corrupting sense of exceptionalism and entitlement to a disproportionate amount of the world's resources. Israeli-Palestinian tensions were in the mix, as were racism, sexism, class resentments, environmental depredation, 9/11 as an inside job, and, of course, the warrior culture. The faction advocating for a narrower focus didn't necessarily disagree that their goals were intertwined with large global forces, nor were they opposed to making common cause with groups working on similar issues. From its start, members had worked hard to understand the connections and context of the wars they had fought and now opposed and they recognized that those wars were tied to geopolitics, global economics, and American arrogance. So the dissension was less about theory than about how to reconcile an ideal campaign with an effective one. As long as IVAW stuck to its core concerns, it was able to gain traction and move forward. It was when it insisted on going macro and embedding its antiwar message in a larger social-structural critique that it got stuck in the mud-slinging.

A letter VVAW sent to the IVAW board around this time warned about the dangers of factionalism: "When people have an agenda other than that of the organization to which they belong, they are always going to make decisions which further the agenda of their sectarian group. This is the same whether that group is socialist, libertarian or democrat." The letter went on to warn that because it is often the most active members who are recruited to the sectarian group's "divisive position," they not only hijack the mass organization, but are diverted from more constructive activity.[30]

The ISO controversy was particularly heated in the Chicago chapter, where several members straddled the two organizations and others had ties to VVAW, which was based there. Patty McCann had come to IVAW by way of her Campus Antiwar Network at the University of Illinois in

Chicago, which, at that time, she said, consisted of two socialists and two veterans. The veterans were McCann and an IVAW member, so she joined IVAW. Though she didn't join ISO, she had positive feelings about both groups, which is why she found the factionalism so upsetting. After the conflict had abated somewhat, McCann told me, "People don't change a lot after they get out of the military. There's still a lot of -isms that can be created and designating people as the other, the enemy. I think that sort of happened with ISO." She talked of the "gusto" that came from working against the dominant perspective, but complained that such zeal also manifested itself in shooting down other people's ideas. "It doesn't feel very good to feel like you're being called out," she said, "especially about something you really care about."

The board struggled to resolve these internal disputes, but discussions crumpled into snark and flame in supposedly private e-mails and on the members' forum. A consultant enlisted by Action Mill to work with the board said that the kind of infighting she saw was typical of their youth and inexperience, but noted that e-mail and blogs were ways to avoid discussion. You just put your firm opinion up and let everyone else attack it, she observed.

When the consultant had the board brainstorm what they thought they did well, the list included "strategic thinking, taking the time to discuss what needs to be discussed, strong volunteer/member commitment, decentralization of good ideas, legacy of being from a mission-oriented organization, ability to effectively do what you need to do (and rise above your past), youth, energy, and"—in contrast to DHS—"we know what we don't know." For challenges, they listed "relatively inexperienced board and executive director, rapid growth, lingering ambiguity, differing views about and relationships with the military, and inappropriate application of hardheadedness and compassion." Along with hardheadedness, they might have included a tendency to rebuff potential allies, which arose in part from self-protection and in part from arrogance. "Best practices don't apply to IVAW because we are a unique organization," Kokesh argued during a budget discussion at a board meeting.

Dougherty found herself battling what she called "an inherent skepticism among some members of anyone who isn't a veteran—like a 'we're-better-than-you' kind of thing." Most of the board had no prior experience in organizational management, but when she hired consultants for training sessions, she said that some members asked her, "'Why are you bringing in special, fancy people to try to tell me what to do?' Like we can't figure it out ourselves. But," she concluded plaintively, "we couldn't figure it out ourselves." A couple of years later, after Dougherty had left her job and the board's internal problems could no longer be papered over, Jason Lemieux said to his fellow board members, "We need to stop rebelling against all authority and grow up."

∽ *Boston, Massachusetts, 11 November 2007* ∽

Once again, the Smedley Butler Brigade is relegated to marching behind the street sweepers in Boston's annual Veterans Day parade, but they're particularly riled up this year because the American Legion, the parade's sponsor, has refused to include IVAW's Liam Madden on its roster of speakers. That gets Tony Flaherty thinking about Memorial Day 1945, when General Lucian Truscott visited a military cemetery in Italy. As the political cartoonist Bill Mauldin later recalled, Truscott turned his back on the assembled brass and other bigwigs and talked instead to the crosses in the cemetery, quietly apologizing before walking away. Tony urges action, and the Smedleys plot a surprise.

This Veterans Day arrives crisp and clear, showing off the city at its autumnal best. There go the politicians, leading the parade, then the marching bands and JROTC with their flags and spiffy uniforms, the horses and the machines sweeping up their manure. At last it's the Smedleys' turn with their Veterans For Peace banner and "War Is a Racket" flyers and upside-down American flags pinned to the back of their jackets—a distress signal, as they're eager to explain.

Nate Goldshlag, curly hair puffing out around his cap like Howdy Doody's friend Claribel, is at the lead as they march out, shouting the cadence they've shouted for decades:

One, two, three, four

Bring it on down

[beat]

No War!

Behind them, Code Pink and Raging Grannies sashay in living color, while cries of "Traitor!" and "Fuck you!" mix with scattered applause from the sidelines.

As they approach the sprawling plaza at Government Center, a veteran of middle age, with a tight, military haircut and neat beard, screams that they're dishonoring him and begins to cry. A Smedley puts his arm around his shoulder and pulls his head down to comfort him, while another gently rubs his back. "We're not here to hurt you," the Smedley vet repeats over and over. "We're all veterans, we feel strongly about this war. We've thought long and hard about this." The angry vet wipes his eyes and tries to regain his composure, finally calming down enough to shake the hands the other veterans offer.

And then it's time. Lining up in front of the stage where assorted dignitaries have gathered to give their speeches, eighteen Veterans For Peace and a few supporters tie brightly colored bandanas over their mouths. Paul Brailsford, at ninety-two is the oldest, but Severyn Bruyn, eighty, and Tony Flaherty, seventy-six, aren't too far behind. Gagged, they turn their backs to the stage to display to the audience the placards hanging around their necks: "American Legion SILENCES the Message of Peace from Veterans." For a moment, no one seems to know how to respond. A policeman consults with Tony, who has led negotiations with the city. He removes his gag and walks up and down the line, repeating, "We have to move or be arrested." No one moves.

They're asking for trouble, of course; civil disobedience is meant to break the rules. The police, some probably veterans themselves, oblige by flexi-cuffing the protesters, a few of whom flash a peace sign while their hands are still free. Somewhere in the shuffle, Tony is knocked down, and Winston Warfield, who will remain behind to make their case to the press, helps him up, asking, "Are you okay, brother?" "I'm okay. Let me be arrested," Tony replies gruffly and climbs into the paddy wagon with the others. Charged with disturbing a public assembly, the veterans plead not guilty and are instructed to return for a hearing. The only thing that might thrill them more would be Dick Cheney's impeachment.

A few years later, a longtime civilian activist will tell me, "Your first arrest is kind of like the first time you have sex. It really should be memorable. After that, it's kind of routine." Newbies or jaded, the next day, the Smedleys are abuzz. On their forum, they boast that their protest has gone national—Keith Olbermann!—and Tony offers to buy the police commissioner a drink, a generous gesture from a recovering alcoholic.

But for all their heartfelt commitment to peace, this is a fractious bunch, and within hours someone gripes on the Smedley forum that he's been told the police are claiming that the vets chanted during the speeches, which, he writes indignantly, is an obvious lie. Plus, his cuffs were too tight. Can it, someone writes back; the cops aren't our enemy, the system is. Stop making statements on a public website which could be used against you in court, a lawyer advises.

It's so hard to let any of this go: the insult of the official parade, the high of the protest, all they remember and all they're still trying to forgive themselves for all these many years after their wars ended. Because all wars go on too long.

10

MAD BAD SAD

Well into the fifth year of U.S. troops in Iraq and the start of the seventh in Afghanistan, it's all about the halt and the lame. On HBO, James Gandolfini, aka Tony Soprano, interviews badly wounded veterans who have (barely) escaped death. On Boston's ABC affiliate, Andy and Anne Sapp tell how his PTSD pains their young daughter. In response to press queries, the army admits to its highest rate of desertion in twenty-seven years. There's the usual gauzy glory we swath our soldiers in as we wave them off to battle, but now we're getting story upon story about the damage that's been done to our guys in uniform—drinking, divorce, homelessness—and nothing about preventing that by ending the war and bringing them home.

Laura Kent calls in to a National Public Radio talk show on the crisis in military mental health care. Her son, Phillip, committed suicide in September 2005 after returning from Iraq, and the host encourages her to tell her story. When she says—twice—that Gold Star and Military Families Speak Out have given her the strength to talk about it, he ignores her. He's not being unsympathetic, he just wants to know, "What's the lesson you've taken from your experience?" But what if there is no lesson—or what if the lesson isn't for a grieving mother, but for the people who put her son in that unbearable position? And when it comes to veterans, why is it that the only response we can imagine is to feel sorry for them?

"PTSD is going to color everything you write," MFSO's Nancy Lessin warned me back in the fall of 2005. Post-traumatic stress disorder wasn't yet getting much attention, but the lucky IVAW members who were well enough (at least on some days) knew that it was impossible to talk about resistance without talking about what ailed them. From its start, the group had highlighted what came to be called the breakdown of the military, and by the end of 2007, the problem was hard to ignore.

The army and marines had been forced to lower standards and offer ever-more enticing promises to fill their ranks, while those already in uniform were sick of repeated deployments, sick of feeling duped, and sick of the hoary mythologies of war, which were growing increasingly hollow and dangerous. On top of that, many were plain old sick, suffering from wounds that didn't heal, ailments without names, brain injuries, and the repercussions of sexual abuse.[1] The *Washington Post* had exposed the appalling conditions at Walter Reed, the army's flagship hospital; the military was reporting an alarming surge in suicide; and everyone, it seemed, was talking about PTSD.

It was around this time that I began to wonder if working to end a war you took part in, as atonement, enlightenment, or reparation, was a healthy response to the psychological stress of battle. I had heard variations on that theme far too often to discount it. "The only way that I've been able to come to terms with what I've been through and everything that I'm now dealing with is by being a member of this organization and doing everything that I can to educate the public about the realities of this war," Eli Wright told me, as he worked to keep IVAW's first active-duty chapter going. "IVAW has literally saved my life."

Homefront Battle Buddies, a peer-support project of IVAW, was based on the belief that "the political is inherently tied to the emotional." That sounded good to me; if you're going to spend the rest of your life repenting what you did in war, working for peace is probably as good a way as any to do it. But maybe I had it backward; maybe mental health *leads* to civic and political involvement. Or maybe the link isn't mental health, but going through the destabilizing process of reevaluating your beliefs, as these antiwar veterans had, and emerging a different person at the other end.

I began to look for research—measurable findings from controlled experiments—that examined the interaction of PTSD and political activism. I didn't expect a direct cause and effect, but I suppose I did hope to find that political activism (at least the activism I approved of) could act as an antidote to some of the misery and self-destructive behavior associated with emotional injury. I never did find any directly related studies, but along the way, I came across an array of tantalizing thinking on the therapeutic, political, moral, spiritual, and economic issues swirling around the psychic and emotional distress of soldiers and veterans.

To get beyond the theoretical, I ask Andy and Anne Sapp to talk with me about his PTSD. It's winter 2012 now, and Andy looks older than I remember him: grayer, shaggier, his shirt less starched than when he was home on R and R in 2005 and he and Anne weren't yet reckoning with his affliction. Now they have lived with PTSD for six years—seven, if you count the year he refused to admit he had it because he had never left the base or fired his weapon, and who was he to suffer when others had it so much worse? Nearly fifty when he deployed, he was older than most of his National Guard unit, had a stable family life, strong religious beliefs, a good education, and a solid teaching career, things he cared deeply about. He expected all that to insulate him, so it took a while to realize that the whole time he was in Iraq, he was numb.

A few years earlier, he had told me, "I remember one day, I was asleep and a mortar came in. It must have landed twenty or thirty meters from my room. It was loud enough that it woke me up, the building shook, the dust was coming down. I just rolled over and went back to sleep. I was startled more when I came home and was hearing the imaginary mortars than the real ones there."

Now he says of the ever-present danger he felt in Iraq, "It reshapes your whole psyche, knowing any moment may be your last. My error beforehand was thinking these things could turn off. It's frustrating to think that ten months out of my life could completely change my life." And yet, he admits, "There's a part of me that still wants to be in that environment because that environment, shitty as it was, made sense." He didn't want to go to war, but after seventeen years of military training, he knew he would go when he was called up. "There was this part of me that was a soldier, there was this little-boy part of me that wanted to play war." Today is the seventh anniversary of his unit's entry into Iraq, and the date is one of the times during the year when his symptoms kick in. He's learned to manage them and function reasonably well. "But functioning becomes so exhausting," he says.

Andy is lucky; the Veterans Administration system has worked for him. He was diagnosed with PTSD and given an 80 percent disability rating, which ensures him free medical care and monthly disability checks, and he is working with a psychologist whom he credits, along with Anne, with keeping him alive. Putting a name to a misery or dysfunction can be helpful in making you feel less aberrant and in holding out hope of a cure. The downside is that you can get stuck in that diagnosis and hang on to PTSD as a substitute for complex, root causes of your pain. Andy struggles with that dissonance. "It's so difficult to get my mental hands around this because there's a part of me that cannot let go of it. People say, just get over it. I don't want to be the wounded vet, and yet on some level I am. How do you acknowledge that this is who you are and at the same time try to build something out of that?" Andy and Anne, eager to add their voices to the antiwar movement when he got home from Iraq, gave numerous interviews and speeches, but after a while, they stopped because the futility of antiwar activities fueled his anger, and repeating their stories interfered with their healing. "We did not want to become what we were talking about," Anne says.

Can a whole society suffer from PTSD, columnist James Carroll asked; he then went on to argue that the United States was doing just that in relation to its ongoing wars.[2] It's a safe bet that when a specific medical condition is generalized to an entire population, it has lost its diagnostic value, but, as Anne points out, theoretically whole countries go to war, not just their soldiers. "Why should the soldiers be the only ones to suffer?" she demands. Which leads Andy to sit up straight and wave his arms and interject, "I just had an epiphany here. If we're going to go with the metaphor of sacrifice, sacrifices are meant to be done in public. We've turned sacrifice into something hidden."

"I don't want the public to suffer," Anne adds quietly. "I just want them to know."

Soldiers have long told war stories, but earlier generations didn't talk much about how they felt about war.[3] Now we put such faith in talk therapy, bearing witness, and sharing our innermost thoughts with legions of Facebook friends and Twitter followers that it's little wonder we half-expect the marine corps to sound like StoryCorps. According to Stephen Soldz, founder of Psychoanalysts for Peace and Justice, repeating one's story over and over is common in PTSD patients and in whistleblowers who expose government or corporate misdeeds. Soldz pointed me to the work of C. Fred Alford, who writes that whistleblowers keep retelling their story so they won't have to relinquish "the stock stories we all draw upon to make at least superficial sense of our lives." The problem for whistleblowers—I'd say for antiwar veterans too—is that these "stock stories" are inadequate to the task.

Many whistleblowers, Alford observes, get stuck in "a frozen narrative,"

a recounting of events that hews to chronology and doesn't allow for character development—that is, insight—instead, repeating itself over and over,
so that it never ends. Whistleblowers have "seen what one is not supposed
to know," he writes. In exposing a wrong, they have risked and lost much—a
job, status, security, friends. To come to a resolution, they would also lose
their faith in the adages we buy into as the currency of the social order:
life is fair, the system isn't stacked against us, the individual matters, and
the truth shall set us free. Like disillusioned veterans, whistleblowers can
become committed to keeping their story going because, otherwise, there is
only emptiness. Yet, when Alford attended a whistleblower support group,
he found that its appeal may have been precisely that the whistleblowers
could keep hearing the same old stories with their soothing mix of mean-
inglessness and paranoia.[4] So could it be that for antiwar veterans, who try
to blow the whistle on the myths of war, the saying *is* the doing? And is
some of what erupts as PTSD a hedge against the emptiness of life after war?

What we now call PTSD goes way back as a consequence of war. The
idea that a soldier may continue to be haunted by wartime life has had
a name since at least the Civil War, when it was called "soldier's heart," a
lovely name for a terrible affliction. In World War I, it went by the names
"shell shock" and "war neurosis" and was so widespread that Great Brit-
ain devoted nineteen hospitals solely to treating soldiers who suffered
from it.[5] During World War II, it was called "battle fatigue," "combat neurosis," or "gross stress reaction," and the problem was severe enough in
the U.S. Army that, at one point, psychiatric discharges outpaced conscription.[6] The Vietnam War gave us the term "post-Vietnam syndrome,"
or PVS, which in time evolved into "post-traumatic stress disorder," or
PTSD.

PTSD's status as an anxiety disorder was established in 1980, when it
was included in the third edition of the *Diagnostic and Statistical Manual
of Mental Disorders* (*DSM*), the bible of psychiatry. Diagnostic criteria
include flashbacks or intrusive memories, avoidance of anything associated with the trauma, emotional numbness, and heightened tension, such
as being quick to startle or anger. The sufferer must have been involved
in or witnessed a traumatic event—what is called the "stressor criterion,"
or sometimes the "gatekeeper"—making it the only mental health condition defined as being caused by a single, external event. Symptoms must
last longer than a month and interfere significantly with social, occupa-
tional, or other core areas of functioning.[7]

It is now widely accepted that PTSD changes the structure and chemistry of the brain, at least temporarily, affecting the parts that channel emotion, manage fear, and maintain memory and make it coherent. Recent research has found that some brains may be genetically more susceptible to PTSD than others, which could help predict the level of risk to an individual. Although the research didn't raise that issue, genetic testing might also weed out particularly vulnerable soldiers.[8]

Since PTSD was first codified, the diagnostic criteria have grown more expansive. That troubles many therapists treating the ailment, but the problem is probably more basic. As Katherine Boone, writing about the paradoxical nature of the diagnosis, put it, "If you react normally to trauma, you have a disorder; if you react abnormally, you don't."[9] A major shortcoming of this approach is the stigma in military culture of admitting weakness, which is how the bulk of servicepeople see PTSD. In addition, there appear to be racial, gender, and ethnocultural differences in how the disorder manifests itself and how patients respond to treatment.[10] It is also possible that indicators of war trauma change from era to era, so that, in assuming that PTSD in today's veterans will look like PTSD in Vietnam veterans, for instance, we may misdiagnose it. All this adds up to a muddle. As Roy Clymer, a psychotherapist consulting with the Defense Department, charges, when PTSD was included in the *DSM*, "life-altering changes in psychological functioning that resulted from the grotesqueries of combat were simultaneously normalized and pathologized."[11]

When the military started monitoring Iraq and Afghanistan veterans for PTSD, estimates of the extent of the problem were all over the place. In 2008, a RAND Corporation study estimated that three hundred thousand postdeployment service members had mental problems.[12] That served as the benchmark figure for a while, but it soon became apparent that the numbers were much larger. Because the onset of PTSD may be delayed and because its diagnosis and treatment are diffused, it is probably impossible to come up with an exact count of sufferers. The RAND study also found that only about a third of veterans with PTSD received even "minimally adequate care." The Pentagon's own figures showed that less than 1 percent of those deployed in 2007 had been referred to a mental health specialist as part of their predeployment screening, although a significant portion of soldiers sent to Afghanistan then had mental health issues serious enough to warrant medication.[13]

Most PTSD is short term, but perhaps one-third of cases become chronic, and it is here that the diagnosis is most contentious, in part because the military uses it to determine eligibility for government-funded health care, and in part because that care costs a lot. By 2012, the VA was estimating that 11 to 20 percent of the 2.3 million troops who had cycled through Iraq and Afghanistan suffered from PTSD. The Congressional Budget Office calculated a cost of $8,300 per patient for the first year of treatment, which means that care for PTSD sufferers could amount to as much as $3.8 billion a year for some time to come.

The Veterans Administration says it takes a "rule-out approach" to diagnosing PTSD; that is, whenever a veteran who has seen combat comes to the VA, even for something as routine as a flu shot, his or her file is flagged for possible PTSD and follow-up. That follow-up begins with a few simple questions—Do you have trouble sleeping? Are you angry a lot?—the sort of thing soldiers are asked when they demobilize and tend to gloss over so as not to delay their getting home. The assumption that PTSD is present until proved otherwise apparently has been in place for some time at the VA, and veterans frequently cite individual caregivers at various VA facilities as dedicated and skilled. Nonetheless, the VA is routinely cast as the villain in the piece, portrayed as insensitive, poorly equipped to meet the mounting need for mental health services, and worse, as a barrier to adequate care.[14]

Many problems begin on base, where the goal of medical practitioners is to get soldiers ready to deploy. Ailing soldiers and their advocates charge that doctors overmedicate them, officers sabotage medical appointments and stigmatize those who seek help, and commanders override doctors' advice and clear soldiers for deployment when they are unwell. An anonymous survey the army conducted in 2007 found that about 12 percent of combat troops in Iraq and 17 percent of those in Afghanistan were taking prescription antidepressants or sleeping pills (this apparently didn't include off-label use of psychotropic medicines).[15] Data obtained from the Defense Department's health-care program showed that prescriptions given to troops for psychoactive drugs ballooned by 682 percent between 2005 and 2011.[16] It's enough to give the term "War on Drugs" a whole new meaning. Little wonder then that horror stories abound: A roommate taken off suicide watch just before family day, then sent to Iraq, where he blew his brains out a few weeks later. Pressure to apply for a diagnosis of depression, rather than PTSD, to keep statistics down. A rape victim cowed into silence despite a written confession from her rapist.[17]

In 2007, *The Nation* documented that the army had discharged thousands of soldiers because of a personality disorder, rather than PTSD.[18] The distinction is significant because a personality disorder is considered a preexisting condition and precludes eligibility for subsidized health care and disability benefits. The army responded to the ensuing outcry by significantly decreasing personality disorder discharges, while increasing adjustment disorder discharges, which often also rule out eligibility for benefits.[19] The advocacy groups Veterans for Common Sense and Veterans United for Truth filed a class action lawsuit alleging that the Veterans Administration had systematically denied veterans the treatment and benefits they were entitled to. A federal court in California, which heard the case in 2008, eventually determined that the VA's "unchecked incompetence" violated soldiers' constitutional rights and ordered a complete overhaul of its mental health care system. The case stretched on through negotiations and appeals for years, until the court eventually bounced the decision back to Congress.

Meanwhile, the Dignified Treatment of Wounded Warriors Act of 2008 gave veterans who had been medically discharged with disability ratings of 20 percent or less the right to challenge the determination and receive benefits they were entitled to. While the VA continued to deny that it had misdiagnosed the cases, it did ease its rules on PTSD disability claims, including some that discriminated against noncombat troops and, therefore, against women, who couldn't officially serve in combat until 2013. However, the final determination of disability remained within the VA, rather than with private doctors, leaving the process vulnerable to the manipulation that had prompted the lawsuit.

Since the early days of diagnosis, when you either had PTSD or you were fine, the medical response to it has gained in nuance and depth, which has brought beneficial funding for research and treatment. In the public mind, though, PTSD still scoops up everything from risky behavior and aggression to substance abuse and suicide—kind of like Alzheimer's as a catch-all label for forgetfulness over fifty—and that does a disservice to veterans who aren't sick, but aren't fine either.

Not surprisingly, what we think is important about injuries to the minds and hearts of soldiers depends on what we think is important in general.

Researchers, military officials, veterans, politicians, mental health workers, philosophers, and political activists all approach the definition and
treatment of PTSD differently. Everyone wants to ease the pain—that
comes first—but some of the more probing thinkers and therapists have
misgivings about overmedicalizing a natural reaction to fighting shad-
owy, relentless wars, and some of the more political argue that patholo-
gizing that reaction is a way to keep dissidents in line. (In diagnosing any
"disorder," political and cultural norms are invoked to reinforce what is
orderly.) It also allows everyone to ignore that the best way to prevent
PTSD and other war-related distress is not to send people into that kind
of war in the first place.

Mike Zacchea, forty-three, was a major in the marines and a self-described "gung-ho," career officer when he deployed to Iraq in March 2004
as the first American adviser to the Iraqi army. Zacchea didn't believe in
preemptive attacks, and he understood that Iraq had nothing to do with
the 9/11 events, but he wasn't against the war and entered it with his eyes
wide open. "I knew with absolute certainty what the rules of engagement
were," he tells me, then launches into a series of morally ambiguous stories about what he felt was required of him there. This included sledge-
hammering the wrists and elbows of captured Iraqis to prevent them
from returning to the battlefield on their release. "I'm haunted by things
I did in war. I didn't do anything wrong," he insists, "but I'm haunted."

Zacchea was wounded by a rocket-propelled grenade in the second
battle of Fallujah, but declined to be evacuated. He was later diagnosed
with a traumatic brain injury, though not PTSD, and was medically retired in 2010. He doesn't remember most of his first year home, but he
does recall in detail the night he tried to set fire to the bathroom where
his wife had sought refuge from his violence. Since then, he has learned
that a brain switched into a fight response is hard to switch off, that the
chemicals released during combat can create a thrilling high.[20] "I look at
everything now as veterans going through their own odyssey," he says
with some bitterness. "There is no happy homecoming."

Like many veterans, Zacchea needed to retrieve some value or use
for all the suffering he saw in Iraq and felt on his return. Soon after he
got home, he read an interview with Paul Rieckhoff, which inspired him
to join Iraq and Afghanistan Veterans of America (then called Operation Truth). "I was going to explode," he reports. "I finally had an outlet."
When we talk, he is less active with IAVA, focusing instead on earning

an MBA and directing the Entrepreneur Bootcamp for Veterans with Disabilities at the University of Connecticut. "My goal is to help people whose lives have been shattered by this war," he says, "To make it make sense."

Barbara Van Dahlen, a psychologist and founder of Give an Hour, a national network connecting mental health workers to veterans, is convinced that part of the healing process for veterans is doing something meaningful when they return from war. "Veterans report, to a person, how incredibly important it is to have something productive to do," she says. The gains to individuals from working toward the betterment of society have long been recognized. In the late 1920s, the psychotherapist Alfred Adler emphasized that "social interest," or concern for the welfare of others, was basic to psychological health, and psychologist Erik Erikson coined the term "generativity" in 1950 to describe the desire to do something to benefit future generations. More recently, Alice Perry, a pastoral counselor, and John Rolland, a professor of psychiatry, concluded from their individual practices that social-justice activism—what they describe as "reaching out . . . to repair the hurts and harm of social injustices and to make things better for others"—has distinct therapeutic benefits. "Thoroughly woven into activism is hope that what is amiss can and will be set right," they write.[21] Using a much broader definition of political activism, a 2010 study found a correlation, though not necessarily cause and effect, between engaging in political activism and "higher levels of well-being."[22]

The connection between working with a supportive group toward a socially constructive goal and mental well-being is hardly straightforward, however. During a particularly tempestuous period for IVAW, Selena Coppa, then an active-duty army sergeant and member of the board, pointed out that while the emotional needs of members bound them to IVAW, those needs also undermined the group's effectiveness. In an open letter to the membership, she wrote: "Thus you have a population which is desperately needing a safe space from conflict, as well as a population which is generally incapable of providing that safe space. . . . This is why IVAW has historically been both the thing that pulls people out of mental health breakdowns and the thing that puts them into it."

Among those who question the conventional wisdom on psychological distress in veterans, there seems to be more agreement about what PTSD is not than about what it is. The several therapists I talked with recognized that returning from war is as indelible as going off to war, but they were adamant that labeling the problems that arise a "disease" is not a constructive approach. What we value and fear in warriors shifts when they become veterans, Jonathan Shay writes in *Odysseus in America*, his exploration of the homecoming of war veterans and their discontents. The fears include what he recognizes as an ancient version of PTSD, which apparently hasn't changed much over the millennia. One thing that has changed is the speed of travel. Odysseus fought for ten years and journeyed for another ten before coming home to Ithaca; American soldiers flew home to the States from Baghdad or Kabul in twelve to fourteen hours. Yet Shay found from his long experience as a psychiatrist at the VA Outpatient Clinic in Boston that today's soldiers have similar difficulties in making the transition.

Three weeks after he got home, Andy Sapp was back at his high school, teaching *The Things They Carried*. His colleagues, civilians all, had put Tim O'Brien's unsparing book about American grunts in Vietnam on the syllabus, excited that Andy would bring his fresh war experience to teaching it, which he did—at a cost to his sanity.

"Yes, war itself will do this to people. It's an uncomfortable truth," Shay says of PTSD when we speak by phone in 2008. He thinks soldiers can be partially protected when the right unit structure and support are in place, but observes, "The more the war goes on and people are overstretched, the more this stuff frays." Shay speaks slowly, carefully, fluently; he's been over this terrain before. He applied what he learned as a therapist to a focused reading of the *Iliad* and *Odyssey*, Homer's epics about the Trojan War and the aftermath, to write two books, which have won him wide acclaim and a coveted MacArthur "genius" award. Shay is adamant that PTSD is not a disorder, but a psychological injury, one that destroys social trust. "The veteran has lost *authority* over his own process of memory," he writes. Recovery includes restoring that authority.[23]

I've called to ask him my question about the interaction of PTSD and political activism, and he responds with a measured approach, suggesting that it depends on the kind of activism and the point where it comes in a veteran's healing. He thinks the recovery process eventually involves reconnecting selectively with others, which may include community work and the company of fellow veterans, who offer the pleasure of shared jargon, jokes, and special knowledge. Yet he's not totally convinced. "Political activity is like art," he tells me. "It's not ethically good or bad, but a fact of human nature. Usually when people are saying, this will be good for you, it's something they approve of."

He sees two extremes on the veteran-activist spectrum. At one end, a person who returns from war drowning in rage and a sense of betrayal gloms onto a group or cult promising violent revenge, which is a way of staying in combat. The kind of examples he cites—Weimar Germany, Trotskyite gangs, the Irish Republican Army—are not in the United States. "Yet," he adds. But he thinks most veterans draw a bright line between military-sanctioned killing and murder, so this way of reenacting communalized trauma doesn't strike him as particularly therapeutic. At the other end are patients who report that, in the final stages of their recovery, they get involved in a political activity because they want to stop the government or society from doing what has led to the bad things they've experienced. This, he thinks is constructive and he often encourages it.

When Shay and I meet face-to-face a couple of years later in New York, serving on the Truth Commission on Conscience and War, and I remind him of our conversation, he replies that he hopes he said something like, the Vietnam vets I've worked with who do antiwar work are among the most adjusted. He shrugs and adds, "But maybe it helps to be a little crazy. Maybe that's what keeps activists going in the face of more frustration than success."

Barbara Van Dahlen agrees with Shay that PTSD is not a disease. To her, it's a continuum on which the brain is trying desperately to make sense of an overpowering experience. "From a psychological perspective, activism is a continuum too. Activism can be very positive if [veterans] feel things that were done need to be looked at and changed," she says when I catch up with her somewhere on her frequent travels for Give an Hour. She too cautions that much depends on what role the activism plays. It can provide the structure veterans miss ("They come from probably the most structured place in our society, then we cut them loose.") and offer an outlet for their anger. For those who can't set boundaries, however, it can mire them in what she calls "overresponsibility."

I phone Roy Clymer, who is now working with veterans in Austin, Texas, after reading his contrarian view on treating PTSD patients in *Psychotherapy Networker*.[24] There he argues that the very diagnosis of PTSD—a line drawn between healthy and sick—hampers veterans' ability to come to terms with their experiences. By labeling it post-traumatic stress disorder, he writes, a condition is turned into a disease, leading sufferers to see themselves as passively damaged victims in need of help. "Of the elements which lead to people expressing [PTSD] symptoms, the most common is a strong sense of betrayal," he tells me. "When you combine that with the inevitable sense of entitlement that a veteran returns from combat with, which he can't acknowledge to himself directly . . ." He breaks off, leery of saying anything that could be construed as discrediting veterans, then begins again. "When you put all that together, it's easy to see how these people who started as committed patriots come back with a very different view of things. Frequently that view gets expressed as protest and resistance. I think that's the other side of the coin in which a veteran can then spend the rest of his life fighting against a system that did him wrong." He concludes, "I think there's a great risk to living out that umbrage the rest of their lives."

Clymer is a Vietnam veteran who took part in rallies against that war, so in his nonprofessional capacity, he has some sympathy for political protest and sees value in the testimony about the realities of war emerging from groups like IVAW. "Personally, I think it's important to tell stories," he says, "but I think it's important not to sit around with buddies and b.s." That echoes something Mike Zacchea said: It was important to remember, but it was hard for him to remember without getting angry, and it was hard to let his anger go. "If I stop being angry," he asked, "what else is there?"

Is political activism no more than displaced anger? I ask Clymer, who reminds me that, as a therapist, his goal is to help his patients heal, and that process is undermined when we assume a linear cause-and-effect or some unifying principle of vulnerability underlying PTSD. "How do you come to terms with this?" he asks me, his patients, himself. "How do you make sense out of a world that has such horror and outrage and mayhem and viciousness that you've seen and nobody else has? Seeing yourself as damaged is a very high price to pay as a way to understand something that's otherwise very difficult to understand."

All these tensions suffuse veteran Michael Uhl's assessment of his years of antiwar work and late onset PTSD. Uhl served in Vietnam as a first lieutenant of military intelligence, cofounded Citizen Soldier with Tod Ensign, and helped organize the first Winter Soldier investigation in 1971. Decades later, he wrote in an e-mail:

I have argued over the years, but not systematically, that activism—anger directed at the source of my discomfort, i.e., the military—was a balm to my ptsd. . . . Certainly, my involvement in the war crimes work contributed to the fact that I never had nightmares . . . on the premise that we made our involvement with atrocities public and didn't repress those memories. That sounds right . . . but it's also a story I've been telling myself for decades now. The truth is, where I'm concerned, that activism—from which I have only recently backed away after forty years—exposes the ptsd vet to a continuous stream of conflict. And so, activism may be healthy in some ways and not in others.

Jerry Lembcke, a sociologist and veteran of the Vietnam War and its antiwar movement, has examined the ways political dissent was associated with mental disorders to discredit radical veterans. In *The Spitting Image*, he argues that these activists were cast first as bad boys—deviant, antisocial, rebellious, adolescent—then as madmen, unknowable and pushed beyond reason by grief and survivors' guilt. While both images were threatening, the latter seemed like progress because it could elicit civilian sympathy, but in Lembcke's reading, conflating badness and sickness for political and cultural reasons was a trap, ensnaring thousands of veterans in a PTSD diagnosis.[25] According to Lembcke, we're doing it again. "The military is using diagnostic categories to manage the tensions created by the wars in Iraq and Afghanistan," he has written more recently. "It's a nasty strategy with the potential to stigmatize the soldiers and veterans opposed to war and isolate them from friends, family, and the antiwar movement with which they have a natural affinity."[26]

The occupations of Iraq and Afghanistan are not the same as the war in Vietnam, though they share many characteristics. Nor is the military today the mix of recruits and draftees that fueled its dysfunction during the Vietnam War. As professionals, contemporary soldiers are supposed to be ready to fight, but as counterinsurgents, they're supposed to be tenderhearted—at least to kids, their buddies, and the village elders they're fated to drink endless cups of tea with. (Every veteran has a kid story, and mourning lost friends with tattoos, rituals, and drunken sorrow is one of the few ways they're allowed to grieve publicly.) They're supposed to be anguished when they hear about the "bad apples" who tortured Iraqi prisoners at Abu Ghraib; or who gang-raped, then murdered and set fire to a fifteen-year-old Iraqi girl; or who photographed themselves pissing on dead Afghans. Maybe it's the confusion of these mixed signals that makes us treat soldiers as if they're tainted by some special, unwanted knowledge, something that *should* drive them over the edge with grief and guilt and remorse. Maybe we think our soldiers are supposed to suffer—to be not just bad or mad, but searingly sad.

All this mad-bad-sadness has contributed to an unprecedented incidence of suicides among active-duty personnel and veterans. In 2012, the number of active-duty servicepeople who killed themselves peaked at 349, more than the number killed in combat that year. The rate for army suicides was about one every thirty-six hours in 2008, a statistic that, little changed over succeeding years, gets cited endlessly for its shock value.[27] One response to this alarming rise in suicide is the army's Comprehensive Soldier Fitness program, which is intended to build emotional, mental, and spiritual resilience in soldiers before they go to war. Unfurled in 2009, the program grew out of research linking optimism to greater emotional resilience; the hope was that such training would prevent PTSD and depression. Martin Seligman, a leading advocate of "positive psychology," who worked closely with the Pentagon to create the program, told the *New York Times*, "The idea here is to give people a new vocabulary, to speak in terms of resilience. Most people who experience trauma don't end up with P.T.S.D.; many experience posttraumatic growth."[28]

The program was controversial from the start and not just because it was slated to cost about $125 million over five years. Critics raised a number of ethical, political, and conceptual concerns, including that the training might lead soldiers to underestimate dangers or do something in an ambiguous situation they would later regret, thus increasing the risk of physical and emotional harm to themselves and others.[29] They also pointed out that such training doesn't solve the larger moral problems many soldiers grapple with or obviate the need for moral reconciliation. Nonetheless, by 2010, all soldiers were taking a resilience assessment survey, followed by online training in specific areas.

Post-traumatic growth—the idea that you can be revitalized by working through the kind of pain that makes you challenge your most cherished assumptions—is not a new concept. The term itself was coined in 1995 by two psychologists at the University of North Carolina, Charlotte, who studied six hundred survivors of traumatic events. Most post-trau-

matic growth research has been retrospective—that is, people reflecting
on how they felt from a distance in time—and similar programs involving various civilian populations were only modestly and inconsistently
effective. In addition, some therapists are skeptical that preventative
measures that aim to desensitize healthy people will later do much to
block PTSD or suicidal impulses.[30]

There is more than a whiff of Pollyannaism in this approach, with its
denial of the moral hazards of war, though it is hardly surprising that it
would appeal to the military, which isn't about to stop sending soldiers
into hazardous situations. But there is also honest recognition that, like
it or not, what may be the most intense period of your life is irrevo-
cably part of who you are. It may not blight your entire life, but it is
an experience with consequences that stay with you. Some people think
they should. So when a radical approach to preventing PTSD emerged
from a small pilot study involving the beta-blocking drug Propranolol,
it didn't take long for philosophers and medical ethicists to raise alarms
about this kind of pharmacological intervention. The study, taking place
at Harvard Medical School in 2002, suggested that Propranolol could
reduce symptoms that lead to chronic PTSD when administered within
hours of a traumatic event. By stopping the stress hormone adrenaline
from flooding the brain, the drug blunts its impact, or, in technical terms,
interferes with the consolidation of memory.[31] As a treatment for PTSD,
Propranolol costs vastly less than therapy and has a more immediate effect. Within a few years of the study, the army was funding research into
the drug's potential use.

"If you could be given a drug that would erase your PTSD, would you
take it?" I ask Andy Sapp.

"I don't know," he answers tentatively. "That would be really tempting."

Tempting and unnerving. Roy Clymer reports that many veterans
tell him they want to forget what happened—to which he replies, "Why
would you? It's a valuable experience, both to yourself and society at
large."

If Propranolol can block the onset of PTSD, it could be administered
prophylactically to soldiers before they are sent to battle to inoculate
them against the emotional shock of war. And if so, what would be the
costs, not only to soldiers, but to a society in which war has little lasting
adverse emotional effect on those fighting it? Healing and moving on
probably require some measure of forgetting, or at least not obsessing

over negative experiences, but, what is gained by robbing soldiers of a moral compass, save a salve to civilian conscience?

Paul Outka, a literature professor concerned about the ramifications of such memory-manipulating drugs, points to the relationship between individual and societal healing and notes the important role veterans play in that interaction. "War exists precisely at the intersection between individual and communal suffering," he writes. By bearing witness to the horror of war, veterans contribute to societal memory and remind us that war is not something to be entered into heedlessly. Summing up the dire warnings about the promise and peril of Propranolol, Outka concludes, "Ultimately, the difficulty of predicting the effect of an end to PTSD arises from the fact that such a cure represents a fundamental change in what it means to be human."[32]

Andy recalls a 1985 BBC series called *Soldiers*, where, as he remembers it, a marine commander says, "It's not that we can't take a man who's forty-five years old and turn him into a good soldier. It's that we can never make him love it." Like many soldiers, Andy had assumed that his role would be to protect his country when it was threatened, but instead, he says, "The way I look at it, I was part of something that was evil, something that did evil to other people, people who have done nothing to me and nothing to my country." He adds bitterly, "If I look at the price I paid for Iraq, I see absolutely no justification for it." So when his therapy stalled and his psychologist pointed out that his spiritual pain was exacerbating his psychological problems, it clicked.

Seeking the right words, he says, "I think you have to bear some level of guilt"—for what he was a part of in Iraq and what his absence did to his family. "Having faced that and acknowledged it, it's put me morally in a place I wouldn't have been otherwise. It's not that I'm a better person for it. It's sort of my penance." He calls the spiritual part his "sacred wound." Others call it "moral injury."

Moral injury, a concept in progress, is defined as the result of taking part in or witnessing something of consequence that you believe is wrong, something that violates your deeply held beliefs about yourself and your role in the world. For a moment at least, you become what you never wanted to be. While the symptoms and causes may overlap with PTSD, moral injury arises from what you did or failed to do, rather than from what was done to you. It's a sickness of the heart more than of the head. Or, possibly, moral injury is what comes first and, if left unattended, congeals into PTSD.

A couple of decades ago, Dave Grossman, a West Point psychology professor and former Army Ranger, wrote an eye-opening, bone-chilling book called *On Killing*. It begins with the premise that people have an innate resistance to killing other people and goes on to examine how the military tried to overcome that inhibition.[33] Grossman cites the now-controversial work of Brigadier General S.L.A. Marshall, who determined that the firing rate in World War II—the percentage of American riflemen who actually pulled the trigger—was 15 to 20 percent. And Grossman suggests many who did fire "exercised the soldier's right to miss."[34] Displeased, the U.S. military set out to redesign combat training so that firing a weapon became a reflexive action. The military (and most police forces) switched from using bull's-eye targets to using realistic, human-shaped silhouettes, which pop up and fall down when hit, as trainees chant bloodthirsty cadences. Grossman calls this kind of Skinnerian conditioning "modern battleproofing." Later, the army added video simulators for the recent generation of soldiers raised on virtual reality. Combined with increased efficiency in weaponry, this training upped the firing rate steadily—to 55 percent in Korea, about 90 percent in Vietnam, and close to 100 percent in Iraq and Afghanistan.[35] Despite challenges to his methodology, Marshall's numbers have been repeated so often that they've become accepted fact, but does it really matter if the firing rate is 90 percent or 99 percent? The point is that soldiers are trained to shoot first and evaluate later. "Killing comes with a price," Grossman writes, "and societies must learn that their soldiers will have to spend the rest of their lives living with what they have done."[36]

Grossman didn't use the term "moral injury." It was probably coined by Jonathan Shay, and it wasn't until the end of 2009 that it began to register in therapeutic communities. That was when Brett Litz, the associate director of the National Center for PTSD at the Boston VA, and several colleagues involved in a pilot study for the marines published "Moral Injury and Moral Repair in War Veterans," a paper aimed at other clinicians.[37] The authors found that it was less fear of personal harm than the dissonance between what soldiers had done or seen and their previously held ideas of morality that caused widespread emotional distress. This echoes Marshall, who believed that "battle failure" came more from fear of killing than of being killed, and Grossman, who concluded that danger is not the greatest cause of psychological injury in soldiers; it is face-to-face aggression and the realization that there are people out there who really want to kill you.

In highlighting moral injury in veterans, the authors' stated purpose was not to create a new diagnostic category, nor to pathologize moral discomfort, but to encourage discussion and research into the lingering effects on soldiers of their moral transgressions in war. Moral injury seems to be widespread, but the concept is something of an orphan. If it's an injury, then it needs treatment, which puts it in the domain of medicine, but its overtones of sin and redemption place it in the spiritual realm. IVAW's Joshua Casteel reported that "when soldiers raise moral issues, shrinks usually send them to chaplains." Chaplains, however, are no more trained to deal with such problems than clinicians, as their essential job is to patch up soldiers, albeit spiritually, to fight another day.

Yet the idea has traction. The military began to consider moral injury as a war wound and possible forerunner of PTSD when Litz presented his research at the navy's Combat Operational Stress Control conference in 2010. The following year, a small, preliminary survey of chaplains, mental health clinicians, and researchers found unanimous support for adding the concept of moral injury as a consequence of war. And in 2012, the Soul Repair Center was established at Brite Divinity School in Fort Worth to conduct research and education about moral injury in combat veterans.

Patriotism and moral imperatives play a role in most soldiers' motivation, and service to one's country and its ideals are mainstays of recruitment pitches and unit cohesion, but the realities of the wars-turned-occupations in Iraq and Afghanistan quickly upended those assumptions. When your job requires you to pull sleeping families from their beds at midnight thousands of miles from your home, or to shoot at oncoming cars without knowing who's driving, or to refuse medical care to decrepit old men, you begin to question what doing your job means. When the reasons keep shifting for what you're doing in someone else's country with a bad attitude and a gun, both aimed at people who want you to go home even more than you do, it's hard to maintain any sense of rectitude. When someone going about his daily life is regularly conflated with someone who means to kill you, everyone becomes the enemy. And when you're trying to make sense of a precarious situation, which nothing could have trained you for, the enemy can move inside and stay there for a very long time. For a combat veteran, writes veteran Stan Goff, "the sense that the world is not a safe place is not a 'disorder.' It is an accurate perception."[38]

Under pressure, decent people do bad things—that's not news—but moral injury shares with PTSD an inability to forgive oneself and a concomitant fear of being judged and shunned by others. This may account, in part, for the defensive, civilians-just-don't-get-it stance of many veterans: some fear their hero status will be revoked, others reject that status as undeserved. Guilt can be constructive when it prevents you from repeating incorrect behavior or spurs you on to ameliorative action; IVAW members attest regularly to being motivated by it. And if we subtract the discomfort of guilt from warriors and war, we're in danger of creating a sizable group of sociopaths and a society I don't want to live in.

Shame, on the other hand, can turn self-destructive and violent—the vet-going-postal stories that make headlines—or it can be internalized in self-harming or risky behaviors. Elizabeth Spradlin, an IVAW member who worked as a nurse at a hospital in Colorado Springs after serving in Iraq, said, "I see a lot of the Fort Carson soldiers because we have the biggest trauma unit in this area. So when the violence happens to soldiers—when they try to take their lives, or motorcycle accidents when they're completely inebriated and just back from Iraq—I see that pretty much every day. Our ICU has twenty-six beds. There's always a soldier in one of them."

Guilt, resilience, hope—words that keep popping up in these discussions about the hearts and minds of soldiers and veterans—imply some sense that the world is a place where justice eventually prevails, but moral injury challenges that belief. Faith in a rightly ordered world is probably hard for anyone who has been through war; it is particularly elusive for soldiers mired in a war they think was unjust and unjustified, a war they have come, actively or passively, to oppose and resent.

In response to an article I wrote about moral injury, I received a long e-mail from David Cortright, the Vietnam veteran and lifelong peace activist who helped create the Appeal for Redress. After writing about his time in the army, he finished:

I had been placed in a situation that went against every moral fiber of my being, a fate I could not accept. The decision to speak out, once I had finally made the commitment to do what was necessary

regardless of the consequence, turned out to be enormously liberating. . . . I felt almost reborn—'radicalized' is what we called it in
those days—but it was much more than a political conversion. It
was a deeply rooted spiritual awakening.

I don't mean to imply any moral purity in describing what I
did. I only mean to say that it was that fundamental underlying
sense of right and wrong—probably drummed into my brain by
nuns during my Catholic education—that somehow broke through
the excruciating dilemma of the time and helped me to make what
proved to be a life-saving and life-affirming decision to resist.

In trying to heal from a moral injury, people struggle to restore their
sense of themselves as moral beings, but the stumbling block for many
veterans of recent wars is that their judgment about the immorality of
their actions may well be correct. When you've done irreparable harm,
feeling bad about your actions—haunted, sorrowful, distraught, dimin-
ished, unhinged—is human. Moral repair is linked to moral restitution,
and taking responsibility for your actions is a step toward maturity. In an
effort to waste neither their past, nor their future, many veterans work to
help heal their fellow veterans or the civilians in the countries they once
occupied. Others work for peace so the next generations of soldiers won't
have to know the heartache of moral injury.

Maybe that's the way the army makes a man of you after all.

∾ *Phone call from Washington, DC, January 2008* ∾

It's early January, about two months into IVAW's planning for Winter
Soldier, and I've volunteered to help out on the media team. So far, the
planners have a title they're defensive about, no set venue, not enough
money, and a testifier who ditched a journalist who schlepped up from
Washington to Vermont for an early, important interview. The reporter
(sympathetic, fortunately) tracked the vet down at a ski lodge, where he
was doing bong hits, and gamely began the interview, only to be treated
to an increasingly stoned diatribe about how all journalists are agents of
the CIA.

This is before press work begins in earnest under the steady guidance
of Emilie Surrusco, IVAW's civilian media consultant—and, all too
obviously, before testifiers are vetted for stability of their psyche, as well
as accuracy of their testimony.

"It couldn't get worse than that, could it?" Surrusco asks me,
hopefully.

11

WINTER SOLDIERS' STORIES

"We come home and everyone shakes our hand and calls us heroes, but no one wants to listen to us," Kelly Dougherty complained on behalf of her fellow veterans. So when Aaron Hughes and Fernando Braga proposed convening something like a truth commission to tell Americans what was really going on in Iraq and Afghanistan, the idea caught fire. It would build on the activities IVAW had undertaken in its four years of existence, and they would call it Winter Soldier: Iraq and Afghanistan.

The title echoed a similar event staged by Vietnam Veterans Against the War in 1971, which had drawn on Thomas Paine's laudation of soldiers who served their country, not just in the relative ease of summer, but also in its darkest hour. "These are the times that try men's souls," Paine wrote in the winter of 1776, in his well-known call to arms. "The summer soldier and the sunshine patriot will, in this crisis, shrink from the service of their country; but he that stands by it now, deserves the love and thanks of man and woman." Two centuries later, IVAW decided to issue a call to disarm, and they deemed that the new patriotism.

The first Winter Soldier investigation had taken place before Hughes or Braga, then in their early twenties, were born, so they knew about it only by reputation and archival film footage. It stood out in the annals of GI resistance as the first time in American history active-duty soldiers had so publicly questioned the morality of military policies while a war was going on. It was also the moment that the Vietnam veterans resistance movement became visible to the public. The newer veterans had reason to believe the second Winter Soldier event would be a turning point for them too. Polls showed the American public opposed the war in Iraq by about two-to-one, but civilians' grasp of the problems there was limited largely to "strategic mistakes" and the headline-grabbing barbarity of "a few bad apples." Winter Soldier could provide evidence of something different and, to the nation's shame, something more typical: wrongdoing that was systemic, pervasive, and the result of official policies.

The veterans knew their wars would end someday. All wars do. But the United States, with its bloated defense budget and conviction that all international problems are military problems, appeared to be settling into a state of perpetual war.[1] Now it seemed crucial to the antiwar veterans that the public know what they had done in Iraq and Afghanistan and imperative that their country heed the consequences. Through their testimony, they would stake a claim on the historical record and, in a reverse of what would later be the slogan of the Occupy Movement, call on the 1 percent—the American military—to challenge the 99 percent—American civilians—to help end the occupations. Most important, IVAW members could speak with the authority of having been there. "We've heard from the politicians, we've heard from the generals, we've heard from the media," Dougherty would soon announce. "Now it's our turn."

Hughes and Braga had each mulled over this kind of event separately, and in the spring of 2007, they met with veterans and filmmakers who had been involved in the first Winter Soldier inquiry. According to Hughes, the older veterans basically told the younger ones that they were crazy, but he and Braga weren't easily discouraged. Liam Madden joined the conversation a little later, and the trio hatched a plan to conduct interviews at IVAW's national convention in August and hold the event a few months later. The interviews didn't happen, but they identified some potential testifiers and enlisted other members for an organizing team. In November, the staff persuaded the team to reschedule the event for March to coincide with the fifth anniversary of the invasion of Iraq. Planning began in earnest and proceeded for the next five months in a mix of dead seriousness, caution edging into paranoia, and let's-put-on-a-show-in-the-barn enthusiasm. Winter Soldier was IVAW's most elaborate undertaking, and as a project both inspired and seat-of-the-pants, it was anyone's guess if they would pull it off. They did, with integrity and panache, but, as with all things IVAW, preparations soared to operatic levels of drama, brinkmanship, and near-disaster.

Leadership of the project was fluid. An early flow chart shows Hughes and Braga as coordinators, but Braga, then a student at CUNY, was pressed for time and soon cut back on his involvement. Perry O'Brien, a conscientious objector who had been a medic in Afghanistan and was now studying government at Cornell University, stepped in. In December, the organizing team met in Philadelphia and determined that the main focus of Winter Soldier would be building IVAW's membership and efficacy. Defining specific aims for the event proved more daunting. History was part of the problem, as the first Winter Soldier investigation—or at least the younger veterans' perception of it—loomed large. IVAW members worried that they would be perceived as a bunch of latter-day hippies who would be resented by the latter-day troops and discredited by their decidedly unhip opponents. At some point, someone prepared a list of "hard questions," which eventually led to a list of talking points, and as the new Winter Soldier event began to take shape, the anxiety of influence eased somewhat.

It helped that IVAW could learn from VVAW's mistakes. VVAW had staged its Winter Soldier in Detroit, largely at the insistence of Jane Fonda, the event's primary funder, who believed this would put the veterans close to "working-class America."[2] Unfortunately, the choice of Detroit gave the mainstream media (which, in 1971, pretty much *was* the media) an excuse to ignore the hearings. Since much of IVAW was already working-class America, the new Winter Soldier planners looked instead for a venue close to a center of power and media interest. They settled on Washington, DC.

Like the planners of the earlier event, IVAW recognized that the heart of their undertaking would be gathering evidence of transgressions against official policy, international law, humanitarian principles, and human decency. This became the responsibility of the fourteen-person testimonial team, led by O'Brien. A call for testifiers went out to members, and about 120 people came forward. Each potential testifier was interviewed, usually in person, for an hour or two. Questions covered war crimes, including torture, rape, and mutilation of dead bodies; misdeeds, such as disregard for rules of engagement or reckless endangerment of civilians; and routine misbehavior, for example, use of illegal drugs or racist epithets. The interviews were designed to elicit specific details, including dates, locations, and military units involved, and interviewers collected corroborating material, such as photographs and videotapes, which, given the ubiquity of recording devices, were plentiful. Whenever possible, interviews were recorded and transcribed and, if the testifier agreed, archived with IVAW.

The testimonial team took care to protect the rights and sensibilities of the testifiers, especially those who were still on active duty and vulnerable to retaliation. "This is not a trial," interviewers were instructed. "Individual soldiers should not be made scapegoats for policies designed at the highest levels of government." Legal and mental health services were made available, and everyone was given the option of confidentiality, but a consent form was mandatory. The entire enterprise rested on the integrity of the testimony, so to ensure that all the assertions were accurate and would stand up to scrutiny, a subgroup created a strict verification system. This was led by army veteran Jose Vasquez, then a graduate student in cultural anthropology at CUNY, which no doubt helped him in the authentication process. Verification began with the requirement that every testifier submit proof of military service: a DD 214 (record of separation) or a military ID. This was an obvious first step, but this time, spotting impostors wasn't hard. Vasquez illustrated this with a story about someone who wanted to testify to atrocities his unit had committed in Iraq, but who disqualified himself the minute he opened his mouth. It had nothing to do with what he said; it was the condition of his teeth. Apparently, anyone who has ever been in the U.S. military knows that they fix your teeth before they send you to war. It turned out the guy hadn't even finished basic training.

As testimony came in, Vasquez's team, composed of veterans and journalists, cross-referenced each incident with service records, military orders, media reports, and other documents, and contacted other soldiers or marines who had been at the site. They followed up with more questions and legal and mental health reviews, then helped shape and edit the stories for coherence and brevity. Testifiers weren't under oath (it's unclear what oath that would be), but the team apparently did its job well, as no credible challenges to the evidence emerged.

"Ladies and gentlemen, I hate guns. I think they should be melted down into jewelry," announces Jason Hurd, a bearded, self-described Tennessee mountain man. He spent ten years in the army and the National Guard, enlisting over the objection of his father, a World

War II marine. According to Hurd, his father was "one of the most warmongering, gun-loving people you could ever meet." Yet he knew the psychological toll war takes on warriors, and he wanted to spare his son.

Hurd became a medic; the incident he recounts took place while he was patrolling a Baghdad neighborhood. The area was relatively calm, but car bombs were an ever-present danger, so when a car kept approaching, despite his increasingly frantic signals to stop, he prepared to shoot. His finger was on the trigger—he extends one arm and cocks the other, as if sighting down a weapon—"And the car kept comin'," he repeats.

Suddenly, a man appeared, as if by magic, from a side street. He waved the car down, getting it to stop, and out popped the driver: a very old woman who, Hurd learned, was a highly respected member of the community. "I am a peaceful person," he says, "but I drew down on an eighty-year-old, geriatric woman who could not see me."

In *Home to War*, Gerald Nicosia writes that Jane Fonda dissolved into sobs at a private screening of a film about the first Winter Soldier investigation because only then, long after the event, did she understand that its purpose was to offer Vietnam veterans the catharsis of telling their stories together.[3] The Iraq veterans were similarly determined to speak primarily to their brothers and sisters in the military, but, as with Fonda and her cohort, it took some of IVAW's civilian allies a while to understand this. They argued that IVAW should use this opportunity to address politicians and other policymakers. The veterans demurred. They knew that they had special credibility with active-duty personnel and figured their testimony would raise IVAW's profile and amplify veterans' voices. That way, they could galvanize resistance within the ranks, make GI resistance feel inevitable, and ramp up pressure from within the military to end the war. Besides, they asked, whose event is this, anyway? Some other antiwar groups were already trying to horn in by calling for activities the same weekend, though the Winter Soldier planners had asked them not to. Let them make speeches and spin theories; IVAW had something else in mind.

It wasn't that simple, of course. Winter Soldier was to be a big event, and the planners wanted the public and the press to take notice, even as they fretted over what that would mean. Some organizers were concerned that making individual testifiers available for media interviews beforehand would leave them exposed, and they threatened to jettison the entire media strategy. The media team was equally concerned that no one be exploited, but its leader, Emilie Surrusco, pointed out that reporters were unlikely to do a story without access to the people at the center of it. The issue came to a head in mid-January, when Surrusco sent a memo to the organizers, urging them to resolve that and other basic issues. "If we ask the media to cover the event and then do not provide the stories they need, they will find their own, and we will have lost control of the message," she reminded them. The memo was collegial, but firm, and it pushed the organizers to clarify their aims. That process continued at a meeting in early February, when Doyle Canning of SmartMeme, a social-change strategy group, was brought in to work on "messaging." SmartMeme believed that, framed correctly, stories could be game changers, so Canning and Surrusco encouraged the organizers to think in terms of a compelling narrative with protagonists, conflicts, obstacles, actions, and consequences. The meeting was long and excruciatingly slow as the veterans debated intangible "values" and the connotation of descriptive taglines for the title. Everyone had an opinion and everyone defended it fiercely—proof that arguments over words are often stand-ins for tensions people don't want to talk about. Messaging was always central to what IVAW did, and Winter Soldier did need a clear and unified vision, but at this point, it felt as if they were all getting PhDs in meetings.

In the end, they reaffirmed that their primary audience would be veterans and active-duty troops, followed by journalists and historians, antiwar groups and other allies, and policymakers, probably in that order. Their message was equally straightforward. Slightly paraphrased, it went: We, the veterans of Iraq and Afghanistan, know firsthand what is happening there, so we are following in the tradition of GI resistance and taking matters in our own hands. We are convening a public investigation because the truth is not being told, and without truth, our democracy is a sham. Join us for four days in March to hear eyewitness accounts, and then act.

In Chris Arendt's junior year in high school, a teacher gave him two contradictory gifts: a copy of *On the Road*, Jack Kerouac's ode to rebellion and the American itch to move on, and the suggestion that he join the marine corps. "I took his advice in both ways," Arendt tells me by phone from Chicago.

Arendt grew up "in a trailer in a cornfield on a dirt road in Charlotte, Michigan" and arrived at basic training with blue hair and bracelets halfway up his arms, having switched from the marines to the Army National Guard a couple of months after 9/11. (He usually lied about the date, because he didn't want it to seem as if he had enlisted out of a momentary spurt of patriotism.) He was at college when his Guard unit was called up for the first time since the Civil War. He told his classmates he was going on a business trip.

Arendt was sent to guard prisoners at Guantanamo. When he arrived in January 2004, he was nineteen years old and had never seen the ocean before. It looked so majestic when the sun rose over the cliffs, but it was a confusing beauty smack up against the ugliness of his daily routine. At first, he worked the blocks, guarding prisoners and bringing them food and toilet paper. He was supposed to keep his distance, but the work was boring and he was curious, so he chatted—about their lives, families, schooling, what they thought of America, what he thought of the Middle East. After two months, he was yanked off prison duty, apparently for being too friendly, and given a desk job. He was also occasionally assigned to videotape the operations of a Quick Reaction Force, a rotating, five-person team called in to subdue recalcitrant prisoners with pepper spray and body blows. He doubts the government will be releasing those tapes any time soon.

When Arendt appears at Winter Soldier, he is long and rangy and generously tattooed. He has a baby face, ears that stick out, bangs that flip up, and an outbreak of acne. He leans into the microphone and rambles a bit, but delivers his story in a steady voice and finishes with a shout-out to his buddies in the imaginary motorcycle gang they had dreamed up at Guantanamo to keep themselves sane. "Via our oath to each other to make sure that we pissed off as much brass as possible," he deadpans, "I would like to say that I think I am in the lead now."

It's a surefire applause line, but a single, quieter sentence in his testimony stands out for its perfect blend of naïveté and truth. He had heard of an official list of what did and did not constitute torture. "I can't believe a human being could even write a list like that," he says.

After the February meeting, things moved quickly. The logistics team found a suitable venue at the National Labor College in Silver Spring, Maryland, just over the line from DC, with a verdant campus, appropriate meeting space, and adequate housing. The testimonial team organized panels and determined who would testify. The outreach team arranged travel for the 220 members who planned to attend. Amadee Braxton raised a significant portion of the projected $225,000 cost from foundations and individuals.[4] The organizers drew up a code of conduct prohibiting weapons, disruptive or violent behavior, and illegal drugs, and permitting alcohol only at designated times. The legal team, led by the Military Law Task Force of the National Lawyers Guild, advised testifiers on how to protect themselves as best they could. The mental health and peer-support teams planned debriefing sessions after each panel and arranged for mental health professionals, peer counselors, and an array of traditional and nontraditional therapists to be on hand that weekend. Because the event would not be open to the public, IVAW planned to live stream the panels on its website and post videos there and on YouTube afterward, while civilian allies organized broadcasts over local cable TV stations. Pacifica Radio, which had been at the first Winter Soldier, prepared to cover this one too. An edited version of the testimony would later appear in *Winter Soldier Iraq and Afghanistan: Eyewitness Accounts of the Occupations*, edited by Jose Vasquez for IVAW and journalist Aaron Glantz.

All this activity raised suspicion in some quarters. Briefings from the Washington [DC] Regional Threat and Analysis Center, an intelligence-collecting center aligned with the Department of Homeland Security, alerted area police and national security agencies that Winter Soldier, a "possible non-violent action," was planned for that weekend.[5] Prowar groups also spread the word: the Gathering of Eagles arranged a small counterprotest, and right-wing bloggers resurrected earlier fiascos, such as the Jesse MacBeth fake-vet affair, to undermine IVAW's credibility.

This Winter Soldier gathering would be smaller and more tightly organized than the first, when some one hundred veterans testified, more than five hundred attended, and panels and unscheduled talks stretched for hours. For IVAW's Winter Soldier, most panels were composed of seven or eight testifiers and a moderator, who was charged with keeping speakers to their time limit. (When one moderator, an active-duty sergeant, was unsuccessful in her attempts to keep a retired captain from running overtime, she announced, "I'm going to exercise a privilege many enlistees can only dream of and ask an officer to wrap it up quickly." He ignored her.)

As testimony came in, patterns emerged. It was clear that the core panels would document disregard for the rules of engagement, dehumanization of the enemy, and breakdown of the military. Other recurring issues—suicide, military sexual trauma (MST), deployment of sick troops, profiteering by military contractors, hostility from native security forces—also made their way onto the agenda.[6] These problems, underreported and barely acknowledged then, would soon slither to the surface and become lasting legacies of the militant decade, but Winter Soldier was among the first to address them publicly.

Inevitably, the focus of the panels raised questions. Some members asked why the hearings wouldn't also investigate atrocities by Iraqi or Afghan insurgents. (Answer: Individual atrocities are an element in any war, but IVAW could speak most accurately about the consequences of its own government's policies.) Others questioned the lack of testimony from Iraqi and Afghan civilians, who were the primary victims of the war. (Answer: Organizers tried to include them, but the U.S. government denied visas to most of the Iraqis they invited. In the end, two Iraqis spoke in person, and their testimony was supplemented by videotaped statements from several others.)

A few members, notably Patty McCann and Jen Hogg, pushed successfully for a separate panel on sexism and homophobia, rather than lumping those problems into what were termed "minority issues." (It would be almost five years before women were officially allowed in combat roles, and the "don't ask, don't tell" policy on homosexuality would be in force until September 2011, so only veterans could testify openly about their same-sex experiences in the military.) Aaron Hughes also remembers a heated debate about racism related to antiwar work. That touched a nerve within the largely white antiwar movement, but the racism that had infused interactions with Iraqi and Afghan civilians and prisoners was much on the mind of many IVAWs. In his testimony, Michael Prysner pointed out that "without racism, soldiers would realize that they have more in common with the Iraqi people than they do with the billionaires who send us to war." Despite good intentions about creating diverse panels, however, testifiers ended up being mostly white, young, and male.[7]

The first time Wendy Barranco encountered sexual harassment, it was from her recruiter the night he made her accompany him to a recruiting session, then got too drunk to go home, and came on to her in his hotel room. She was seventeen. Barranco was able to get out of it, but she wasn't so lucky when she got to Iraq.

As a combat medic, she wanted to learn more about medical procedures, so she asked a surgeon if she could transfer to an operating room. He arranged it, then apparently assuming a sexual quid pro quo, cornered her in the hallway almost daily. He stayed just this side of touching her, but the threat was clear. "It's extremely difficult to do your job proficiently, efficiently, and correctly when you have to look out for one of your own supervisors," she testifies.

Barranco is diminutive, but she's no pushover. She grew up in Los Angeles, the daughter of Mexican immigrants, and enlisted in the army reserves after high school, mostly for the educational benefits, but also because she wanted to give something back to the country that had given her family real opportunities. "I joined trying to be patriotic, I joined trying to do something for my country. The last thing I expected was to join an organization that would do this to me," she says, the betrayal stinging anew.

"Crap!" she mutters into the microphone, as she begins to cry. "I hate being the girl."

Winter Soldier: Iraq and Afghanistan opens on 13 March 2008. At least 50,000 Iraqi and Afghan civilians have been killed, 4,800 American soldiers have died,[8] Congress has appropriated about $666 billion for the two wars,[9] and the situation in Iraq has improved from truly awful to merely bad, while Afghanistan is stuck somewhere between a stalemate and an afterthought. For everyone who has been sent to conduct these wars/occupations/counterinsurgencies/nation-building exercises, regardless of how right or wrong they believe their actions to be, the futility of both campaigns must be overwhelming.

The BBC has predicted that Winter Soldier "could be dominating the headlines around the world this week," and seventy-five media outlets have registered to attend, with many more showing up unannounced. Reporting appears as far away as Slovenia, Iran, Japan, and Australia. Domestically, Fox, CBS, AP, Reuters, and MTV set up cameras, and NPR and "Democracy Now!" interview testifiers. The progressive press carries reports, of course, but so do *Time*, the *Washington Post, Newsday, Boston Globe, Buffalo News, Christian Science Monitor*, and other mainstream papers. The *International Herald Tribune* mentions the event, but its parent company, the *New York Times*, ignores it, which rankles IVAW and its supporters for months.[10] ("The *Times* doesn't cover rallies," a reporter for that paper informed me, as he dismissed an invitation to attend with a verbal wave of the hand.[11]) Most important, Winter Soldier is covered in the military publications, *Stars and Stripes* and the four *Military Times* weeklies.

To deal with this onslaught of cameras and notepads, at least a score of volunteers hunkers down in a back room to augment the media team. A political organizer from Pennsylvania has brought two high school girls, who create a system of formidable efficiency to pair journalists with testifiers and track the nearly two hundred interviews that take place over the weekend. A radical librarian from Massachusetts organizes allies around the country to alert the team to local coverage. An army sergeant from New York mediates when a faction of the media team wants to kick out a hostile blogger who has registered under false pretenses. (To everyone's credit, he's allowed to stay.) SmartMeme flies in from California and Vermont to churn out press releases and convene meetings, which verge on pep rallies. A man from Virginia with a day job creating technology for the Defense Department ("The stuff you don't want to know about," says Jethro Heiko) oversees technicians from who knows where, who are recording the testimony. When he starts talking about IVAW in the first person plural, the Action Mill guys chant, "You drank the Kool-Aid. You drank the Kool-Aid."

A press conference at the National Press Club on Thursday afternoon is standing room only, and that evening, Dougherty, poised and elegant in black blouse and slacks, launches the opening panel. "Iraq Veterans Against the War is going to be a force that ends the occupation of Iraq," she announces.

The next day, the National Labor College is ajangle with anticipation, as some fifty veterans of Iraq and Afghanistan, plus a few doughty active-duty service members, begin to testify. It's a scene worthy of Hunter Thompson, except that the drugs of choice are sincerity and remorse. A friend asks me if the veterans talk about how they got ready to testify, but it seems as if most have been ready for a very long time and are relieved to be getting their chance at last. They like to think that what they're doing here is daring and slightly dangerous in the way that challenging orthodoxy is supposed to be, and the sense of urgency is contagious. You half-expect someone to grab you by the lapels and shout, "Listen, goddamn it!" Shalom Keller, IVAW's high-octane membership coordinator, teeters on the edge of a meltdown, but composes himself enough to observe, "You get two hundred veterans with PTSD together to talk about the horrors of war and you don't expect us to go crazy?"

"That's when I knew he was okay," Heiko says.

The gang's all here, gathered once again for this much-anticipated reunion: Lessin and Richardson from MFSO; Gold Star parents Elaine Johnson, Fernando Suarez del Solar, and Carlos Arredondo with his ever-harder-to-miss truck-memorial; Tod Ensign of Citizen Soldier; Barry Romo of VVAW; and author Gerald Nicosia, who reads a message of support from Vietnam veteran Ron Kovic. There are the indy journalists, the good-looking French photographer, the guy with the shaved head and long Mao beard, at least seven veterans who attended the 1971 Winter Soldier investigation, and a host of Smedleys and other VFPs. The older veterans provide security, monitoring the small group of prowar veterans who demonstrate near the entrance to the college and keeping order inside the hall. When a protester tries to storm the stage during a Friday morning panel, yelling, "Kerry lied while good men died, and you guys are betraying good men," they bum-rush him out.

Michael Hoffman, the only founder of IVAW in attendance besides

Dougherty, looks a little lost amid all the new members he doesn't recognize, but he talks generously about their work and the attention they attract with their larger numbers. He finds a difference between the veterans who enlisted before 9/11 and those who enlisted after, because the latter knew what they were signing up for. Both groups feel betrayed, he explains, but the ones who joined up later feel "more righteous anger."

What unites them is a common and indelible experience and a hope to salvage something from it. As people who have grown into their fuller selves under duress relatively few of us know, they have come to believe that there is honor in refusing to make any more compromises with their conscience. This may not be the first definition of patriotism that leaps to mind, but it will serve.

The testifiers have been told to spiff up for the panels, and in the final days of preparation there has been a flurry of e-mails about a dress code. It's hard to tell how much is tongue-in-cheek. Someone gives a rousing defense of IVAW gear; another announces indignantly, "My jeans cost $200!" When the veterans arrive, their appearance runs the gamut from scruffy to freshly barbered, freaky to military dapper. Some faces still carry baby fat, others are lined and leathery. Everyone looks tense. And what an attractive bunch they are as they mount the platform to testify: America's youth in fighting trim, beribboned and crisply uniformed or sporting one of the black suit jackets that seem to get passed from panel to panel. They've brought photos and videos to illustrate their testimony, and I find myself staring into the faces of heavily armed men and women I know only in mufti. They wear uniforms and helmets and sunglasses, they're tanned in funny patterns, they clutch their weapons, they stare back at me fiercely, as if trying to reconcile the sense of immortality that comes with being young with the reality that they could die at any minute. I think: all soldiers look the same age, and it isn't young, and they aren't innocents.

The room where the panels are held is large, windowless, wider than deep. Testifiers file in from a side door opening onto a back corridor, which is off-limits to anyone without an identifying badge. They take their places at a long, skirted table with a box of Kleenex at each end. Behind them, a shiny blue-and-white banner catches a little too much reflection from the bright lights required for broadcasts and filming. Audience members listen solemnly, take notes, rest their heads in their hands, applaud enthusiastically, and rise to their feet with numbing regularity.

Outside, there are rolling lawns and a pleasant patio where people gather between sessions, but the event feels intensely enfolded, as if the world beyond has stopped and no one remembered to rewind it.

Some speakers sit ramrod straight, others slump with the weight of their testimony. Moral ambiguity could be these wars' middle name, but many here admit to doing irredeemable acts that can't be excused or forgiven. Most have not forgiven themselves, and that is one of the reasons they're here, telling what they are most ashamed of. They talk of courage and duty and truth-telling, but perhaps the worst truth they have learned is that under enough pressure, ordinary people will do horrible things to other human beings.

John Turner was a lance corporal, a machine gunner with Kilo Company, 3rd Battalion, 8th Marines in Fallujah and Ramadi. With a scruffy beard and clump of blond hair falling over one eye, he looks all-American and haunted as he begins his testimony. "We have a saying, 'Once a marine, always a marine.' We also have a saying, 'Eat the apple, fuck the Corps.'" He hurls his medals into the audience and growls, "I don't work for you no more."

Turner is known to have incendiary testimony, but the organizers are concerned about his stability. That may be why the sense of an explosion barely avoided hovers over what he says. Or it may be that what he says, and backs up with photos and videos, is horrific. His testimony comes the closest of any to war porn. Actually, it probably crosses the line. It certainly focuses your attention like a slap.

What Turner offers:

A photograph of his first confirmed kill, an Iraqi man he shot in front of his family. First kills are cause for congratulations, he informs us, and as further incentive, his commanding officer promised a four-day pass to whomever got his first kill by stabbing an Iraqi in the back.

A photograph of his third confirmed kill. This man was on a bicycle when Turner shot him. His body was left in the street for a while before someone—a marine? a neighbor?—dragged it behind a wall and threw his bike on top. The CBS reporter who was usually embedded with them was with another squad that day. "Anytime we did have embedded reporters with us, our actions changed drastically," Turner explains. "We were always on key with everything, did everything by the book."

And another photograph, this one of a face peeled off an Iraqi corpse and stretched over the curve of a Kevlar helmet. You wouldn't know what it was if you weren't told, but you look and look and try to remember to breathe. A man's face. Christ.

"I am sorry for the things that I did," Turner tells his hushed audience. "I am no longer the monster that I once was. I just want to say that I'm sorry."

"Every war constitutes an irony of situation because its means are so melodramatically disproportionate to its presumed ends," wrote Paul Fussell.[12] Winter Soldier's centerpiece is its two "Rules of Engagement" panels, where fourteen young men document how nearly everyone, from GIs on up the chain of command, stretched, ignored, and broke the rules governing what was and was not permitted in combat. Their detailed and specific testimony amounts to a damning, grunt's-eye view of the routinization of wrongdoing. The rules of engagement (ROE) started out to be quite strict, but they were relaxed in the summer of 2003, when attacks on U.S. soldiers reached as many as a thousand a day. Originally, the troops were told to identify hostile action before they opened fire; the new rules required them only to identify hostile intent. Jason Lemieux (marine sergeant, Iraq, three tours) sums it up: "The rules of engagement were broadly defined and loosely enforced to protect U.S. service members at the expense of the Iraqi people. And anyone who tells you differently is either a liar or a fool."

The panel's moderator, Jabbar Magruder (National Guard sergeant, Iraq) observes that when you're being shot at, the rules go out the door, and clearly the ROE shifted often. With his flair for the apt image, Adam Kokesh (marine reserves sergeant, Iraq) announces, "During the siege of Fallujah, we changed rules of engagement more often than we changed our underwear." Whereupon, Logan Laturi (army sergeant, Iraq) testifies, "When Adam Kokesh flashed [an ROE card] in front of everybody this morning, that was the first time I saw one. I didn't think they existed."

The testimony could serve as a crash course in military tactics, as speakers take pains to note context, clarify terms and methods, name weapons, and explain the damage each does. They translate the military's jargon, the sly twisting of language for propaganda purposes, and the jazzy, Orwellian names for weaponry, tactics, and missteps. People jailed at Guantanamo are not prisoners, but "detainees"; "Haji," the epithet flung at all Iraqis, is basically a synonym for "not us." A "weapons free zone" signifies not an area free of weapons, but a situation in which soldiers are permitted to use weapons freely—which apparently translates into shooting at anyone who might pose a danger. There's "dry hole"— a raid that yields nothing—and "recon by fire," which means starting a firefight if you feel threatened. A "drop weapon" is the extra AK-47 you carry in case you accidentally kill an unarmed Iraqi, so you can put it next to his corpse to make him look like an insurgent. When you "light someone up," you're shooting him; when you "butt-stroke," you're poking him with a weapon; and when the Iraqi army engages in "spray and pray," they're shooting wildly in the hope they'll hit their target. "Death blossom" is self-evident.

As testimony accumulates, themes recur. Nighttime house raids, a common tactic, were intended to be frightening and destructive, but they turned especially harrowing when the wrong house was targeted, which seemed to be most of the time. "We never went on a raid where we got the right house, much less the right person, not once," testifies Hart Viges (army specialist, Iraq). He describes the night his patrol arrested two young men at the wrong house while their mother wept and begged for an explanation. "I can't speak Arabic, I can speak human," he says quietly, leaning into the microphone and speaking as if he still marvels at what went down. "The place you put yourself in, when you're looking back at it, it's almost alien."

Except that it isn't alien; it's you. Testifying about ransacking the wrong house, Steve Casey (army specialist, Iraq) says, "I can't blame the people who did it. I was one of them."

Critics of Winter Soldier have argued that this is what happens in war, but as details mount and so many testifiers repeat, "This was not an isolated incident," it becomes clear that that's the point. All these blunders and violations are standard operating procedure, or at least procedure everyone knows will be tolerated. Infractions are seldom reported, because at the end of a long night, getting back to your cot trumps any moral imperative, and because no one wants to tattle on brothers-in-arms for doing what nearly everyone is doing. Maybe that's why multiple speakers make sure to mention good intentions and praise battle buddies: "squared away," "honorable." Cliff Hicks (army private, Iraq), a cavalry scout in the same unit as Casey, attests, "We were there because we thought that we were going to make things better, because these people wanted us to be there. We showed up and realized that there's a whole bunch of people that wanted to kill us."

To avoid blaming the lower ranks, testifiers have been instructed not to name anyone below the rank of captain. The policy is practical—it makes it easier to testify candidly—but it also reflects the ambivalence many of the veterans feel about their role in the wars. Their testimonies may be, as the Winter Soldier tagline says, eyewitness accounts, but they are also participant accounts. Many speakers begin by acknowledging the idealism with which they embarked on their mission, and more than one identifies a "turning point," when he stopped shooting or realized with shame that he cared more about a single American death than multiple Iraqi ones. Yet the testimony is a study in disillusion, even as testifiers sound amazed that this could have happened. To them. With them. By them. Steve Mortillo (army specialist, Iraq), a former cavalry scout, who is haunted by the death of good friends in combat, tries to explain. "You do what you have to do so you don't have to listen to 'Amazing Grace' played on bagpipes one more time." At a loss for words, he asks rhetorically, "Do you really think I'm going to pull out the card and say 'stop' before people get it?'"

The ROE changed because the political and military goals shifted, but there is a simpler explanation: it is impossible to be an occupying force without becoming an oppressive, and inevitably, a corrupt one. "I could not understand how an entire nation like mine, an enlightened nation by all accounts, is able to train itself to live as a conqueror without making its own life wretched," the Israeli novelist David Grossman wrote of his country's treatment of Palestinians.[13] So too for Americans in Iraq. In a war that is fought while driving down the wrong side of the road, anyone unfortunate enough to be driving in the opposite direction becomes a target to be lit up. The Iraqi driver is killed, the American shooter is wretched, and the occupation goes on.

In two panels called "Dehumanization of the Enemy," thirteen veterans detail the toll their lack of understanding, training, and common language took on Iraqis, Afghans, and, ultimately, themselves. They provide exhaustive evidence of good intentions thwarted by official indifference, casual racism, and brutish behavior sanctioned from above. Moderator Joshua Casteel (army Arab linguist and interrogator, Iraq) observes, "Moral slippery slopes have to go from top to bottom. They don't go from bottom to top."

Camilo Mejia (National Guard staff sergeant, Iraq) contends, "We didn't wake up one morning as monsters"—but if you consider reflexive killing monstrous, that's what they're trained to become. Testifiers recognize that casting the enemy as subhuman is an imperative of military preparation and war propaganda: a conquered people must be portrayed as different (they look odd, talk funny, pray strangely) and lesser (they treat women badly, don't value life, can't be trusted). This kind of disdain is tied to arrogance—Mike Totten (army military police, Iraq) describes a photo he had taken of himself standing in one of Saddam's palaces, pointing to an American flag and thinking, Good job!—and it is also tied to power. A few testifiers admit uneasily to the frisson that comes from the power to harass and humiliate. No one calls it bullying, but that's what it is: bullying with guns.

When disdain and arrogance combine with the inability, or disinclination, to overcome cultural or language barriers, you get cultural transgression. More than one medic describes the American military's practice of cutting up Afghan and Iraqi cadavers as teaching tools, although mutilation of the dead deeply offends Islamic beliefs. The misunderstandings that arise can have tragic consequences. Cliff Hicks tells about the night his unit mistook wedding festivities for hostile fire and ended up killing a child. He recalls, "That was the first time that I had ever seen a six-year-old girl dead. She had been shot by a bunch of teenage American kids." They didn't have a translator with them and didn't speak Arabic, so they couldn't even say they were sorry. "We just hopped in our vehicle and rode off."

Mixed in with the recitation of facts are the sense memories the testifiers can't shed—the stink of dead bodies floating in sewage, the weight of an old man dying in a medic's arms—but Mejia counters with a story about the "blank spaces," the self-protective amnesia he found himself creating. "Your own body erases certain memories to erase the face of a child whose father was decapitated next to him in a car at a control point," he says. "It is necessary to become dehumanized."

Then there's the boredom. Mike Leduc (marine corporal, Iraq), who was eighteen when he deployed, wears a half-embarrassed smile, as if to say, "This stuff happens." When the intense fighting he experienced in Fallujah died down, he and his fellow marines did target practice on dead bodies left in the street. "We'd be holed up in houses . . . and we'd get bored," he recounts. "We ran out of people to shoot, so we turned to dogs and cats, chickens, whatever's moving." But he becomes less offhand as he finishes. "For the most part, I was just doing what I had to do . . . whether it was doing what I thought was right or doing what I knew was wrong."

Even when they thought their actions were justified, most of the testifiers are haunted by them—because they aren't bad people, are they? Andrew Duffy (National Guard specialist, Iraq), one of several medics and, at twenty-one, among the youngest testifiers, tells of being mocked by other soldiers for giving mouth-to-mouth resuscitation to a dying detainee. "A lot of people call them hajis," he says. "To me, this detainee was just an old man that could've been somebody's father, grandfather, or uncle. . . . But as a medic, and as a professional, I needed to treat these people the same. They are human beings and I couldn't treat them like subhumans."

So there are moments of clarity when something breaks through the conditioned response, and warriors refuse to let their training dehumanize them as well. Hart Viges testifies frankly about sending mortar rounds into apartment buildings, following instructions to fire on all oncoming taxis, and declining to be in a photo with a dead Iraqi only because the kill wasn't his. Yet, the day he sighted his weapon on "a dude with an RPG on his back," he found himself looking into a face he recognized as a mirror of his own. "He was scared and confused, probably the same expression I had on my face," he admits. "He was probably fed the same b.s. I was fed." Viges didn't pull the trigger, and the man got away.

Saturday morning gets under way with a groundbreaking panel, "Divide and Conquer: Gender and Sexuality in the Military," where testifiers document how women in the military are preyed upon by the men who are supposed to have their back. It's apparently one of those things everyone knows about and no one wants to talk about. At the Veterans For Peace convention the previous August, a group of women, led by the indefatigable Ann Wright, held a press conference to highlight sexual assault in the military, and a few months later, the Service Women's Action Network (SWAN) formed to address discrimination and violence against women there, but this is probably the first extended, public discussion of what will come to be called military sexual trauma, or MST.

This panel feels different from the others and not just because it is composed mostly of women or because it ends ahead of schedule. While other panels are equally emotional, the level of vulnerability is especially high here; that it involves sex only ups the anxiety, as that topic usually does. The focus is on sexual predation, but panelists also report that women service members are routinely blocked from doing their jobs, isolated from their peers, and promoted more slowly than their male counterparts, which translates into lower pay and benefits—all because of their gender. For women who served in Iraq, add in the dangers of a war zone, where they were sometimes unofficially attached to a combat unit and exposed to the same dangers as male combatants, but without the same training. When women soldiers get home, their needs come as an afterthought—if at all.

The testimony, alarming and raw, depicts a world where sexist and sexually abusive behavior is routine, pervasive, and tolerated. There is, after all, little incentive to deal with a situation that makes everyone look bad. By the end of the year, the Department of Defense will have recorded 2,908 reports of sexual assault, but nobody believes that statistic, not even DoD, which subsequently estimates that fewer than 14 percent of assaults are reported.[14] Three years later, nearly a quarter of women serving in combat areas will say they have been sexually assaulted by other members of the military.

So it hardly sounds like an understatement when Patty McCann (National Guard specialist, Iraq) begins her testimony by saying, "I'd like everyone to acknowledge that there's lots of things we're not going to talk about." Some things there isn't enough time for, some things are too hard to say, and some things they've been told not to say because the hearings are being broadcast live. "It's unfortunate, the FCC . . . ," she complains when she tries to quote an officer from the army's Criminal Investigation Division, who stumbled drunkenly into her company area at Baghdad airport on Christmas Day 2003. "He was, 'Who will s-word my d-word?'" It's funny, but McCann isn't amused. "I thought the military was supposed to protect us," she concludes dolefully, "but obviously they don't."

In keeping with what can't be said, the most specific testimony is anonymous. Tanya Austin (army Arab linguist) delivers it on behalf of a woman who was raped in 2006 by a shipmate four months into her tour at a Coast Guard station on Lake Champlain in Vermont. She didn't report the rape immediately, fearing she would be blamed and also blaming herself for not being strong enough to fight off the attack. When she did try to report it to her superior officers, they discouraged her from talking to an Equal Opportunity officer, barred her from seeing a civilian therapist, ignored and later denied having seen a written confession from her attacker, and browbeat her into silence. The story continues miserably—death threats, rape jokes, involuntary confinement on a VA psych ward, relentless pressure to drop the charges—until she was finally discharged too early to receive the GI benefits or bonus her recruiter had promised.

The woman later reveals herself to be Panayiota Bertzikis, and when we talk a couple of years later, she tells me that at the time of her rape she thought she was the only one this had happened to. She went online to look for help and found almost no information, but when she blogged about her experience, similar stories poured in. She responded by setting up the Military Rape Crisis Center in Cambridge, Massachusetts, to provide counseling, advocacy, and case management to servicepeople who are sexually abused.[15] Bertzikis's story turns out to be typical. Those who are raped in the military are usually low-level enlistees, and their rapists are often their superiors, making it especially hard to report the abuse. Those who do report it are routinely ignored, scolded that the sex was consensual, or ordered not to pursue action because it might ruin their attacker's career. Retaliation is common (sometimes to the extreme of murdering the rape victim and making it look like suicide) and punishment is rare.[16] By the Pentagon's reckoning, fewer than 21 percent of reported cases make it to court-martial and only a little more than half of those result in convictions.[17]

Because the military is a world unto itself, commanders have control over enlistees' work, career, living situation, medical care, community standing, safety, and, to an alarming degree, sanity. Victims of sexual abuse are often forced to continue working under their attackers or to live nearby, giving them no safe place to recover. When a rape survivor meets her attacker daily in the military, Bertzikis tells me, "the only options out are going AWOL or suicide." In the ultimate insult, as a result of their trauma, many victims are deemed unfit to serve and get kicked out of the military. "Every case I get," Bertzikis says, "it's always, they blame the victim, the perpetrator never gets punished, and the survivor is the one who ends up losing her career."

For three days, the damning testimony pours out at Winter Soldier, and for three days, the military brass ignores it. On Saturday, after the *Washington Post* quotes a Defense Department spokesman as saying that he has not seen the allegations raised at Winter Soldier but is confident that the incidents reported there aren't representative, IVAW creates a quick response team to craft an answer, and veterans and civilians try out phrases, polish prose, cut to the nub.[18] With many writers and even more editors, the process is inefficient, but the result is a succinct and pointed message from Winter Soldier to the Pentagon:

> These service members and veterans' testimonies are ultimately not about individual conduct, but about the nature of occupation. The military is being asked to win an occupation. The troops on the ground know this is an impossible task. Their commanders know this is an impossible task. We're asking the Department of Defense to stop saying that it can achieve the impossible. We have a political problem that cannot be solved with a military solution. This is not a war that can be won. It is an occupation that can only be ended.

The Pentagon's defensiveness is hardly surprising. The American military advertises itself as the greatest fighting force since the Roman Legions,[19] yet a marine testifies that, while he was lucky enough to get both front and back protective armor before deploying to Iraq, he had to give one piece to a battalion that had been issued none. Another marine reveals that he spent $300 of his own money on a holographic sight because the scope on the rifle he was issued kept falling off. He has just lent the sight to another marine who is about to deploy.

Stop-loss, multiple deployments, broken recruiter promises, benefits denied on specious grounds, a mission that changed, as one testifier puts it, "depending on who was riding with us," and civilian contractors making three to four times what enlisted personnel earn: the list of complaints is long and detailed. Someone says the last on the list is adding insult to injury. As if the injuries weren't plentiful enough, and as if the available medical care were adequate to the need. All this comes out in the penultimate panel, "The Breakdown of the Military," where veterans and active-duty personnel attest to a collapse of bodies, minds, and morale. These are not whiners or malingerers—to the degree that several testify they continued to perform their duties despite their injuries. Eli Wright (army sergeant, active duty, Iraq) tells us that when he had a damaged shoulder and probable brain injury, what worried him most was that he would be unable to do his job as a medic and others might die as a consequence.

The problems aren't confined to the lower ranks. Junior officers are especially important in counterinsurgencies, where action is decentralized, yet their retention rate plummeted to historical lows in 2006, as many of the most promising young officers abandoned their military careers.[20] One of them is Luis Montalván (army captain, Iraq, two tours), who, after seventeen years, has recently left the military with a Purple Heart, two Bronze Stars, post-traumatic stress disorder, possible brain injury, and the need of a cane to walk. He provides exhaustive testimony about his attempts to establish a system to track border crossings at the post on the Iraq-Syria border where he was in charge, then claims that his best efforts were stymied by the incompetence, neglect, and arrogance of his superiors.[21]

No wonder a sense of betrayal hangs thick in the air as the veterans count the ways the military is falling apart. The journalist Chris Hedges will later write that for working-class kids, the military is often the only option that doesn't "break their spirit and their dignity."[22] Maybe so, but the wars in Iraq and Afghanistan did.

"I joined the army to kill people," announces Kristofer Goldsmith (army sergeant, Iraq), who grew up on Long Island, close enough to see the smoke from the collapsing World Trade Center towers. As a forward observer in Iraq, he saw his share of killing, but when he was ordered to photograph the corpses his unit was charged with exhuming in Sadr City, he had to look away. That didn't stop the image from burning in his brain, nor the blood from spurting onto his shoe, nor the flies from crawling up his nose. He was told the pictures were to help with identification, but he thinks they were really "trophies of war for people who didn't experience that death." Goldsmith says that the one thing he had to look forward to was going to college when his contract was up, but he got stop-lossed and ordered back to Iraq a second time. That's when he tried to kill himself—pills, vodka, it didn't work—after which he was given a general discharge, which lost him his college benefits. He had been a sergeant, he reminds us, an accomplished leader, a squared-away soldier. Now he delivers pizza on Thursdays "because that's the only job where I can call in a couple of hours before and say, 'I'm still at the VA. I'm waiting in line.'"[23]

Ah, yes, the Veterans Administration. Huge, bureaucratic, under-staffed, and underfunded, it's an easy target.[24] Lars Ekstrom (marine lance corporal, USS *Ponce*)—big, blond, young—scowls and stares straight ahead, as if transfixed by his memories. He joined the marines in 2003 in full support of the military and its policies in Iraq, but after what sounds like a disproportionate punishment for mildly sassing an officer, he fell into a depression. For months, he was thwarted in his efforts to get help from the VA, especially on its toll-free number, which he imitates in a robo-call voice: "If you require an ass-chewing, press one. If you know someone else who needs an ass-chewing, press two. If you require some sort of empathy or understanding, please hang up and grow a ball sack." The place explodes in laughter of recognition.

Tales of the VA's shortcomings at an earlier panel, "The Crisis in Vet-erans' Healthcare," range from exasperating to alarming. Eric Estenzo (marine reserves corporal, Iraq) praises the care he got while he was stationed at Camp Pendleton, but now, three years after leaving the ma-rines, he hasn't progressed past the paperwork stage with the VA. With embarrassment, he describes his downward spiral, which ended with his becoming one of the thousands of homeless veterans. (He told himself he was couch surfing.) His lowest moment came, he says, when "I looked at myself and I thought, I'm now an Iraq war vet, I'm standing in a line with homeless people being served free food, and this is actually happening to me."[25]

As the VA struggles to keep up with demand, increasing numbers of traumatized soldiers and veterans are dying by their own hand. Joyce and Kevin Lucey, whose son, Jeffrey, committed suicide in June 2004, charge that many of them are denied the medical help that might have saved them. When Jeffrey killed himself, military suicide was barely spoken of, but the Luceys were determined to raise awareness of the problem.[26] They filed the first wrongful death lawsuit of its kind against the Veterans Ad-ministration and later joined a class-action suit against Prudential Insur-ance that charged the company used deceitful practices with its payment of survivor benefits.[27] The Luceys are in their late fifties and live in a small town in western Massachusetts. Kevin, a big man with a soft, jowly, expressive face, is a therapist for sex offenders. Joyce, who dons reading glasses apologetically before she testifies, is a nurse, but she hasn't worked since suffering a stroke a few weeks before her son returned from Iraq. With their plain-folks manner, eagerness to inform, and mournful story, they've become the go-to family for journalists reporting on military suicide, and they have burnished their story over many retellings.

Jeffrey Lucey was a twenty-three-year-old in the marine reserves when he killed himself. A part of the initial invasion of Iraq, he served as a convoy driver for four months. Like his parents, he had opposed the war, but, like most marines, when he was called up, he went. In the photo his parents have projected over our heads at Winter Soldier, he is good-looking, young, and smiling. After he came home in July 2003, however, he began drinking heavily, sleeping badly, acting erratically, and raging at himself for what he had seen and done. "He was slowly dying in front of our eyes and nobody knew what to do," Joyce tells me when we talk a couple of years after Winter Soldier. Despite his symptoms of PTSD and an inability to function, the Veterans Administration adhered to its policy to withhold help until he was alcohol-free. For his part, Jeffrey didn't want the marines to know what was happening to him because he didn't want the stigma of a PTSD diagnosis or psychiatric discharge. The story of his decline goes on, from repeated pleas to the VA for help, to a car crash, which may have been a suicide attempt, to Jeff's request to crawl onto his father's lap the night before he died. The next day, Kevin found his son hanging by a garden hose from a rafter in their basement. "Neither our veterans nor their families should ever have to beg for the care they should be entitled to," Joyce insists.

The army doesn't count suicides as casualties of war, but Joyce argues, "If [officials] don't recognize suicide, then how do you expect to get rid of a stigma that comes from boot camp right up the ranks?" As she winds up her Winter Soldier testimony, she begins to read the note Jeffery left. "I am truly embarrassed of the man I became," she begins, but her composure crumples and she pushes the paper toward Kevin, who finishes, " . . . and I hope you can try to remember me only as a child, when I was happy, proud, and enjoyed life." It's awful and sad, and many in the audience, who have been listening to awful and sad stories all weekend, dissolve into jagged sobs.

There's much more, too much more. In assessing the legacy of the first Winter Soldier investigation, Nicosia suggests that the depth of emotion in the testimony obscured its political impact, and a similar hazard arises these thirty-seven years later.[28] You listen, you laugh, you scribble notes, you clap, you cry. It's cathartic, but it doesn't change anything—at least, not enough—and that breaks your heart.

The veterans are far from heartbroken, though. They're drained, hungover, running on too much adrenaline and too little sleep, but they've accomplished what they set out to do, and it feels very good. On Sunday afternoon, at the last panel, Dougherty, Reppenhagen, Mejia, and a few other IVAW stalwarts address the potential of GI resistance in rhetoric both hopeful and urgent. Ronn Cantu (army staff sergeant, active duty, Iraq, two tours) wraps it up by announcing that today is his thirtieth birthday. "I'm doing this for the soldiers over there right now," he says, "so they could one day see thirty as well." The audience, ready to celebrate, breaks into a full-throated rendition of "Happy birthday to you."

And then it's over. People start to pack up and head home, but not before the veterans gather one last time. It's billed as a final debriefing, but it feels more like the love child of Yoko Ono and Elmer Gantry. About a third of the IVAWs find their way to the chapel, which served as an all-night dance floor only hours before. Maybe fifty veterans sit in a circle, others crowd in the doorway. Liam Madden, as master of ceremonies, paces the center of the room and recognizes veterans as they indicate that they want to speak, testifying this time about the glory and legacy of the weekend, about brother- and sisterhood, and about being sent by Providence. Madden calls for a moment of silence for those who are no longer here, and as heads bow, someone nearby inhales deeply, gulping back tears. Then more thanks, cheers, hugs, offers of a place to crash—Colorado, LA, DC, the door's always open—and exhortations to keep at it.

"This is so sixties!" whispers Nick Jehlen's father, Alain, who has helped out all weekend. He can barely suppress a giggle.

"Yeah," agrees his son, also laughing, "but don't ever let them hear you say that."

In the days that follow, it becomes clear that Winter Soldier was more than an exercise in bonding and nostalgia. It added valuable evidence to the record, attracted media attention worldwide, and fostered discussion of critical issues for the military. For civilians, it offered a way to understand veterans' wartime experiences without reducing them to a sickness or a smiley face. IVAW brought together a third of its membership, engaged hundreds of supporters, and added fifty new members over that weekend alone, including a group of soldiers who e-mailed from Baghdad that they were following the hearings online. It probably also enabled other soldiers and veterans to speak honestly about their experiences for the first time.

For a while, the momentum continues. IVAW will finish out 2008 by testifying at an informal hearing on Capitol Hill at the request of the Congressional Progressive Caucus, staging a dozen regional Winter Soldier hearings around the United States, visiting several military bases on another national bus tour, and spearheading the largest protest at the Democratic National Convention in Denver. There, Liam Madden and Jeff Key, leading the march in full dress uniform, will deliver a letter to the Obama campaign, asking the candidate to endorse their points of unity on the convention floor, and Obama's people will respond with an offer to meet and discuss the demands in the letter. It's all heady stuff, but the meeting never happens (it's unclear who dropped the ball), nor does the war in Iraq end—at least not for another three years, another 7,000 or more Iraqi civilian lives, and another 356 American combatant lives.[29]

And so, with Winter Soldier and the bold action in Denver, IVAW's year of living large comes to an end.

In the aftermath, the organization will grow in size but contract in activity, unity, and resources. Both Winter Soldier and the summer base tour go over budget, and by late fall, the organization is broke. The board lays off staff, ends the contract with Action Mill, borrows from Veterans For Peace to stay afloat, moves toward decentralization, and squabbles so regularly that Dougherty and more than half of the board quit or are pushed out before the next election.

Then slowly, Iraq Veterans Against the War regenerates itself under new and stable leadership. It embarks on Operation Recovery, a multi-year project to promote what it believes is "a soldier's right to heal," and later joins with the Center for Constitutional Rights and Iraqi human rights groups to try to make that right to heal an international one. When the Occupy Movement captures the American imagination, it will be an IVAW member who becomes a symbol of the resistance after his skull is fractured by a kind of ammunition called a beanbag round during a melee with police in Oakland. Pundits will discuss at length whether it is ironic, tragic, or shameful that he survived a tour in Iraq, only to be beaned by cops in California, but in the *plus ça change* category, no one spends much time discussing what he was doing in either place.

So did IVAW accomplish anything significant in its heyday? Clearly, it made a difference to its members, helping them move back into civilian life, educating them, giving them a sense of mission when they most needed it, and honing their skills in organizing, planning, negotiating, articulating their ideas, and advocating for themselves—in addition to creating joyful and abiding friendships and a community of shared experience. Members went on to run for political office; work on environmental advocacy, alternative energy, and veterans affairs; conduct scholarly research on veteran culture; connect with international peace, social justice, labor, and women's groups; and write about and create art arising from their military life.

The group's activities also had a spill-over effect, reminding others that it is possible to resist orders that are wrong and wars that are wrongheaded. In campaigning for the rights of high-profile resisters, IVAW reinforced the argument that dissent can be as principled as military service, and in doing counterrecruiting, it showed some soldiers alternatives to reenlisting and some students alternatives to enlisting in the first place. IVAW highlighted crucial issues before most Americans were talking about them: the psychological distress of veterans, deployment of sick soldiers, military sexual trauma, abuse of people in occupied countries, and the effects of the war economy on domestic policy. Its members experimented with different forms of grassroots political protest, such as petitioning the government directly, conducting eye-opening street theater, and using individual stories, rather than a centrally controlled narrative, to demonstrate the basis of their convictions. And, not least of all, they kept showing up, which put the government on notice that veterans would not be ignored and demonstrated that they could play other roles than hero or victim.

But after the storytelling and swarming and spectacle-making comes the hard part. For campaigners, it's on to the next action or pressure tactic, because revolutions aren't won in a day and because once they are won, there's that thorny question of what comes next. Sometimes it's important to act without any guarantee of success. With something as unpredictable as politics or social change, you can't know how it will turn out, and symbolism does matter. Still, while antiwar movements throughout history may have whittled away at support for a war, they've seldom stopped one. Because democracy keeps rebellion in check? Because the power equation is so lopsided? Because no one wins a war against a war?

So the real legacy of Iraq Veterans Against the War may be its story, as what began as a tale of men at war—a genre we never seem to tire of—evolved into one of men and women working together at peace. And that? Ah, that's a life's commitment.

NOTES

1 MAIMED FOR BULLSHIT (WITH GALLANTTRY ON THE SIDE)

1 IVAW's founding members were Michael Hoffman, Kelly Dougherty, Jimmy Massey, Tim Goodrich, Alex Ryabov, Diana Morrison, Rob Sarra, and Isaiah Pallos. Ivan Medina, a chaplain's assistant, whose twin brother was killed in Iraq, was also listed as a founder in early records, but according to Hoffman, he was an early member. Sarra, Pallos, and Medina were not at the launch in Boston.

2 Taylor Branch, "The Last Wish of Martin Luther King," *New York Times*, 6 April 2008, doi: 2008/04/06/opinion/06branch.html.

3 According to *Networks and Netwars*, a RAND Corporation monograph analyzing emerging political resistance movements, "the narrative level of analysis may matter most." John Arquilla and David Ronfeldt, *Networks and Netwars: The Future of Terror, Crime and Militancy* (Arlington, VA: RAND Corporation, 2001), xi.

4 This stop-loss policy was authorized by an executive order signed by President George W. Bush on 14 September 2001. On 1 July 2003, the marines were the only branch of the military to issue stop-loss orders to all of its service members, active and reservists.

5 Charles W. Hoge, M.D., et al., "Combat Duty in Iraq and Afghanistan, Mental Health Problems, and Barriers to Care," *New England Journal of Medicine* 351 (1 July 2004): 13–22.

6 Operation Iraqi Freedom Mental Health Advisory Team (MHAT-11) Report (30 January 2005), http://www.comw.org/od/fulltext/0501mhatreport.pdf.

7 In an ABC News/Washington Post poll (20 June 2004), sentiment was fifty-fifty on the question "Was the war worth fighting?" Other polls asking "How well is President Bush handling the situation in Iraq?" found more disapproval than approval. CBS/New York Times poll (11–15 July 2004): 37 percent approve, 58 percent disapprove. ABC News/Washington Post poll (25 July 2004): 45 percent approve, 53 percent disapprove. USA Today/CNN Gallup poll (9–11 August 2004): 45 percent approve, 52 percent disapprove.

8 See David Vins, "The Lily-Pad Strategy: How the Pentagon Is Quietly Transforming Its Overseas Base Empire and Creating a Dangerous New Way of War," TomDispatch.com, 15 July 2012, http://www.tomdispatch.com/blog/175568.

9 Andrew Bacevich argues that this massive military buildup leads to the belief that if you have the weapons, you use them. This, in turn, has led to "the normalization of war." Bacevich, *The New American Militarism* (New York: Oxford University Press, 2005), 18.

10 "Do you approve or disapprove of the way George W. Bush is handling the situation with Iraq?" 63 percent yes, 20 percent no. "Should the United States have gone to war in Iraq?" 60 percent yes, 21 percent no. "How long do you think the United States will need to stay in Iraq to achieve its goals?" 1 percent less than a year, 7 percent one-to-two years, 38 percent three-to-four years, 49 percent five-to-ten years. *Military Times* annual year-end poll 2004, http//www.militarycity.com/polls/index.php.

11 Available at *Z Magazine* http://www.zmag.org/znet/viewArticle/10712.

12 Ron Harris, "Is Jimmy Massey Telling the Truth about Iraq?" *St. Louis Post-Dispatch*, 6 November 2005.

13 Massey went on Venezuelan television in 2007 and made six "pledges" to the people of that country, purportedly on IVAW's behalf. When IVAW's board declined to back him up, he resigned from the organization in anger.

14 Sarra's mother, Fran Johns, was already a member of Military Families Speak Out and had been featured as an antiwar mother of a marine in a series of articles in the *Chicago Tribune* from 16 March 2003 to 2 July 2004.

15 Sean Dougherty, a Vietnam vet and VFP member, told the *Boston Globe*, "The day George Bush sent my daughter to war was the day I declared war against Bush." Alonso Soto, "Antiwar Veterans, Vying to Be Heard at Meeting, Group Airs Iraq Criticism," *Boston Globe*, 25 July 2004.

16 Cynthia Peters, "Veterans Speak Out," *Z Magazine*, 1 April 2005.

17 Michael Taylor, "Back from the War, Forever Transformed," *San Francisco Chronicle*, 11 November 2005.

2 BOOTS ON THE GROUND

1 At its 2005 convention, Veterans For Peace passed a resolution encouraging fireworks-free celebrations because the explosions triggered war-residue anxiety in many veterans.

2 The idea is expanded in Cohen's book, *Speaking to History: The Story of King Goujian in Twentieth-Century China* (Berkeley: University of California Press, 2008).

3 Jerry Lembcke considers the question at length in *The Spitting Image* (New York: New York University Press, 1998). He finds no credible evidence that veterans were spat on, although it is probably impossible to resolve the issue beyond doubt.

4 David S. Meyer, *The Politics of Protest* (New York: Oxford University Press, 2007).

5 Andrew E. Hunt, *The Turning: A History of Vietnam Veterans Against the War* (New York: New York University Press, 1999), 191.

6 David Cortright, *Soldiers in Revolt* (Chicago: Haymarket Books, 2005), 150–151.

7 Ibid.

8 Howard C. Olson and R. William Rae, *Determination of the Potential for Dissidence in the U.S. Army*, Technical Paper RAC-TP-410 (McLean, VA: Research Analysis

Corporation, March 1971). R. William Rae, Stephen R. Forman, and Howard C. Olson, *Future Impact of Dissident Elements within the Army*, Technical Paper RAC-TP-441 (McLean, VA: Research Analysis Corporation, January 1972). Cited in Cortright, *Soldiers in Revolt*, 269–271.

9 Gerald Nicosia, *Home to War* (New York: Three Rivers Press, 2001), 86–88.

10 Nicosia writes of the encampment, "The daily count of veterans remained fairly consistent at around 1,200," but estimates that more than 3,000 veterans may have taken part or observed the activities during the five days of events. Ibid., 108.

11 Hunter S. Thompson, "From *Fear and Loathing on the Campaign Trail '72*" (1972), in *Reporting Vietnam, Part Two: American Journalism 1969–1975* (New York: Library of America, 1998), 393.

12 "Legacy of GI Resistance" panel, Winter Soldier: Iraq and Afghanistan, Silver Spring, MD, 13 March 2008.

13 The most consistent resistance by enlistees during World Wars I and II, Korea, and Vietnam may have come from black service members rebelling against racism, segregation, and severe mistreatment in the military and in communities surrounding military bases. Cortright, *Soldiers in Revolt*, 148–149. Black soldiers and marines were also disproportionately involved in the limited resistance during the Gulf War. See Nan Levinson, *Outspoken: Free Speech Stories* (Berkeley: University of California Press, 2003), chapter 2.

14 David Cortright described a variation on fragging known as "signaling," where a grenade would be left on the bed of a particularly gung-ho career soldier as a warning. Phone interview with the author, 12 October 2007.

15 Hunt, *The Turning*, 106. Cortright confirms that members of the 82nd Airborne Brigade told veterans they would refuse these orders. Cortright, *Soldiers in Revolt*, 81. Nicosia documents the refusal of twenty-six marines at Quantico to participate in riot control. Nicosia, *Home to War*, 106.

16 Hunt, *The Turning*, 191.

17 Most accounts date the start of the Vietnam War at the Gulf of Tonkin Resolution on 7 August 1964, but there was significant U.S. military involvement long before then. The first U.S. combat troops arrived in 1965.

18 About 1.5 million U.S. troops served in Iraq over the ten years of the war.

19 The first draft lottery since World War II, which established the order of call for induction, took place on 1 December 1969, but the draft became increasingly unproductive: by 1972, for every 100 men inducted into the military, 131 others received exemptions, Richard Nixon stopped draft call-ups at the end of 1972, and the last American soldier was drafted on 30 June 1973.

20 "The Listening Process," War Resisters League, http://www.warresisters.org/node/410.

21 Cortright, *Soldiers in Revolt*, 182.

22 Hunt, *The Turning*, 88.

23 Gerald Nicosia filed a Freedom of Information request with the FBI in 1988 for surveillance files on Vietnam Veterans Against the War. When the agency, probably only one of several that had kept records on VVAW, finally complied ten

years later, it sent fourteen boxes that stood twelve feet high and contained about twenty thousand files. http://www.geraldnicosia.com/html/geraldframeset2.html.

24 The Secret Service did keep track of antiwar protests against Iraq, recording, for instance, that sixty-five thousand people marched in Washington, DC, on 24 September 2005. *PRISM Demonstration Abstract* case # 127–673–0083443, obtained through FOIA request.

25 An earlier Veterans For Peace, composed primarily of veterans of World War II and Korea, was founded in Chicago in 1966. It played a small role in the formation of Vietnam Veterans Against the War, when it gathered some Vietnam vets under a banner proclaiming, "Vietnam Veterans Against the War!" at the Spring Mobilization in New York City in 1967. The group had a national presence, but it was defunct by 1970. Hunt, *The Turning*, 9–10. It apparently had no relationship to the current Veterans For Peace, beyond the shared name.

26 VFP membership is hard to pin down, in part because there are two categories of members: veterans and associates (i.e., civilians). In a phone interview with the author, Michael McPhearson reported between 800 and 900 members before 11 September 2001, while Lee Vander Laan said there were 1,200 members then and 1,000 more in 2002. Woody Powell, in the VFP winter 2004/2005 newsletter, reported 550 paid members in 2001 and 5,000 paid members in fiscal year 2003–2004. However, a VFP report from its national convention in 2006 noted 4,842 members, including associate members, in September 2005.

27 Robert J. Lifton, "Made in Iraq: The New Antiwar Veteran," *Boston Globe*, 25 August 2004.

28 Smedley Butler, "In Time of Peace," *Common Sense* 4, no. 11 (November 1935).

29 Ibid.

30 Quoted on Federation of American Scientists Military Analysis Network, http://www.fas.org/man/Smedley.htm.

31 Smedley Butler, *War Is a Racket* (New York: Round Table Press, 1935), 1.

32 Joanna Griffin, "Veterans' Peace Convoy Heads to Managua," UPI, 20 July 1988. In September 1988, the Center for Constitutional Rights, representing the veterans, got the courts to overturn licensing requirements for humanitarian aid under the International Emergency Economic Powers Act. *Veterans Peace Convoy v. Schultz*, Customs Service 722 FSupp 1425 (SD TX 1988).

33 Christina Silva, "Veterans Cancel Their Parade," *Boston Globe*, 12 November 2005.

34 The U.S. Supreme Court ruled in 1995 that the parade's sponsor, the Allied War Veterans, was within its First Amendment rights in refusing to allow a gay and lesbian group to participate in the parade. The sponsors interpreted that to allow them also to exclude VFP and their message of peace. In later years, VFP organized an inclusive, alternative parade and marched behind the city-subsidized street sweepers.

3 EXIT A FREE MAN

1 The army calls absence without leave AWOL; the marines and navy call it unauthorized absence or UA; and more than thirty days absence is classified as deser-

NOTES TO PAGES 46–49

tion. Desertion can be a serious infraction, especially in times of war, but the army has usually considered it more trouble than it's worth to track down deserters, so if they are caught, it is often inadvertently—when they're stopped for a traffic violation, for instance—or because they turn themselves in.

2 From the invasion of Iraq in March 2003 through late 2007, the army reported an 80 percent increase in desertion. Lolita C. Baldor, "Army Desertion Rates Rise 80 Percent since Invasion of Iraq in 2003," AP, 16 November 2007. Army records showed 4,698 desertions in 2007, which did not include the National Guard or reserves. E-mail from Nathan Banks, OCPA, U.S. Army headquarters, 11 July 2008. Military counselors believe official figures are considerably understated. In an October 2009 phone conversation, Adam Szyper-Seibert, a counselor at Courage to Resist, estimated that thirty-five thousand service members were AWOL or UA. He based his figures on army reports that 1.8 percent of troops fell into those categories, double the percentage before the war began.

3 "Search and avoid" is a term used in Iraq to describe bogus missions, for example, when a team of soldiers parked at the end of a patrol route and called in to base to report falsely that they were searching for weapons caches. Eli Wright, of IVAW, reported that it was a common tactic: "We'd just hang out, listen to music, smoke cigarettes, and pretend." Dahr Jamail, "US-IRAQ: Ill-Equipped Soldiers Opt for 'Search and Avoid,'" Inter Press Service, 14 September 2007.

In October 2004, nineteen members of the 343rd Quartermaster Company reportedly refused to go on a convoy mission because they considered it too dangerous. John J. Lumpkin, "Platoon Reported to Refuse Mission," AP, 16 October 2004. According to an e-mail dated 5 November 2004, from army spokesman Major Richard Speigel, they received minimal punishment.

Soldier-on-soldier murder may be interpreted as an extreme form of dissent. The deadliest incident during the Iraq conflict took place on 5 November 2009, when Major Nidal Hasan, an army psychiatrist, opened fire in a predeployment processing center at Fort Hood, killing thirteen and wounding at least thirty others. In other multiple murders, Sergeant John Russell killed five soldiers at a counseling center on a military base in Iraq in May 2009, and , Sergeant Hasan Akbar killed two officers with a grenade in Kuwait in 2003. National Guard Staff Sergeant Alberto Martinez was acquitted in June 2005 of killing two army officers with an antipersonnel mine in Iraq.

4 The first recorded instance of pacifist resistance was in Maryland in 1658. Among its first acts, the Continental Congress granted exemption from military service on the basis of conscience.

5 David Cortright, *Soldiers in Revolt: GI Resistance during the Vietnam War* (Chicago: Haymarket Books, 2005), 4–17.

6 Major Nathan Banks, e-mail to the author, Office of the Chief of Public Affairs, 11 July 2008.

7 Captain Jeff Landis, media officer, U.S. Marine Corps, e-mail to the author, 29 October 2004.

8 Ted Ladd at Websense, a website blocking service, confirmed in an e-mail to the

author on 13 March 2003 that the army and other branches of the military had contracts with his company. SmartFilter, another blocking service, reported in a public announcement on 16 April 2003 that the army had selected its product for use on its computers. In a phone conversation on 24 March 2003, Lieutenant Colonel Ken McClellan declined to name which blocking software the army used.

9   The Military Task Force of the National Lawyers Guild offers a succinct review of the speech rights of GIs at http://www.nlgmltf.org/leaflets/G Rights free speech .html.

10 Philosophical differences between CCCO and other GI Rights Hotline members in 2009 led to a reorganization, a split among member groups, and a new phone number.

11 Camilo Mejia, *Road from Ar Ramadi* (New York: New Press, 2007), 300.

12 Robert Finnegan, "US Army Sergeant Refuses Redeployment to Iraq; Two Soldiers Attempt Suicide at 2–7 Infantry, 17 Go AWOL," *Southeast Asia News*, 14 January 2005; and David Zucchino, "Breaking Ranks to Shun War," *Los Angeles Times*, 7 February 2005.

13 When Hinzman's petition to remain in Canada was denied, the Canadian appeals court wrote, "The ordinary foot-soldier such as Mr. Hinzman is not expected to make his or her own personal assessment as to the legality of a conflict in which he or she may be called upon to fight." *Hinzman v. Canada.* Federal Court decision. Paras (157) and (158). Hinzman's case worked its way through the courts; as of 2010, he was still living in Canada.

14 Until 30 June 1973, when the last American was drafted, more than fifty thousand American draft resisters and deserters were sheltered by supportive Canadian governments, and about half stayed on, even after then-President Jimmy Carter issued a blanket pardon in 1977.

15 A June 2008 survey by Angus Reid Strategies found that 64 percent of Canadians agreed that U.S. soldiers should be allowed to stay as permanent residents. However, the legislature voted down Bill C-440, which would have granted resisters permanent residence in Canada, by a small margin in September 2010.

16 Robin Long, an army private who had fled to British Columbia to avoid deployment to Iraq three years before, was sentenced to fifteen months in a naval brig near San Diego.

17 Sarah Olson, one of the journalists subpoenaed to testify at the trial, explained why she would refuse to cooperate with the government in "Why I Object to Testifying against Lt. Watada," *Editor and Publisher*, 30 December 2006. The subpoenas were eventually dropped.

18 Jeff Paterson, "Lt. Watada Mistrial Clear Victory," Courage to Resist, 8 February 2007.

19 Adam Szyper-Seibert, of Courage to Resist, believed the number might be as much as 50 percent higher, but documentation was scare. Phone conversation with the author, 9 October 2009.

20 For eleven low-ranking soldiers charged with mistreating detainees or failing to report mistreatment at Abu Ghraib, seven were sentenced to less than a year in

jail. Sentences ranged from ninety days hard labor, a fine, and no prison time to ten years imprisonment. "Soldiers Convicted in the Abu Ghraib Prisoner Abuse Scandal," AP, 1 November 2008. On the sniper case, see "US Inquiries into Iraqi Deaths," BBC News, http://news.bbc.co.uk/2/hi/americas/5105284.stm.

4 HOME FIRES BURNING

1 Polls taken by the Defense Department showed that parents became obstacles to enlistment. Parents of children between the ages of twelve and twenty-one who said they were likely to recommend military service fell from 70 percent in 2001 to 20 percent in June 2006. Kristin Roberts, "US Military Sees Parents as Big Recruiting Barrier," Reuters, 11 May 2007.

2 Amy Swerdlow, *Women Strike for Peace* (Chicago: University of Chicago Press, 1993). Gerald Nicosia, *Home to War* (New York: Three Rivers Press, 2001), 109.

3 The case was *Drinan v. Nixon*, 502 F2nd 1158, decided on 8 October 1973.

4 The military sociologist Charles Moskos found that the class structure of the U.S. Army remained essentially unchanged since the Revolutionary War, when soldiers were poor or working class and officers were middle class. Steve Gilliard, "The Draft: No Solution to Social Inequality," AlterNet, 22 November 2006, http://www.alternet.org/story/44556/the_draft%3A_no_solution_to_social_inequality.

5 Drew Brown, "Guard Chief Says Recruitment Woes to Pass," *Boston Globe*, 13 July 2005. The National Guard as a percentage of troops in Iraq varied widely, falling as low as 7 percent in January 2008. Between September 2001 and November 2007, 254,894 Army and Air National Guard were deployed to Iraq and Afghanistan. Michael Waterhouse and JoAnne O'Bryant, *National Guard Personnel and Deployments: Fact Sheet*, Congressional Research Service, Order Code RS22451, 17 January 2008, http://www.fas.org/sgp/crs/natsec/RS22451.pdf. By late 2005, the National Guard and reserves accounted for one-quarter of U.S. deaths since the invasion of Iraq, and the proportion was on the increase. Robert Burns, "Death Toll Rises for U.S. Military Reservists as Their Role Grows in Iraq," AP, 10 October 2005.

6 Ann Scott Tyson, "Shortages Threaten Guard's Capability," *Washington Post*, 2 March 2007.

7 Suicides of Iraq and Afghanistan veterans doubled between 2004 and 2006. Pauline Jelinek, "Army Suicides at Year High," AP, 29 January 2009. Robert Weller, "Experts: Repeat Deployments Hurt Care Efforts," AP, 23 June 2007. A study by the RAND Corporation estimated that, as of October 2007, approximately three hundred thousand troops who had deployed to Afghanistan or Iraq were suffering from PTSD or major depression. Terri Tanielian and Lisa H. Jaycox, eds., *Invisible Wounds of War* (Santa Monica, CA: RAND, 2008).

8 Susan Jones, "Anti-War Groups Protesting US Troops Instead of Decision-Makers," CNSNews.com, 17 March 2005.

9 In the *plus ça change* department, a leader of the Moratorium organized in 1969 to protest the Vietnam War told a journalist, "Demonstrations were a minority tactic that were good for '66 and '67. . . . The days of symbolism are over." Francine du

Plessix Gray, "The Moratorium and the New Mobe," *New Yorker*, 3 January 1970.

10 Stan Goff, "Operation (Un)Truth: A Trojan Jackass for the Anti-War Movement," *CounterPunch*, 2/3 April 2005, http://www.counterpunch.org/goff04022005.html.

11 Ellen Barfield, "Bring Them Home Now—Or Not?" *Nonviolent Activist: The Magazine of the War Resisters League* (July–August 2005).

12 Reported on National Public Radio, 14 August 2005.

13 Andrew J. Bacevich, *The New American Militarism* (New York: Oxford University Press, 2005), 35.

5 WHAT NOBLE CAUSE

1 Gold Star Families for Peace founding members were Cindy Sheehan, Celeste Zappala, Sue Nederer, Bill Mitchell, Jane and Jim Bright, and Lila Lipscomb.

2 From 1991 until March 2009, when the Obama administration lifted the ban, the government prohibited the press from photographing coffins of dead soldiers as they returned to the States. In June 2004, Nadia McCaffrey, a member of Gold Star Families for Peace and Military Families Speak Out, defied the ban by inviting the press to Sacramento Airport to cover the arrival of the flag-draped coffin of her son, Patrick, who was killed in Iraq on 22 June 2004.

3 Demographic sources: http://www.usbeacon.com/population/Texas/Crawford.html; http://www.crawfordchamberofcommerce.com/members.htm#2; http://www.citydata.com/city/CrawfordTexas.html.

4 The Peace House, which was almost broke before the protest began, raised enough money within the first week to pay off its $40,000 mortgage. Michael A. Fletcher, "In Texas, a Time to Circle the Minivans: Activists Protest the War, or Protest the Protesters," *Washington Post*, 13 August 2005.

5 *Democracy Now*, 19 August 2005.

6 Larry Northern, of Waco, was later charged with the felony of criminal mischief and was released on $3,000 bail. "Crawford Protest Moves Nearer to Bush: Neighbor Lets Demonstrators Use Land," CNN, 17 August 2005, doi: 2005/POLITICS/08/17/ crawford.protest.

7 Sociologist Sarah Sobieraj has analyzed the differing norms news media observe in reporting on what she calls political "insiders" and "outsiders." For outsiders, she found that "good sources" establish their authenticity through amateur status and sharing personal, emotional, and seemingly unscripted stories, among other things. Sarah Sobieraj, *Soundbitten* (New York: New York University Press, 2011).

8 The shooter, Larry Mattlage (who said he was preparing for dove hunting season), had a longtime deal that allowed NBC News to use his land for a view of the Western White House. G. Robert Hillman, "Protesters near Ranch Counter Mom's Message," *Dallas Morning News*, 14 August 2005.

9 Fred Barnes on *Special Report with Brit Hume*, Fox News Channel, 11 August 2005.

10 Christopher Hitchens on *Hardball with Chris Matthews*, 17 August 2005.

11 Rush Limbaugh on *Rush Limbaugh Show*, 15 and 16 August 2005.

12 Howard Kaloogian, cofounder of Move Forward, quoted in "Anti-War Protest Draws Other Side to Texas," UPI, 28 August 2005.

13 Michael A. Fletcher, "Cindy Sheehan's Pitched Battle: In a Tent Near Bush's Ranch, Antiwar Mother of Dead Soldier Gains Visibility," *Washington Post*, 12 August 2005. Peter Canellos, "She Strikes a Chord for Military Families," *Boston Globe*, 16 August 2005.

14 Frank Rich detailed the administration's failed attempts to deflect attention from the failures of the war in "The Swift Boating of Cindy Sheehan," *New York Times*, 21 August 2005.

15 ABC's *Nightline* received an e-mail, purportedly from Sheehan, on 15 March 2005, saying in part that her son "was killed for lies and for a PNAC Neo-Con agenda to benefit Israel." She maintained that it was doctored by "a former friend" and did not reflect her views. The original e-mail was lost, and the controversy echoed throughout the blogosphere without resolution. David Duke, "Why Cindy Sheehan Is Right," http://davidduke.com/whycindysheehanisright.

16 A bus tour titled "You Don't Speak for Me, Cindy" culminated near Camp Casey toward the end of August.

17 The northern route stopped in Oklahoma City, Wichita, Kansas City, Des Moines, Minneapolis, Madison, Milwaukee, Chicago, Toledo, Detroit, Buffalo, Rochester, Syracuse, Albany, Amherst, Boston, New Haven, and New York City. The southern route went from Austin to Houston, New Orleans, Mobile, Tallahassee, Montgomery, Atlanta, Savannah, Columbia, Fayetteville, Raleigh-Durham, and Richmond. The central route followed from Dallas to Little Rock, Memphis, St. Louis, Indianapolis, Cincinnati, Columbus, Cleveland, Pittsburgh, Harrisburg, Philadelphia, Trenton, and Baltimore. A fourth bus carried relief workers to New Orleans. All four buses arrived in Washington, DC, on 21 September.

18 The death toll for U.S. forces reached 1,927 at the end of August, as per icasualties. org. According to *The Cost of Iraq, Afghanistan, and Other Global War on Terror Operations since 9/11*, by Amy Belsco (Congressional Research Service, 28 September 2009), the Defense Department's estimated funding for operations in Iraq for FY 2003 and FY 2004 totaled $106.4 billion, and the estimate for FY 2005 was $83.4 billion. Most of that fiscal year's funding would have been spent by the end of August, so for a rough estimate, I used five-sixths of the FY 2005 figure.

19 Jennifer Loven, "Bush Gives New Reason for Iraq War," *Boston Globe*, 31 August 2005.

20 Estimates put the size of the march between one hundred thousand and three hundred thousand. The National Park Service reports that of the approximately three thousand permits it issues each year for demonstrations on the National Mall, only about twelve attract more than five thousand people.

6 ONE PARAGRAPH IN

1 The interim board, formed in early 2005, included VFP members Dave Cline, Dennis O'Neil, Frank Corcoran, and John Grant; MFSO's Patricia Gunn; and later, post-9/11 veterans Anita Foster, Camilo Mejia, Garett Reppenhagen, Jimmy Massey, and Michael Hoffman.

2 Ward Riley, "Mobile to New Orleans: Resistance Defined in Epic Action," *Veteran* (Spring 2006), http://www.vvaw.org/veteran/article/?id=592.

3 Music was a moneymaker for IVAW: in 2007, Sire Records donated $100,000 in the name of Tomas Young, a severely wounded Iraq veteran who would become the subject of the documentary film *Body of War*. Profits from a CD compilation selected by Young, with cover art donated by graffiti artist Shepard Fairey, were donated a few months later.

4 For example, in an LA Times/Bloomberg Poll (8–11 December 2006), 56 percent thought the situation in Iraq was not worth going to war for, and 66 percent thought neither side was winning. A CNN/Opinion Research Corporation Poll (11 January 2007) found 67 percent opposed the war, 50 percent thought it would end in stalemate, and 20 percent in defeat. An ABC News/Washington Post Poll (11 December 2006) was even more pessimistic: 11 percent thought it would end in a tie, and 46 percent thought the United States would lose.

5 "U.S. Troops in Iraq: 72% Say End War in 2006," Zogby International, released 23 February 2006.

6 Office of the United Nations High Commissioner for Refugees update on the Iraq situation, *Relief Web*, 30 November 2006, doi: report/iraq/unhcrupdateiraqsituation.

7 Clousing describes his training in *Breaking Ranks*, by Matthew Gutmann and Catherine Lutz (Berkeley: University of California Press, 2010), 42–43. According to Joshua Casteel, who spent five months as an interrogator at Abu Ghraib, the average age of interrogators there was twenty-one or twenty-two. Most of the men he interrogated were in their late twenties, but his subjects ranged from schoolboys to imams to old men.

8 Laurie Goodstein, "A Soldier Hoped to Do Good, but Was Changed by War," *New York Times*, 13 October 2006.

9 David Cortright, *Soldiers in Revolt: GI Resistance during the Vietnam War* (Chicago: Haymarket Books, 2005), 33.

10 Cortright was part of a class-action lawsuit challenging his transfer orders, which were found unconstitutional by a federal district judge in 1971. The decision was overturned on appeal and rejected for review by the Supreme Court. Ibid., 69.

11 Ibid., 82.

12 Some papers lasted no more than a few issues, but they were still sources of information and agitation and an outlet for their writers, who gave them names both tart and cheeky: e.g., *Fatigue Press, Attitude Check, Rough Draft, Spread Eagle, Whack!* (by women), *Kill for Peace, Star Spangled Bummer, Harass the Brass, Kitty Litter* (from USS *Kitty Hawk*), and *Hunley Hemorrhoid* (from USS *Hunley*).

13 In September 1971, Vietnam Veterans Against the War collected hundreds of signatures from service members in Vietnam for a petition of protest to be sent to Congress. Military officials swiftly stifled the campaign, so it is unclear how many actually signed. Cortright, *Soldiers in Revolt*, 34.

More successful was the first, and apparently only, officially sanctioned petition drive, which took place at Fort Huachuca in Arizona in July 1971, when 811 active-duty soldiers signed an antiwar petition to be presented to Congress. Cortright, *Soldiers in Revolt*, 86.

14 In *Rules of Disengagement*, Marjorie Cohn and Kathleen Gilberd note that the directives addressing the rights soldiers have do so primarily by describing the rights they don't have. *Rules of Disengagement* (Sausalito, CA: PoliPoint Press, 2009), 79.

15 Hutto also noted Department of Defense directive 1344.10, Political Activities by Members of the Armed Forces on Active Duty, which concerns electoral politics, but states, "It is DoD policy to encourage members of the Armed Forces to carry out the obligations of citizenship."

16 Lizette Alvarez, "Service Members Sign Appeal Calling for Troop Withdrawal," *New York Times*, 28 February 2007.

17 http://www.appealforcourage.org.

18 Andrew Bacevich, "Warrior Politics," *Atlantic* (May 2007).

19 Liam Madden, "Silence Is Not an Option," IVAW website, 10 July 2007, http://www.ivawarchive.org/membersspeak/silencenotoption.

20 Liam Madden, letter to the editor, *Atlantic* (May 2007).

21 In *The New American Militarism* (New York: Oxford University Press, 2005), Bacevich warns against isolating soldiers from civilian society and argues that a return to citizen-soldiers would foster a beneficial cross-fertilization of ideas. He expanded on those ideas in a 2013 op-ed, where he charged that in rebranding enlistment as an opportunity and individual right, military service has been removed "from the realm of collective obligation and converted . . . into an issue of personal preference" (Andrew Bacevich, "Once a Duty, Military Service Recast as a Right," *Boston Globe*, 2 February 2012).

22 Madden, letter to the editor, *Atlantic* (May 2007).

23 Gene Sharp, "The Role of Power in Nonviolent Struggle," Monograph Series no. 3 (Boston: Albert Einstein Institution, 1990).

24 Helen Benedict examines conditions for women in the military in *The Lonely Soldier* (Boston: Beacon Press, 2009).

25 The battle-of-the-story trope comes from a RAND Corporation paper, which posits that organizations cohere around narratives that "provide a grounded expression of people's experiences, interests, and values." John Arquilla and David Ronfeldt, eds., "Networks and Netwars: The Future of Terror, Crime, and Militancy" (Santa Monica, CA: RAND, MR1382OSD, 2001).

26 See, for example, Mark Memmott, "Soldier, Reporter Teamed Up for Question Asked Rumsfeld," *USA Today*, 10 December 2004.

27 In May 2007, the Defense Department cut off access to Myspace, YouTube, and other social networking on its computers, but servicepeople followed them on nonofficial computers.

28 The army launched an Online and Social Media Division in January 2009, a month after it created an iPhone app.

29 New York National Guardsman Jason Christopher Hartley, one of the first soldiers demoted and fined for security breaches on a blog, was quoted as saying of a caption he added to a photo of an Iraqi's corpse, "It leaves a bad taste in your mouth? That's sorta the point." Joseph Mallia, "U.S. Military 'Hunts Down' Soldiers' Blogs," Newsday.com, 2 January 2006.

30 It would be hard to dream up a better display of tone deafness than a video sent to all soldiers overseas in August 2005 of the army chief of staff warning that "Loose blogs may blow up BCTs" (brigade combat teams). The *Army Times* reported a couple of years later that the regulations were revised to spell out policy and to include e-mail and postings on message boards, though the army admitted that it would be impossible to monitor these. Michelle Tan, "Bloggers Beware: Army Tightens Regulations," *Army Times*, 4 May 2007.

7 WE'LL BRING 'EM ON

1 Whyte's first name never appears in the exchange of e-mails or other documentation of Kokesh's separation hearing.

2 Kokesh got into the convention using his credentials from the Ron Paul campaign. His banner read, "You Can't Win an Occupation" on one side and "McCain Votes Against Vets" on the other. According to Project Vote Smart, McCain had voted four times in the previous six months against funding for veterans' health care.

3 The article, "Far from Iraq, a Demonstration of a War Zone," by David Montgomery (*Washington Post*, 20 March 2007) is included in Kokesh's marine corps file with an arrow pointing him out in a photograph. File obtained through FOIA request.

4 "Virtual Roll Call," 25 January 2007, obtained through FOIA request.

5 The regulations cited were Department of Defense directive 1334.01: Wearing of the Uniform, and Art. 134 of the Uniform Code of Military Justice: Disloyal statements.

6 U.S. Army Human Resources Command, doi: staff/individual%20ready%20reserve.

7 Jim Garamone, "Army to Recall Thousands of Individual Ready Reservists," *American Forces News Service*, 30 June 2004. In FY 2007, the army reported that of its approximately 111,000 IRRs, 3,400 were called up. Some served stateside, but most were sent to Iraq or Afghanistan.

8 Courage to Resist, http://www.couragetoresist.org/x/content/view/658/1.

9 See, for example, Dick Foster, "Troops Feeling Strain: GI Discontent Grows as Uncle Sam Struggles to Find Enough Forces," *Rocky Mountain News*, 22 November 2004.

10 *Doe v. Rumsfeld* L.E. 1–10, 435 F.3d 980.

11 *Qualls v. Rumsfeld*, 357 F. Supp. 2d 274, 284 (D.D.C. 2005).

12 Monica Davey, "Eight Soldiers Plan to Sue over Army Tours of Duty," *New York Times*, 6 December 2004.

13 Monica Davey, "Soldier Protesting Extended Deployment Drops Suit and Re-enlists," *New York Times*, 6 February 2005.

14 Cheryl Pellerin, "Gates Urges Servicemembers to Claim Stop-Loss Pay," American Forces Press Service, 5 October 2010.

15 Cloy Richards, who also received a warning, suffered from PTSD. Worried about losing his health and disability benefits, he agreed to stop speaking publicly. His

mother, Tina Richards, a member of MFSO, spoke in his stead, telling everyone how messed up her son was. Keeping it in the family, when Kokesh ran for Congress three years later, Richards served as his campaign manager.

16 Brian Montopoli, "Is Adam Kokesh the New Cindy Sheehan?" CBSNews.com, 1 June 2007, doi: news/isadamkokeshthenewcindysheehan.

17 "Summarized Record of Board Hearing: Adam C. Kokesh," 6 June 2007. Obtained through FOIA request.

18 RAND cited Mexico's Zapatistas as an example of an extreme group and Burmese monks as an example of civil society activists. John Arquilla and David Ronfeldt, eds., *Networks and Netwars: The Future of Terror, Crime, and Militancy* (Arlington, VA: RAND Corporation, 2001), ix.

19 Notes from Nowhere, eds., "Networks: The Ecology of the Movements," in *We Are Everywhere* (London: Verso, 2003).

20 A related RAND study reports, "This second principle—swarming—has not been explicitly espoused or adopted by the actors we have looked at, but it is implicitly there, awaiting refinement in many of them." John Arquilla and David Ronfeldt, *Swarming and the Future of Conflict*, RAND, DB311OSD, 2000.

21 The Yellow Rose of Texas bus was destroyed by fire at a New Jersey rest stop on 11 January 2008. The cause was undetermined, but Internet buzz labeled it "suspicious."

22 At Fort Hamilton, the security posture was raised, and at Fort Drum, the veterans' names were placed on "No Access" lists. A Fort Campbell report, labeled "for official use," included a copy of an *Army Times* story about the Fort Benning arrests, although Campbell was not on the tour itinerary.

23 Two other coffeehouses opened afterward: Coffee Strong, outside Fort Lewis in Washington State, in 2008, and Under the Hood in Killeen, Texas, in 2009.

24 Dahr Jamail, "Ill-Equipped Soldiers Opt for 'Search and Avoid,'" Inter Press Service, 25 October 2007, Antiwar.com, http://www.antiwar.com/jamail/?articleid=11806.

25 Dana Priest and Anne Hull, "Soldiers Face Neglect, Frustration at Army's Top Medical Facility," *Washington Post*, 18 February 2007; "The Hotel Aftermath," *Washington Post*, 19 February 2007; "Hospital Investigates Former Aid Chief," *Washington Post*, 20 February 2007; and "Swift Action Promised at Walter Reed," *Washington Post*, 21 February 2007.

26 Recognizing the difficulty of getting a diagnosis, the IVAW national office sponsored internships for members so they could be evaluated at the VA's Philadelphia office.

27 Kimberly Hefing, "Injured Soldiers Trying to Leave Military Slowed by Red Tape," AP, 19 August 2011.

28 Lisa W. Foderaro, "Report Faults Mental Care for Iraq Veterans at Upstate Base," *New York Times*, 13 February 2008.

29 "2005 Department of Defense Survey of Health Related Behaviors among Active Duty Military Personnel," December 2006, RTI/7841/106-FR.

8 ART HEART DREAM PEACE

1 IVAW members were also featured in others' films. Kelly Dougherty, Jimmy Massey, Camilo Mejia, Charlie Anderson, Demond Mullins, Rob Sarra, Mike Blake, and Perry O'Brien appeared in Patricia Foulkrod's 2006 documentary *The Ground Truth*. Two other members were the subjects of films that got significant notice: Tomas Young, who was severely injured in Iraq, was the subject of *Body of War*, produced by Phil Donahue and Ellen Spiro in 2007. Robynn Murray, a former army sergeant and machine gunner in Iraq, was the focus of *Poster Girl*, a documentary short by Sara Nesson, which was nominated for an Academy Award in 2011.

2 Paul Fussell, *The Great War and Modern Memory* (New York: Oxford University Press, 1975), p. 31.

3 Photographs of dead Afghans played a role in a trial of soldiers accused of killing civilians for sport near Kandahar in 2011, but after they appeared in the German magazine *Der Spiegel*, the army restricted them. Calling them "repugnant," officials worried publicly that they could damage U.S. relations with the Afghan government. William Yardley, "Soldier Is Expected to Plead Guilty in Afghan Killings Case," *New York Times*, 23 March 2011.

4 The army considered whether posting photos on NTFU.com constituted a felony in September 2005, but suspended its inquiry without reaching a conclusion. The site's administrator, Chris Wilson, was later charged with possessing obscene material. He agreed to close the site and turn control of the address over to the sheriff's office in Polk County, Florida. Kari Andén-Papadopoulos, "Body Horror on the Internet: US Soldiers Recording the War in Iraq and Afghanistan," *Media, Culture & Society* (2009): 925–926.

5 Ibid.

6 Stephen Duncombe, *Dream* (New York: New Press, 2007), 174.

7 Make Drag, Not War was launched by Stephen Funk, the first marine to publicly refuse deployment to Iraq. (He came out as gay at the same time.) Funk cofounded Veteran Artists, a San Francisco–based collective for recent veterans interested in making art.

8 Charlie Anderson, of IVAW, and Tamara Rosenleaf, an army wife, launched Bake Sales for Body Armor in February 2006 in response to a secret Pentagon finding that up to 80 percent of the marines who died from upper body wounds in the first two years of the Iraq War could have been saved by protective armor, which the military failed to supply to all combatants. (Though the study was completed the previous June, the military apparently had data indicating that heavier armor was needed two years earlier.) Their project raised enough money through actual and virtual bake sales to fill requests for eighteen sets of armor.

9 Gerald Nicosia, *Home to War* (New York: Three Rivers Press, 2001), 56–73.

10 Drew Cameron, foreword to *I Hacky Sacked in Iraq*, by Nathan Lewis (Burlington, VT: Combat Paper Press, 2009).

11 A study requested by the Veterans Administration in 2011 was inconclusive about the long-term health effects of the burn pits. Leo Shane III, "Burn Pit Study Inconclusive on Health Effects," *Stars and Stripes*, 31 October 2011.

12 Key created the Mehadi Foundation to use art to help Iraqi citizens and American veterans.

13 Walter Benjamin, "The Storyteller: Reflections on the Works of Nikolai Leskov," in *Walter Benjamin: Selected Writings*, vol. 3: *1935–1938*, ed. Howard Eiland and Michael W. Jennings (Cambridge, MA: Belknap Press, 2006).

9 DISGRUNTLED

1 Charley Richardson survived for another six years. He died on 4 May 2013.

2 Air force and navy aircraft dropped five times as many bombs and missiles in Iraq in the first half of 2007 as in the first half of 2006 and three times more than in the second half of that year. MSNBC, 14 July 2007 and CBS News, 15 July 2007, using AP reporting.

   AP reported that the military's reliance on unmanned drones in 2007 "soared to more than 500,000 hours in the air, largely in Iraq," with their use by the air force more than doubling in the first ten months of the year. Conveniently, this allowed servicepeople to conduct the war out of offices in Nevada, Arizona, and California and return home by dinnertime. Lolita C. Baldor, "Military's Use of Unmanned Drones Soars in Iraq," AP, 2 January 2008.

3 U.S. military strength in Iraq reached its peak in October 2007, with 166,300 troops and 505 bases. There were 904 American military fatalities that year, and an average of 58 Iraqis died violently each day. An AP/Ipsos poll in September of that year found that 59 percent of Americans thought history would judge the Iraq campaign a partial or complete failure. Six months later, 66 percent opposed the war and 71 percent linked it to the bad economy. CNN/Opinion Research, 19 March 2008.

4 Letter to the board of directors, chapter leaders, and members of Iraq Veterans Against the War from leaders of Vietnam Veterans Against the War, 2008, author's personal files.

5 Bill Moyer, *Doing Democracy* (Gabriola Island, Canada: New Society Publishers, 2001), 45.

6 The Gathering of Eagles assaulted Carlos Arredondo as he marched past carrying a mock coffin and photos of his dead son.

7 Sarah Sobieraj, *Soundbitten* (New York: New York University Press, 2011), 91.

8 Bryan Bender, "Some See Army Pitch in Preteen Magazine," *Boston Globe*, 3 July 2006.

9 See, for example, Bryan Bender and Kevin Baron, "Fewer High-Quality Army Recruits," *Boston Globe*, 6 July 2007; and Lizette Alvarez, "Army Giving More Waivers in Recruiting," *New York Times*, 14 February 2007.

10 See, for example, "Violations by Military Recruiters Increase," *Boston Globe*, 15 August 2006; and "Report Finds Military Recruitment at Select New York City Public Schools Violates Students' Rights," *US States News*, 6 September 2007.

11 The National Priorities Project calculated that 6.39 percent of recruits came from the top tenth income bracket in 2007, a figure that varied only slightly from 2006 to 2010. Percentages for recruits from the bottom tenth were similar, http://nationalpriorities.org.

12 Sarah Manski, "Nothing Short of Criminal—IVAW Takes on the War," *Liberty Three Journal of the Democratic Revolution* 2, no. 3, http://sarah.manski.org/IVAWArticle.pdf.

13 The army redacted the reports from time to time, changing rates for 2003, for instance, from an original 72 percent reporting low or very low unit morale to 51 percent in later versions. High or very high ratings for individual morale consistently hovered in the mid to high teens. Reports available through U.S. Army Medical Department, http://www.armymedicine.army.mil/reports/mhat/mhat.html.

14 "Mental Health Advisory Team IV, Operation Iraqi Freedom 05–07, Final Report," 17 November 2006, http://armymedicine.mil/Documents/MHATIVReport-17NOV06FullReport.pdf.

15 Jo Freeman, "The Tyranny of Structurelessness" (first presented, 1970), http://www.jofreeman.com/joreen/tyranny.htm.

16 Moyer, *Doing Democracy*, 32–38.

17 A Kokesh stunt that led to publicity, but not arrest, took place at a congressional hearing in April 2007, when he was photographed with a sign keeping count of the number of times Attorney General Alberto Gonzalez said, "I don't remember" or "I don't recall," as he was grilled about the dismissal of U.S. attorneys for what may have been political reasons. Kokesh recorded seventy-four instances. Paul Kane, "The AG Hearing: A Post-Mortem," *Washington Post*, 20 April 2007.

18 IVAW Membership Report, 3 February 2009, author's personal files.

19 Kevin Simpson, "Many Faces of 'Fake Vet' Rick Strandlof Exposed," *Denver Post*, 7 June 2009.

20 The website Stolen Valor has maintained a sizable list of people caught lying about their military involvement, http://www.stolenvalor.com/Target.cfm?.

21 Letter to members from IVAW Board, 12 March 2008, author's personal files.

22 Letter to members from IVAW Board, 4 December 2009, author's personal files.

23 "Executive Director on Flag Burning," 27 March 2010, http://ivaw.org/blog/executive-director-flag-burning.

24 Obtained from Department of Homeland Security by FOIA requests.

25 See Nan Levinson, "US Information Policy: Lock It Up," *Index on Censorship* (June/July 1988).

26 Off Post Event Threat Analysis and Update, 3/2 SBCT Movement from Port of Olympia to FLW, Army Directorate of Emergency Services, Ft. Lewis, 5 November 2007. Obtained by National Lawyers Guild through FOIA request.

27 Nancy Murray and Kade Crockford, "Targeting Dissent," *Truthout*, 15 September 2011, doi: targeting-dissent/1314383265.

28 E-mail from Chris Adamson to Mike Kortjohn, 5 November 2008. Obtained by National Lawyers Guild through FOIA request.

29 IVAW also harbored some distrust toward establishment leftist groups, such as MoveOn, with its faith in liberal democracy and the Democratic Party as its avatar. The wariness seemed mutual, as MoveOn grew impatient with grassroots groups like IVAW, who shunned most partisan politics and were hard to control.

30 Letter to Iraq Veterans Against the War from Vietnam Veterans Against the War, 2008, author's personal files.

10 MAD BAD SAD

1 According to the reliable icasualties.org, as of September 2012, 32,223 U.S. troops were wounded in Iraq, and 17,674 were wounded in Afghanistan. According to the *Boston Globe*, advances in protective armor and battlefield medicine increased the survival rates from one fatality out of every three wounded in World War II to a ratio of one death out of every nine wounded in the recent conflicts. Liz Kowalczyk, "Brigham Gets $3.4m for Face Transplants, Defense Pact Aids Veterans, Civilians," *Boston Globe*, 21 December 2009.

2 James Carroll, "A Nation under Post-Traumatic Stress," *Boston Globe*, 28 June 2010.

3 Psychiatrist Jonathan Shay suggests that the huge psychiatric hospitals the VA built after World War II sent the message that if you talked about your anger or nightmares, you would be locked up forever. Jonathan Shay, *Odysseus in America* (New York: Scribner, 2002), 109.

4 C. Fred Alford, "Whistleblower Narratives," *Narrative* 8, no. 4 (October 2000): 279–293.

5 Adam Hochschild, *To End All Wars* (Boston: Houghton Mifflin Harcourt, 2011), 242.

6 Dave Grossman, *On Killing* (Boston: Little Brown, 1995), 43.

7 *DSM-IV*, Diagnosis & Criteria, 309.81: Posttraumatic Stress Disorder. *DSM-V*, released in 2013, made some changes to the criteria, putting more emphasis on behavioral symptoms. It reclassified PTSD under a new class of anxiety disorders, named Trauma and Stressor-Related Disorders.

8 Lisa M. Shin, Scott L. Rauch, and Roger K. Pitman, "Amygdala, Medial Prefrontal Cortex, and Hippocampal Function in PTSD," *Annals of the New York Academy of Sciences* 1071 (2006): 67–79. Also, Kristina B. Mercer et al., "Acute and Posttraumatic Stress Symptoms in a Prospective Gene x Environment Study of a University Campus Shooting," *Archive of General Psychiatry* 69, no. 1 (2012): 89–97.

9 Katherine N. Boone, "The Paradox of PTSD," *Wilson Quarterly* (Autumn 2011): 18–22.

10 Anthony J. Marsella, "Ethnocultural Aspects of PTSD: An Overview of Concepts, Issues, and Treatments," *Traumatology* 16, no. 4 (December 2010): 17–26.

11 Roy Clymer, "The Puzzle of PTSD," *Psychotherapy Networker* 34, no. 6 (November/December 2010): 26–33.

12 T. L. Schell and G. N. Marshall, "Survey of Individuals Previously Deployed for OEF/OIF," in *Invisible Wounds of War: Psychological and Cognitive Injuries, Their Consequences, and Services to Assist Recovery*, ed. T. Tanielian and L. H. Jaycox (Santa Monica, CA: RAND Center for Military Health Policy Research, 2008), 87–115.

13 Matthew Kaufman and Lisa Chedekel, "Military Psychiatric Screening Still Lags: Few Are Ordered, despite Pressure from Congress," *Hartford Courant*, 9 March 2008. Subsequent studies suggested that the frequently prescribed stimulants

Ritalin and Adderall may promote the onset of PTSD and increase resistance to its treatment. Richard A. Friedman, "Why Are We Drugging Our Soldiers?" *New York Times*, 22 April 2012.

14 Nora Eisenbert, "Leaked Internal Memo Shows How VA Systematically Screws Over Wounded Vets to Maintain Performance Grades," *AlterNet*, 30 June 2010.

15 Mark Thompson, "America's Medicated Army," *Time*, 5 June 2008. See also Martha Rosenbert, "Why Are Suicides Climbing in the Military? Let's Look at the Drugs Being Prescribed," *AlterNet*, 2 February 2013; Andrew Tilghman and Brendan McGarry, "Medicating the Military: Use of Psychiatric Drugs Has Spiked," ArmyTimes.com, 17 March 2010, http://www.armytimes.com/article/20100317/NEWS/3170315/Medicating-military.

16 Richard A. Friedman, "Wars on Drugs," *New York Times*, 7 April 2013.

17 On suicide, see testimony of Sergio Kochergin, 14 March 2008, in *Winter Soldier Iraq and Afghanistan*, ed. IVAW and Aaron Glantz (Chicago: Haymarket Books, 2008), 51. On pressure to misdiagnose, Serena Hayden, phone call with the author, 16 September 2011. On rape victim, Panayiota Bertzikis, interview with the author, 22 April 2011.

18 Joshua Kors, "How Specialist Town Lost His Benefits," *Nation*, 9 April 2007.

19 Anne Flaherty, "Alleging Misdiagnoses, Veterans' Advocates Battle Army," *Boston Globe*, 16 August 2010. Bob Kinder, "The Long Road Home," *Boston Globe*, 11 November 2010.

20 Violent or aggressive behavior is statistically more common in people with PTSD than in their peer group, but the relationship is complex and the aggression tends to be turned inward, erupting in domestic violence, self-destructive actions, and suicide. Combat veterans don't appear to be overrepresented in prisons, where most of the available research concerns Vietnam veterans. See, for example, Margaret E. Noonan and Christopher J. Mumola, "Veterans in State and Federal Prison, 2004," U.S. Department of Justice, Bureau of Justice Statistics, May 2007.

21 Alice deV. Perry and John S. Rolland, "The Therapeutic Benefits of a Justice-Seeking Spirituality: Empowerment, Healing, and Hope," in *Spiritual Resources in Family Therapy*, ed. Froma Walsh, 2nd ed. (New York: Guilford Press, 2010), 379–396.

22 M. Klar and T. Kasser, "Some Benefits of Being an Activist: Measuring Activism and Its Role in Psychological Well-Being," *Political Psychology* 30 (2009): 755–777.

23 Shay, *Odysseus in America*, 38.

24 Clymer, "The Puzzle of PTSD."

25 Jerry Lembcke, *The Spitting Image* (New York: New York University Press, 1998).

26 Jerry Lembcke, "Medicating and Medicalizing Dissent," *National Catholic Reporter*, 6 January 2010.

27 The other much-reported statistic was eighteen veteran suicides a day, or one every eighty minutes. The military doesn't officially track veteran suicides, so these numbers appear to come from an estimate by the Centers for Disease Control that 20 percent of the thirty-four thousand suicides in the United States in 2007 were veterans and a 2008 internal VA memo presented at a trial that year. However, another internal memo, obtained by CBS, cited four or five suicides a day among those receiving care from the VA, and a 2010 article in *Army Times* reported an average of

950 veterans who were receiving some type of treatment from the VA attempting suicide each month, with 7 percent succeeding, which would come to a little more than
two suicides each day. In February 2013, the VA reported that the suicide rate among
veterans was 20 percent higher than previously estimated. The figure was corrected
to about twenty-two suicides a day, or one every sixty-five minutes.

28 Benedict Carey, "Mental Stress Training Is Planned for U.S. Soldiers," *New York
    Times*, 18 August 2009.

29 See, for example, Roy Eidelson, Stephen Soldz, and Marc Pilisuk, "The Dark Side
    of 'Comprehensive Soldier Fitness,'" Truthout, 1 April 2011, http://www.truth-out
    .org/news/item/250:the-dark-side-of-comprehensive-soldier-fitness.

30 Jim Rendon, "The Postwar Attitude Adjustment," *New York Times Magazine*, 25
    March 2012.

31 Intriguingly, another study found that Propranolol may also make people less ra-
    cially biased. Jeremy Laurance, "Heart Drug Can Alter Racial Attitudes," *Indepen-
    dent*, 7 March 2012.

32 Paul Outka, "History, the Posthuman, and the End of Trauma: Propranolol and
    Beyond," *Traumatology* 15, no. 4 (December 2009): 76.

33 The factors Grossman discusses as influencing an individual's relationship to kill-
    ing include the killer's physical, cultural, moral, social, and mechanical distance
    from the victim; the killer's relationship to authority and to his/her peer group; the
    intention of and payoff from the killing; and the killer's training or conditioning.

34 Grossman, *On Killing*, 14.

35 The Veterans Administration website cites a 2006 sample survey of soldiers in Iraq,
    which found that only 36 percent had fired their guns, but this probably includes
    the many who were not in combat roles.

36 Grossman, *On Killing*, 194.

37 Brett T. Litz et al., "Moral Injury and Moral Repair in War Veterans: A Preliminary
    Model and Intervention Strategy," *Clinical Psychology Review* 29 (2009): 695.

38 Stan Goff, "Returning Home Alive," *Truthout*, 20 January 2006.

11 WINTER SOLDIERS' STORIES

1 Defense spending by the United States accounts for upward of 40 percent of defense spending worldwide, more than what is spent by the next fourteen countries
   combined.

2 Gerald Nicosia, *Home to War* (New York: Three Rivers Press, 2001), 80.

3 Ibid., 84.

4 Winter Soldier ran about 40 percent over budget in 1971. The first Winter Soldier
   inquiry cost $50,000 to $75,000, which would put its cost close to the second Winter Soldier's in 2008 dollars. It also ran over budget. Ibid., 89.

5 "Daily Summaries," dated 13, 22, and 25 February 2008, and "Weekly Fire and
   Emergency Medical Service Intelligence Briefing," dated 19 February 2008,
   obtained through a FOIA request. All were very heavily redacted, so it is unclear
   what information about the event, if any, was shared among local police and national security agencies.

6 In 2008, there were 505 military bases in Iraq, which required supplies, equipment, maintenance, and staffing, usually provided by private contractors. By October 2011, when U.S. forces began to leave Iraq, the military had removed 1.6 million pieces of equipment, with another eight hundred thousand still waiting to be taken out. Lisa Daniel, "U.S. Forces Have Met All Obligations in Iraq, General Says," American Forces Press Service, 12 October 2011.

7 Testifiers ranged in age from twenty-one to forty-two, with an average of just under twenty-four. More than half came from the army, including the reserves and National Guard, and a fifth were marines. Their ranks ran from private to a captain, with a preponderance of specialists (E-4) and sergeants (E-6 and E-7). Of the veterans who testified, ten, or about 17 percent, were women, and about 15 percent were people of color.

8 The Watson Institute for International Studies at Brown University calculated in September 2013 that at least 123,000 to 134,000 Iraqi civilians had died as a direct consequence of the war. Many human rights organizations believe the real number is much higher. For U.S. troop casualties, see icasualties.org.

9 Amy Belasco, "The Cost of Iraq, Afghanistan, and Other Global War on Terror Operations since 9/11," CRS Report for Congress, updated 8 February 2008.

10 See "New York Times Explains Winter Soldier Blackout," Fairness and Accuracy in Reporting/FAIR, 8 April 2008.

11 Thom Shanker, phone conversation with the author, 12 March 2008.

12 Paul Fussell, *The Great War and Modern Memory* (New York: Oxford University Press, 1975), 7.

13 David Grossman, *The Yellow Wind* (New York: Picador, 2002), 212.

14 In May 2013, the Pentagon estimated that twenty-six thousand people in the military had been sexually assaulted in the previous fiscal year, recording a 40 percent increase in complaints from the year before.

15 Bertzikis was one of twenty-five women and three men named in a lawsuit charging then–Defense Secretary Robert Gates and his predecessor, Donald Rumsfeld, with mishandling their sexual assault cases while they were in the military. The case, *Cioca et al. v. Rumsfeld and Gates*, was dismissed in December 2011 and appealed in April 2012.

16 Unresolved cases include the deaths of LaVena Johnson in July 2005 and Tina Priest in March 2006, both on army bases in Iraq. See Ann Wright, "Is There an Army Cover Up of Rape and Murder of Women Soldiers?" Common Dreams, http://www.commondreams.org/view/2008/04/28.

17 Legislation, notably the Defense STRONG Act of 2011, championed by representatives Niki Tsongas and Mike Turner, addressed some of the problems then. A high-profile case in 2013, in which an air force general reversed another officer's sexual assault conviction, led to pressure to limit the judicial power of commanding officers in such cases. Congress enacted some reforms, but a stronger measure pushed by Senator Kirsten Gillibrand, which would have removed commanders from the process of deciding which crimes go to trial, ultimately failed.

18 Steve Vogel, "War Stories Echo an Earlier Winter," *Washington Post*, 15 March 2008.

19 William J. Astore, a retired air force lieutenant colonel, examines this assertion in "Freedom Fighters for a Fading Empire: What It Means When We Say We Have the World's Finest Fighting Force," TomDispatch.com, 6 January 2011, http://www.tomdispatch.com/post/175337/tomgram%3A_william_astore,_we%27re_number_one_%28in_self-promotion%29.

20 Andrew Tilghman, "The Army's Other Crisis: Why the Best and Brightest Young Officers Are Leaving," *Washington Monthly*, December 2007. The Center for Army Leadership reported in May 2012 that only 26 percent of officers believed that the army was headed in the right direction, a historic low. The top reason given was that "the army is unable to retain quality leaders." *2011 Center for Army Leadership Annual Survey of Army Leadership (CASAL): Main Finding, Technical Report 2012–1*, May 2012.

21 In *Until Tuesday*, a best-selling book about his service dog, Montalván writes that as the highest-ranking veteran present at Winter Soldier, he felt compelled to accept their invitation to speak in front of "several thousand people," but got through it by doubling up on his meds and being "loaded to the gills on rum." The no-alcohol policy for testifiers was strictly enforced at Winter Soldier, and Montalván appeared composed as he spoke. Luis Montalván, *Until Tuesday* (New York: Hyperion, 2011), 178. After Winter Soldier, as Montalván continued to speak and write about military incompetence and corruption, his version of events in the book was called into question by soldiers who had served with him. The most strident attacks, however, came when he threatened to sue McDonald's for giving him a hard time about bringing his service dog into their facilities.

22 Chris Hedges, "War Is Betrayal: Persistent Myths of Combat," *Boston Review* (July/August 2012).

23 Goldsmith resigned from IVAW about a year after Winter Soldier. Among the reasons he gave was what he perceived as a reflexive anti-American stance, which he believed undermined not the military, but IVAW itself.

24 Between 2002 and 2012, the VA's budget more than doubled and its full-time staff increased by 43 percent, yet the number of pending disability claims in November 2012 was nearly twice that of three years before, and two-thirds had been working their way through the system for longer than four months. Kathleen Miller, "Veterans Home from War Battle V.A.," Bloomberg, 12 November 2012. The VA Watchdog site (http://www.vawatchdog.org) asks, "Is the VA the enemy?" After a long list of complaints, it concludes, "The VA isn't evil. It's incompetent."

25 According to HUD, some seventy-six thousand veterans are homeless at any given time, but about twice as many are homeless during a single year. Nearly one-fifth of homeless people are veterans.

26 In 2004, the suicide rate was beginning to climb and, according to the Army Health Command, had increased 80 percent by 2008, when it rose above the civilian rate among young, healthy adults for the first time. The rate peaked in 2009.

27 *Lucey et al. v. Nicholson et al.* (No. 07–30134-MAP) was settled in January 2009 when the Justice Department determined that, although the VA was not responsible for his death, Jeffrey Lucey had received substandard care. The Luceys had

not asked for recompense, but they received a $350,000 settlement. The suit was filed just after Veterans for Common Sense filed a class-action suit against the VA on behalf of veterans who were denied benefits they were entitled to. See also Nan Levinson, "Mass. Family at Center of Suit: Class Action Alleges Prudential Unfairly Profited from Death Benefits," *Boston Globe*, 4 October 2010.

28 Nicosia, *Home to War*, 93.

29 This low figure of Iraqi casualties comes from icasualties (http://icasualties.org/IraqiDeaths.aspx). The Iraq Body Count (http://www.iraqbodycount.org/database) puts civilian deaths from August 2008 to December 2011 at 15,725. Most sources assume these counts are incomplete.

BIBLIOGRAPHY

Alford, C. Fred. "Whistleblower Narratives: Stuck in Static Time." *Narrative* 8, no. 4 (October 2000): 279–293.

Andén-Papadopoulos, Kari. "Body Horror on the Internet: US Soldiers Recording the War in Iraq and Afghanistan." *Media, Culture & Society* 31 (2009): 921–938.

Arquilla, John, and David Ronfeldt, eds. *Networks and Netwars: The Future of Terror, Crime, and Militancy.* Arlington, VA: RAND Corporation, 2001.

Bacevich, Andrew J. *The New American Militarism: How Americans Are Seduced by War.* New York: Oxford University Press, 2005.

Benedict, Helen. *The Lonely Soldier: The Private War of Women Serving in Iraq.* Boston: Beacon Press, 2009.

Body of War. Directed by Phil Donahue and Ellen Spiro. Distributor, Film Sales Company, 2007. Film.

Butler, Smedley D. "In Time of Peace." *Common Sense* 4, no. 11 (November 1935): 8–12.

———. *War Is a Racket.* 1935. Reprint, Los Angeles: Feral House, 2003.

Calica, Lovella, ed. *Warrior Writers: Move, Shoot, and Communicate.* [Philadelphia]: IVAW, 2007.

———. *Warrior Writers: Re-Making Sense.* [Philadelphia]: IVAW, 2008.

———. *After Action Review.* [Philadelphia]: Warrior Writers, 2011.

Chandrasekaran, Rajiv. *Imperial Life in the Emerald City: Inside Iraq's Green Zone.* New York: Knopf, 2006.

———. *Little America: The War within the War for Afghanistan.* New York: Knopf, 2012.

Clymer, Roy. "The Puzzle of PTSD." *Psychotherapy Networker* 34, no. 6 (November/December 2010): 26–33.

Cohn, Marjorie, and Kathleen Gilberd. *Rules of Disengagement: The Politics and Honor of Military Dissent.* Sausalito, CA: PoliPoint Press, 2009.

Coleman, Penny. *Flashback: Posttraumatic Stress Disorder, Suicide, and the Lessons of War.* Boston: Beacon Press, 2006.

Control Room. Directed by Jehane Noujaim. Distributor, Magnolia Pictures, 2004. Film.

Cortright, David. *Soldiers in Revolt: GI Resistance during the Vietnam War.* Chicago: Haymarket Books, 2005.

Duncombe, Stephen. *Dream: Re-imagining Progressive Politics in an Age of Fantasy.* New York: New Press, 2007.

Filkins, Dexter. *The Forever War.* New York: Knopf, 2006.

Fountain, Ben. *Billy Flynn's Long Halftime Walk.* New York: Ecco, 2012.

Fussell, Paul. *The Great War and Modern Memory.* New York: Oxford University Press, 1975.

Generation Kill. Directed by Susanna White and Simon Cellan Jones. HBO, 2008. TV miniseries.

Gilbertson, Ashley. *Whiskey Tango Foxtrot.* Chicago: University of Chicago Press, 2007.

Goodwin, Jeff, James M. Jasper, and Francesca Polletta, eds. *Passionate Politics: Emotions and Social Movements.* Chicago: University of Chicago Press, 2001.

Graves, Robert. *Good-Bye to All That.* New York: Doubleday, 1929.

Gray, Francine du Plessix. "The Moratorium and the New Mobe" (1969). In *Reporting Vietnam, Part Two: American Journalism 1969–1975.*

Greider, William. "Viet Vets: A Sad Reminder" (1974). In *Reporting Vietnam, Part Two: American Journalism 1969–1975.*

Grossman, Dave. *On Killing: The Psychological Cost of Learning to Kill in War and Society.* Boston: Little, Brown, 1995.

The Ground Truth: After the Killing Ends. Directed by Patricia Foulkrod. Distributor, Focus Features, 2006. Film.

Gutmann, Matthew, and Catherine Lutz. *Breaking Ranks: Iraq Veterans Speak Out against the War.* Berkeley: University of California Press, 2010.

Hedges, Chris. *War Is a Force That Gives Us Meaning.* New York: Public Affairs, 2002.

Hemingway, Ernest. "Soldier's Home." In *The Short Stories of Ernest Hemingway.* New York: Scribner, 1953.

Hidden Battles. Directed by Victoria Mills. Distributor, Filmakers Library, 2010. Film.

Hochschild, Adam. *To End All Wars: A Story of Loyalty and Rebellion, 1914–1918.* Boston: Houghton Mifflin Harcourt, 2011.

Hoffer, Eric. *The True Believer: Thoughts on the Nature of Mass Movements.* New York: Harper & Row, 1951.

Hunt, Andrew E. *The Turning: A History of Vietnam Veterans Against the War.* New York: New York University Press, 1999.

Hurley, Elisa A. "Combat Trauma and the Moral Risks of Memory Manipulating Drugs." *Journal of Applied Philosophy* 27, no. 3 (August 2010): 221–245.

The Hurt Locker. Directed by Kathryn Bigelow. Distributor, Summit Entertainment, 2008. Film.

Hutto, Jonathan W., Sr. *Antiwar Soldier: How to Dissent within the Ranks of the Military.* New York: Nation Books, 2008.

The Invisible War. Directed by Kirby Dick. Distributor, Docudrama, 2012. Film.

Iraq Veterans Against the War and Aaron Glantz. *Winter Soldier Iraq and Afghanistan: Eyewitness Accounts of the Occupations.* Chicago: Haymarket Books, 2008.

Jamail, Dahr. *Beyond the Green Zone: Dispatches from an Unembedded Journalist in Occupied Iraq.* Chicago: Haymarket Books, 2007.

———. *The Will to Resist: Soldiers Who Refuse to Fight in Iraq and Afghanistan.* Chicago: Haymarket Books, 2009.

Jones, Ann. *They Were Soldiers: How the Wounded Return from America's Wars—The Untold Story.* Chicago: Haymarket Books, 2013.

Khatchadourian, Raffi. "The Kill Company." *New Yorker* (6 and 13 July 2009): 41–59.

Kirk, Donald. "Who Wants to Be the Last American Killed in Vietnam?" (1971). In *Reporting Vietnam, Part Two: American Journalism 1969–1975.*

Laufer, Peter. *Mission Rejected: U.S. Soldiers Who Say No to Iraq.* White River Junction, VT: Chelsea Green, 2006.

Lembcke, Jerry. *The Spitting Image: Myth, Memory, and the Legacy of Vietnam.* New York: New York University Press, 1998.

Lewis, Nathan. *I Hacky Sacked in Iraq.* Burlington, VT: Combat Paper Press, 2009.

Litz, Brett T., Nathan Stein, et al. "Moral Injury and Moral Repair in War Veterans: A Preliminary Model and Intervention Strategy." *Clinical Psychology Review* 29 (2009): 695–706.

Mejia, Camilo. *Road from Ar Ramadi: The Private Rebellion of Staff Sergeant Camilo Mejia.* New York: New Press, 2007.

Meyer, David S. *The Politics of Protest: Social Movements in America.* New York: Oxford University Press, 2007.

Moser, Richard. *The New Winter Soldiers: GI and Veterans Dissent during the Vietnam Era.* New Brunswick, NJ: Rutgers University Press, 1996.

Moyer, Bill. *Doing Democracy: The MAP Model for Organizing Social Movements.* Gabriola Island, Canada: New Society Publishers, 2001.

Neale, Jonathan. *A People's History of the Vietnam War.* New York: New Press, 2003.

Nicosia, Gerald. *Home to War: A History of the Vietnam Veterans' Movement.* New York: Three Rivers Press, 2001.

No End in Sight. Directed by Charles Ferguson. Distributor, Magnolia Pictures 2007. Film.

Notes from Nowhere, eds. *We Are Everywhere: The Irresistible Rise of Global Anticapitalism.* London: Verso, 2003.

O'Brien, Tim. *If I Die in a Combat Zone: Box Me Up and Ship Me Home.* New York: Broadway Books, 1999.

Outka, Paul. "History, the Posthuman, and the End of Trauma: Propranolol and Beyond." *Traumatology* 15, no. 4 (2009): 76–81.

Perry, Alice deV., and John Rolland. "The Therapeutic Benefits of a Justice-Seeking Spirituality: Empowerment, Healing, and Hope." In *Spiritual Resources in Family Therapy*, ed. Froma Walsh. 2nd ed. New York: Guilford Press, 2010.

Reporting Vietnam, Part Two: American Journalism 1969–1975. New York: Library of America, 1998.

Rieckhoff, Paul. *Chasing Ghosts: Failures and Facades in Iraq: A Soldier's Perspective.* New York: NAL Caliber, 2006.

Ronfeldt, John, and John Arquilla. "Networks, Netwars, and the Fight for the Future." *First Monday* 6, no. 1 (October 2001): http://ojphi.org/ojs/index.php/fm/article/view/889/798.

Rudd, Mark. *Underground: My Life with SDS and the Weathermen.* New York: Harper-Collins, 2009.

Rules of Engagement. Produced by Arun Rath. *Frontline*, 2008. TV news series.

Saar, John. "You Can't Just Hand Out Orders" (1970). In *Reporting Vietnam, Part Two: American Journalism 1969–1975.*

Schanberg, Sydney H. "The South Vietnamese Retreat" (1972). In *Reporting Vietnam, Part Two: American Journalism 1969–1975.*

Shay, Jonathan. *Odysseus in America: Combat Trauma and the Trials of Homecoming.* New York: Scribner, 2002.

Sobieraj, Sarah. *Soundbitten: The Perils of Media-Centered Political Activism.* New York: New York University Press, 2011.

Soldiers of Conscience. Directed by Catherine Ryan and Gary Weinberg. Distributor, Journeyman Pictures, 2007. Film.

Stone, Geoffrey R. *Perilous Times: Free Speech in Wartime.* New York: Norton, 2004.

Swerdlow, Amy. *Women Strike for Peace: Traditional Politics and Radical Motherhood in the 1960s.* Chicago: University of Chicago Press, 1993.

Tanielian, Terri L., and Lisa H. Jaycox, eds. *Invisible Wounds of War: Psychological and Cognitive Injuries, Their Consequences, and Services to Assist Recovery.* Santa Monica, CA: RAND Center for Military Health Policy Research, 2008.

Thompson, Hunter S. "From *Fear and Loathing on the Campaign Trail '72*" (1972). In *Reporting Vietnam, Part Two: American Journalism 1969–1975.*

The Tillman Story. Directed by Amir Bar-Lev. Distributor, Weinstein Company, 2010. Film.

Weber, Max. "Politics as Vocation." Speech delivered at Munich University, 1918. Available at http://www.ucc.ie/social_policy/Weber_Politics_as_Vocation.htm.

Wood, Trish. *What Was Asked of Us: An Oral History of the Iraq War by the Soldiers Who Fought It.* New York: Little, Brown, 2006.

Wright, Ann, and Susan Dixon. *Dissent: Voices of Conscience.* Kihei, HI: Koa Books, 2008.

INDEX

ABOUT THE AUTHOR

Nan Levinson is a writer and journalist whose work on civil and human rights, technology, and culture has appeared widely in publications in the United States, abroad, and online. Her earlier book, *Outspoken: Free Speech Stories*, grew from her reporting as the U.S. correspondent for the London-based magazine *Index on Censorship*. Levinson teaches journalism and fiction writing at Tufts University and has also taught at the Kennedy School of Government at Harvard University and at Bentley University. Previously, she worked in arts administration, including as an assistant program director at the National Endowment for the Arts and as executive director of the British American Arts Association/US. She lives in Somerville, Massachusetts.